# Nuclear Terrorism

## A Threat Assessment for the 21st Century

Gavin Cameron
*Post-Doctoral Fellow*
*Centre for Nonproliferation Studies*
*Monterey Institute of International Studies*
*California*

First published in Great Britain 1999 by
**MACMILLAN PRESS LTD**
Houndmills, Basingstoke, Hampshire RG21 6XS and London
Companies and representatives throughout the world

A catalogue record for this book is available from the British Library.

ISBN 0–333–74850–6

First published in the United States of America 1999 by
**ST. MARTIN'S PRESS, INC.,**
Scholarly and Reference Division,
175 Fifth Avenue, New York, N.Y. 10010

ISBN 0–312–21983–0

Library of Congress Cataloging-in-Publication Data
Cameron, Gavin, 1972–
Nuclear terrorism : a threat assessment for the 21st century /
Gavin Cameron.
p.   cm.
Includes bibliographical references and index.
ISBN 0–312–21983–0 (cloth)
1. Nuclear terrorism.   2. Nuclear nonproliferation.   I. Title.
HV6431.C35   1999
303.6'25—dc21                                    98–37389
                                                          CIP

This book is printed on paper suitable for recycling and made from fully managed and
sustained forest sources.

10   9   8   7   6   5   4   3   2   1
08   07   06   05   04   03   02   01   00   99

Printed and bound in Great Britain by
Antony Rowe Ltd, Chippenham, Wiltshire

For Maureen and my family
who were with me word for word...

# Contents

# Acknowledgements

I have been greatly assisted in the preparation of this work by a number of people. Dr Bruce Hoffman has continued to be a considerable source of wisdom, good sense and positive criticism, even after his formal obligation to teaching me the rudiments of writing were over. He has also been unfailingly generous with his time and effort on my behalf and consequently deserves special thanks. Professor Paul Wilkinson and Dr Frank Barnaby were both encouraging from an early stage and made many insightful comments on a previous version of the work. Donna Kim Hoffman and David Claridge in the Rand–St Andrews Database were both ceaselessly willing to seek out spurious pieces of information on my behalf. Their efforts made the empirical aspects of this work immeasurably easier than they would otherwise have been. Gina Wilson provided a constant anchor of efficiency, helping greatly with the administrative aspects of my research. At St Andrews, many people offered their friendship, empathy and support. Amongst them have been: Daphne Biliouri, Alex Ashbourne, Paula Briscoe, John and Ollie Hulsman, Mark Humphries, Gabriel Kikas, Wendy Lazarus, Magnus Ranstorp, Guy Sanan, Pritie Sharma, Mike Wesley and Gazman Xhudo.

Throughout my three years as a doctoral student, I was supported by scholarships from the University of St Andrews, for which I am very grateful. The sections of the work that deal with nuclear nonproliferation were significantly strengthened by a visit to the United States in November 1996. This was almost entirely financed by the St Andrew's Society of Washington, DC. I greatly appreciated their generosity and the kindness of James McLeod, the Chairman of the Society's Charity and Education Committee, who facilitated the visit. I also owe a debt of thanks to Richard Falkenrath, Robert Newman and Brad Thayer at Harvard, and to Floyd Clarke, Thomas Cochran, Henry Sokolski, John Sopko and Leonard Spector in Washington, and to others who would prefer to remain unnamed. They provided invaluable insights into the issues, and were uniformly generous with their time, tolerant of my questions, and interested in my opinions.

My family, Alan, Alison, Catherine and David Cameron, Bill and Joan Brindle, and Jack and Sue McCartney, provided me with support of every conceivable nature. They were unstintingly interested, enthusiastic and willing to help in any way that they could.

Their belief in me was a constant source of encouragement. My father was especially helpful in assisting with a first edit of the manuscript, a process that did much to minimise my 'purple prose', for which everyone should be grateful. Finally, Maureen McCartney-Cameron, who in spite of never having known me without a looming thesis or book in tow, agreed to be my friend and wife. This role has also encompassed cheerleader, solace, proof-reader, sounding-board and critic. It is to her that I owe my biggest thanks.

# List of Abbreviations

| | |
|---|---|
| AD | Action Directe |
| ADC | Aide-de-camp |
| ALF | Animal Liberation Front |
| ASALA | Armenian Secret Army for the Liberation of Armenia |
| BCE | Before Common Era |
| BKA | German Bundeskriminalamt |
| CCC | Cellules Communistes Combatants |
| CE | Common Era |
| CIA | Central Intelligence Agency |
| EMETIC | Evan Mecham Eco-Terrorist International Conspiracy |
| ETA | Euskadi Ta Askatasuna |
| FARC | Revolutionary Armed Forces of Colombia |
| FBI | Federal Bureau of Investigation |
| FEMA | Federal Emergency Management Agency |
| FLN | Front de Libération Nationale |
| FLQ | Front de Libération du Québec |
| GDR | German Democratic Republic |
| GIA | Armed Islamic Group |
| HEU | Highly Enriched Uranium |
| INLA | Irish National Liberation Army |
| IRA | Irish Republican Army |
| JDL | Jewish Defense League |
| JRA | Japanese Red Army |
| KGB | Soviet Intelligence Organisation |
| KKK | Ku Klux Klan |
| LEHI | Lohame Herut Israel |
| MLN | Movimiento de Liberacion Nacional |
| MPCA | Material Protection, Control and Accountability |
| MVD | Russian Ministry of the Interior |
| NATO | North Atlantic Treaty Organization |
| NBC | Nuclear, Biological and Chemical |
| NEST | Nuclear Emergency Search Team |
| NNWS | Non Nuclear Weapons State |
| NWS | Nuclear Weapon State |
| OAS | Secret Army Organisation |
| PFLP | Popular Front for the Liberation of Palestine |

| | |
|---|---|
| PFLP-GC | Popular Front for the Liberation of Palestine – General Command |
| PLO | Palestion Liberation Organisation |
| RAF | Rot Armee Fraktion |
| RB | Red Brigades |
| RUC | Royal Ulster Constabulary |
| SAM | Surface to Air Missile |
| SDS | Students for a Democratic Society |
| SLA | Sybionese Liberation Army |
| SRF | Special Rocket Forces |
| UDA | Ulster Defence Association |
| UFF | Ulster Freedom Fighters |
| UN | United Nations |
| USSR | Union of Soviet Socialist Republics |
| UVF | Ulster Volunteer Force |
| U-235 | Uranium-235 |
| WMA | War Measures Act |
| WMD | Weapons of Mass Destruction |
| WTC | World Trade Center |
| ZOG | Zionist Occupation Government |

# 1 Introduction: the Opportunities For Nuclear Terrorism

On 20 March 1995, members of the Aum Shinrikyo cult released a lethal nerve agent, sarin, on the Tokyo underground. The attack killed 12 people and injured over 5,000 others, and was the first major sub-state use of a weapon of mass destruction. Although terrorism using non-conventional weaponry had been the subject of academic and governmental discussion for twenty years prior to the attack, the events in Tokyo gave new impetus to this debate. Aum's actions broke a norm, that terrorists almost invariably limit their attacks to conventional means, and, given the derivative nature of many terrorist tactics, it thus increased the likelihood that there will be further attacks using weapons of mass destruction.

This book concentrates almost entirely on just one part of non-conventional terrorism, nuclear terrorism. Nuclear weapons possess a unique destructive force and still, eight years after the end of the Cold War, remain unsurpassed in their power as a tool towards political legitimacy and in their ability to capture the attention of a wide audience. Furthermore, in the wake of the collapse of the former Soviet Union, the opportunities for rogue states and sub-state actors to acquire fissile material have risen exponentially. Since 1989, the proliferation of the means to acquire weapons of mass destruction has become one of the foremost global issues for the future. As the change has been the greatest in nuclear, rather than chemical or biological, weapons, it is they that are most deserving of renewed study.

Nuclear terrorism covers a broad spectrum, from low-level incidents of threats involving radioactive material through attacks on reactors to a terrorist nuclear bomb. There have been several terrorist attacks on reactors, such as the ETA rocket assault on Lemoniz in northern Spain;[1] and the possibility of sabotage or a siege and hostage situation developing at a facility remains, particularly from single-issue anti-nuclear groups. In most cases, the latter form of terrorism is aimed at highlighting security and safety failures at facilities, and for

1

that purpose, such actions will continue to be a possibility. However, where the objective is to embarrass the government or to gain leverage for a group, then other varieties of nuclear terrorism have become increasingly likely as the feasibility of acquiring fissile material has increased. The result has been that 'the threat of terrorist use of weapons of mass destruction has never been greater; and at the same time, it is never going to be less than it is right now.'[2]


NUCLEAR PROLIFERATION

Easier access to fissile material is largely a result of the collapse of the former Soviet Union and the growth of nuclear trafficking that has stemmed from it. FBI chief Louis Freeh has described the situation as 'the greatest long-term threat to the security of the US'[3] and Graham Allison, former Assistant Secretary of Defense, has stated that 'Russia is a state in revolution...This revolution is shredding the fabric of a command and control society, in a state that houses a superpower nuclear arsenal and a superpower nuclear enterprise.'[4] Russia, too, acknowledges the danger. As early as 1989, then chairman of the KGB, Vladimir Kryuchkov, said:

> The threat of nuclear terrorism is for us very dangerous. The fact is that on the globe several tons of enriched uranium has disappeared from sites where it was produced and stored.[5]

While nuclear weapons remain under tight military supervision, there may have been at least one case where a fissile material component of a weapon was stolen and then recovered.[6] There is also a huge quantity of nuclear materials, dispersed throughout Russia, that is far less secure. One estimate puts the Russian inventory at 150 metric tonnes of weapons-grade plutonium, 1,000 metric tonnes of enriched uranium, and at Chelyabinsk alone about 685,000 cubic metres of radioactive waste.[7] Others put the figures higher, at 165 tonnes of separated weapons-usable plutonium and 1,100 to 1,300 tonnes of highly enriched uranium.[8] However, no one really knows what quantities are involved because, during the Cold War, Soviet facilities were set production targets. When they exceeded these, material was kept aside rather than declared, so as to compensate for any shortfalls in subsequent targets.[9] Keeping an accurate record of existing stocks was therefore not a priority. Furthermore, material was counted in rouble value rather than in weight and inventories could be out by several tons.[10] This obviously all poses immense problems of accounting; and the danger is heightened by poor security, especially at nuclear sites, secret cities and research institutes.[11] One US official, visiting the Kurchatov Institute, found about 160 pounds of weapons-grade uranium stored in lockers secured only by a chain through the handles of the lockers. There was no other security.[12] It is estimated that fewer than 20 per cent of these research facilities have even the most elementary electronic monitoring system as part of the security.[13] The problem is further exacerbated by the fact that there are over 100 such storage sites and civilian research facilities in the former Soviet Union.[14] In March 1994, the Russian Counterintelligence Service reported to President Yeltsin that there had been 900 thefts from military and nuclear plants and 700 thefts of secret technology in the second half of 1993 alone.[15] The Ministry of Internal Affairs reported 900 attempts to gain illegal entry into nuclear facilities in 1993.[16] The German federal criminal police (BKA) reported 267 cases of 'illicit traffic in nuclear or radioactive materials' in 1994, compared to 241 in 1993, 158 in 1992 and 41 in 1991.[17] Much of the theft is insider crime: staff employed within the industry making the most of their access to nuclear material.[18] Furthermore, the amounts of material available for theft will only increase in the near future. Russian-American arms reduction agreements mean that Russia will cut its number of nuclear warheads from 15,000 to 5,000 by the year 2007, increasing its supplies of HEU by hundreds of tonnes and of plutonium by tens of tonnes.

The problem is not limited to Russia; Ukraine, Kazakhstan and the Baltic states are in a similar predicament and there has been leakage from non-members of the former Soviet Union too: 130 barrels of enriched uranium waste were stolen from a facility in South Africa in August 1994,[19] and there have been seizures of illicit nuclear materials in Switzerland, Poland, Turkey, Romania, Hungary, Bulgaria, the Czech Republic, Austria, Belgium, Italy and India.[20]

Worldwide, civilian nuclear material represents a greater smuggling threat than military material, and while reactor-grade material does pose more handling difficulties and has a higher critical mass than weapons-grade material, it would be still usable for a crude nuclear device or radiological terrorism. The global stock of plutonium in 1995 was around 1,500 tonnes, of which 1,200 were civilian, the overwhelming majority remaining unseparated as reactor fuel. The 1996 ratio of used military to used civilian plutonium was 50:50. However, by 2010, 70 per cent of the world's used plutonium will be civilian, much of it in states such as France, Japan, the United Kingdom and Germany as a result of reprocessing, as well as in Russia. By contrast, almost all HEU is military: only about one per cent is classified as civilian. HEU is also relatively easy to dispose of: it is simply mixed with natural uranium. The result, low-enriched uranium, is useful in reactors but extremely difficult to 'weaponise'. Plutonium poses a more difficult disposal problem. Currently there is a considerable debate on what should be done with the material in Russia: using it as mixed-oxide fuel in a closed cycle is the most likely possibility. Other options include burying or vitrifying it: mixing plutonium with radioactive waste to form a glass or ceramic.[21] However, whatever is decided seems certain to take time to implement, adding to the risk of the material falling into the wrong hands. It seems unlikely that the disposal process will begin before 2010, due to the lack of a technological infrastructure and the enormous cost involved. This may be a mixed blessing in the current situation, given the social and economic state of the former Soviet Union, because the transportation of fissile materials at the moment would only increase the opportunities for their theft.[22]

An additional problem in Russia has been a haemorrhage of personnel. The nuclear industry used to support entire cities such as Tomsk, but cutbacks have resulted in thousands of layoffs.[23] Workers often lived in secret cities where they were well paid and highly respected members of Soviet society. Since 1989, they have periodically been unpaid for months at a time; their wages have failed to increase in line with inflation and they have lost their cachet in society.[24] Vladimir Orlov, a Russian nuclear safety expert, stated in July 1997 that: 'The industry is seriously and dangerously underfunded – 70% of security devices at Russian facilities are outdated ... Some of the staff working at these plants are desperately depressed and haven't been paid in months – and the temptation to smuggle nuclear material out is great. The situation is very serious.'[25] Unsurprisingly, some Russian scientists have been tempted to offer their services elsewhere: their wage in mid-1996 was around $150 a month, well below the Russian national average.[26] The problem is exacerbated by the Russian press's publication of alleged prices for nuclear materials in Western countries.[27] Between 1,000 and 2,000 individuals have detailed knowledge of nuclear weapons design and another 3,000 to 5,000 have been directly involved in the production of plutonium and enrichment of uranium in the former Soviet Union.[28] Money is not the only possible way for scientists to be recruited: Aum Shinrikyo attracted Russian scientists' and research students' attention through vast donations to leading facilities. They then attempted to persuade them to join the cult itself. They partially succeeded, having a follower who worked in the I. V. Kurchatov Institute of Atomic Energy and another in the Mendeleyev Chemical Institute, a facility that researched nerve gas, amongst other things.[29] However, the majority of scientists that are moving are doing so to states that already possess a nuclear capability, such as Israel or China, and are intent on upgrading the quality of that capability.[30] Such vertical proliferation is a major global concern, but is not of immediate importance to the issue of nuclear terrorism since it involves a level of complexity and sophistication well beyond any foreseeable terrorist objective. It is also questionable whether terrorist organisations, intent on maintaining tight security, would want to risk using a mercenary scientist, no matter what their expertise or the amount they were being paid since the information required to design and construct a crude nuclear device is so readily available that weapons scientists from the former Soviet Union are almost superfluous.[31] The greatest constraint on micro-proliferation remains the ability of groups to obtain sufficient fissile material.

The extent of nuclear trafficking, the so-called grey market, is much debated: a March 1996 General Accounting Office report linked lax control over fissile materials to several nuclear thefts and the threat of nuclear blackmail, but found no direct evidence of a market operating within the former Soviet Union.[32] This would suggest that the trade is still in its infancy and has yet to be firmly established, that it is still a series of opportunistic bilateral deals, but in fact, there has yet to be a single unequivocal example of stolen nuclear materials reaching a *bona fide* customer.[33] Of 278 radioactive theft incidents recorded by the Russian MVD between January 1992 and December 1995, only eight involved a purchase, in each case to a middleman.[34] When Aum was investigating methods of developing a nuclear device (in 1993 they sought a meeting with Russian Minister of nuclear energy, Viktor Mikhailov, possibly to enquire about the cost of a nuclear warhead, but their request for a meeting was denied), they eventually sought to acquire the fissile material in the form of natural uranium from Australia. Given Aum's vast wealth, and their excellent contacts with Russian security forces and dealers in black-market arms, it seems almost inconceivable that they did not seek an alternative source of the fissile material first, and yet they evidently failed in this quest.[35] However, that there have been no unequivocal cases of a transaction involving stolen fissile material may be as much a reflection of our ability to apprehend these smugglers as the absence of such a market.[36] There clearly are states (and maybe sub-state actors), such as Iran, that would be willing buyers for such material. Equally, there is solid evidence of individuals who have been able to obtain such material, but who have little contact with buyers. It is these individuals that have been caught as they tried to find a market for their product. The real risk, in terms of a market developing, comes from middlemen willing to exploit an individual's access to sources of material and also having contacts with buyers. The obvious candidates for such a role would be ex-KGB or intelligence agents, the military or organised crime in Russia.[37]

It has been suggested that the purported market is composed almost exclusively of non-weapons-grade material or a situation artificially created by journalists and security service personnel setting up sting operations,[38] the notable example being the case of the seizure of 350 grams of atomic fuel at Munich airport on 10 August, 1994.[39] There is little doubt that the quantities of non-weapons-grade material being trafficked are increasing[40] and that it currently forms the bulk of the market.[41] It is also important to note that it is only in bomb-building that the quality of material is crucial; radiological terrorism would be just as effective using industrial-grade material as weapons-grade. While it is possible that the market has been inflated in Germany, where most of these supposed sting operations have occurred, there is increasing evidence that there are several more conduits into the West which have grown in significance, as the profile of the German one has risen and thus decreased its usefulness to nuclear smugglers. Progressively more and more material is being brought through southern routes rather than through Eastern Europe. Traditional routes for smuggling a range of other goods are being utilised for the nuclear traffic. John Deutch, former Director of Central Intelligence, testifying before a Senate Committee on 20 March 1996, stated:

> The countries of Central Asia and the Caucasus – Kazakhstan, Armenia, Azerbaijan, Kyrgyzstan, and Uzbekistan – form transit links between Asia and the West, and the Middle East and the West. The break-up of the Soviet Union has resulted in the breakdown of the institutions that kept many smugglers and questionable traders out of this region...According to anecdotal information from recent travellers to these areas, anything can go across the borders in these countries for a minimal price.[42]

Peshawar, on the Pakistani border with Afghanistan, is one centre for this trade. There is a thriving market for nuclear equipment, some of it of weapons-making calibre, stolen from reactors and military installations within the former Soviet republics. Goods on offer are reputed to include ultra-powerful magnets, catalysts and alloys to make thermo-nuclear devices and enriched uranium. Iran, India and Pakistan are all alleged to be buyers, and there is the added risk of terrorists also making use of the Peshawar market: religious extremists from Algeria, Kashmir, Egypt and Sudan used Peshawar as a back base in the war between the Soviet Union and the mujahedin. Many are still there. A great deal of the material available in the town is fake: worthless but dangerous radioactive waste passed off as enriched uranium.[43] At least some of the smuggling is concealed under legitimate exports, for example, shipments of cesium-137, correctly labelled and with the required paperwork, may also include a quantity of illicit nuclear material. Such practices form an important part of the criminal proliferation in the former Soviet Union.[44]

It would be an exaggeration to suggest that there has been no weapons-grade material trafficked: since 1992 there have been at least six examples of such trade. In 1992, an employee stole 3.7 pounds of HEU from the Luch Scientific Production Association at Podolsk in Russia. Around 1.8kg of material enriched to 30 per cent U-235 was stolen from two fuel assemblies at a facility of the Northern Fleet naval base at Andreeva Guba in July 1993 by two naval servicemen. In November 1993, a Russian Navy captain stole about ten pounds of HEU from the Murmansk submarine fuel storage facility. German police discovered 5.6 grams of supergrade plutonium in Tengen and then 0.8 grams of HEU in Landshut in May and June 1994. In December 1994, Czech police seized six pounds of HEU in Prague.[45] It is worth making two further points, based in part on comparisons with drug trafficking: physical detection measures are not infallible, generally, those caught trafficking drugs are the ones who are less experienced or competent at it, the good ones are much more likely to get through; and drug seizure rates vary between 10 and 40 per cent, even if the nuclear seizure rate was well above that, the probability that some goes undetected is considerable.[46] The strict comparability of the drugs example is debatable: nuclear smuggling is likely to be much smaller in volume and receive a much higher priority than drugs do; but the comparison is at least suggestive.[47]

There are several different varieties of nuclear trafficker currently operating. Most of the detected smuggling so far has been by

amateurs simply trying to make some fast money.[48] These amateurs
are almost invariably opportunists: they rarely have past criminal
records, links to organised crime or illegal business involvement.
Instead, they tend to be employees or former employees of the
nuclear-industrial complex, linked to such an insider, or live in the
vicinity of a vulnerable facility.[49] They also rarely have a customer in
mind at the time of the diversion or theft; rather, they have been
willing to seize their chance and then seek a buyer.[50] They are often
people who are desperate to find a way to maintain their livelihoods.
The situation at the Zvezda repair yard gives a good indication of
their plight. There, striking workers, frustrated at their inability to
force the Russian government to pay their overdue wages, threatened
to sabotage the nuclear submarines at the yard.[51] It would be quite
plausible to believe that these workers might, given the opportunity,
also resort to theft of the available nuclear material. A more sophisticated group are those opportunist entrepreneurs and business
people who regard trafficking as simply an extension of their legitimate activities. The Russian Internal Affairs Ministry Economic
Crimes division has reported that, of the 172 people arrested for
nuclear smuggling in 1993, ten were directors of small commercial
enterprises and two were low-level employees of the same firms.
These dealers have export licences and Western bank accounts and
trade legally and illegally in goods such as oil, weapons or rare materials. Nuclear trafficking is simply a highly profitable sideline, one
done primarily on consignment.[52]

The extent of the Russian Mafiya's role in nuclear trafficking is
hard to assess: it would increase the likelihood of a crackdown on the
sector as a whole and offers relatively low incentives for them, especially while other activities such as drugs smuggling are so lucrative,
providing an easily accessible mass market and little physical danger
from the materials.[53] Although the Russian authorities have made
numerous arrests of individuals with links to organised crime
attempting to smuggle non-weapons-grade nuclear material, there is
little evidence currently that large organised crime groups *per se*, with
established structures and international connections, are involved in
the trafficking of radioactive materials.[54] This appears to have been
a largely economic decision: there is a more clearly established
market for dual-use isotopes and non-fissile material and the mafiya
have been involved in the trade of these. There appears to be only
one clear-cut case of organised criminal involvement with fissile
material trafficking: in 1993 a Volgograd businessman offered 2.5kg

of highly-enriched uranium to a gang based in the Central Volga region to pay off a debt he owed to them. The gang sought buyers in the Baltic states and Europe, but, unable to find any, refused to accept the material as payment for the debt.[55]

These organisations do possess the means to acquire nuclear materials by threats or bribery and, almost certainly, the network to move them out of the country.[56] Russian organised crime is a series of networks encompassing criminals, businessmen, politicians, bureaucrats, security and military personnel, who between them are more than capable of moving stolen fissile material without Western intelligence forces ever being aware of the fact. The relative ease with which this could be achieved suggests that it would be extremely rash to wholly exclude the possibility of organised crime being involved in nuclear trafficking and certainly not as the result of any moral strictures.[57]

Amongst those best able to engage in nuclear smuggling are former Soviet bloc military and intelligence personnel, some of whom spent their Cold War careers moving material and technology from West to East, and now find themselves, using the same methods, able to simply reverse the route.[58] Like the scientists of the former Soviet Union, many military personnel greatly resent the deterioration in standards of living, budgets and social status, and might be willing to exploit the lax security surrounding fissile material.[59] In October 1996, Russian defence minister, General Igor Rodionov warned that the army was demoralised and on the brink of revolt over unpaid salaries and poor conditions. Furthermore, this state of affairs applied equally to the strategic rocket forces (SRF), the section of the army responsible for security of Russia's nuclear armoury.[60] Given their poor work conditions, there is no substantial reason to believe that personnel responsible for Russia's WMD are more reliable than the demonstrably corrupt military officials assigned to other duties.[61] There are already several examples of military personnel using their access to nuclear material for their profit. On 29 November 1993, Lieutenant-Colonel Alexei Tikhomirov of the Russian Navy and Oleg Baranov, deputy administrator of the Polyarnyy submarine base, stole 4kg of uranium from the Navy's nuclear weapons and fuel store in Murmansk, in the hope of selling it for $50,000. Lieutenant Dimitri Tikhomirov, Alexei's brother and in charge of a nuclear reactor, helped them handle the fuel. The thieves walked through a hole in the perimeter fence, forced the padlock on the fuel-store door, and stole three fuel rods containing uranium 235 enriched to 20 per cent. The theft was not discovered until twelve hours later, by which time Tikhomirov and Baranov had smuggled the fuel into the top-security Polyarnyy naval base where it was stored in Baranov's garage for seven months, until Dimitri got drunk and boasted to fellow officers, when the three were arrested.[62] The theft would have taken even longer to detect were it not for the fact that the thieves left the door to the warehouse open. Otherwise, it 'could have been concealed for ten years or longer'.[63]

The main buyers for nuclear material are almost certainly pariah states eager to take a shortcut towards nuclear programmes of their own. Although there is currently little hard evidence to decisively prove the existence of this market, in view of the expense and time required to develop a nuclear capability, it seems unlikely that states would decline the opportunity to ease the process by acquiring fissile material.[64] There is decisive evidence that both Iran and Iraq sought to illicitly obtain other items of use to a nuclear weapons programme, so it is illogical to suppose that they would scorn the opportunity to obtain fissile material.[65] Weapons-grade material is not sold on the open market, so states are compelled to produce their own or to acquire the material illicitly. The purchase of such material would probably save proliferator states between eight and ten years on their weapons programmes and, in view of the time and facilities required for manufacture, improve the chances of maintaining the secrecy of the project.[66] It seems unlikely, though, that this will replace proliferator states' normal process of hidden weapon acquisition; states will use the black market to facilitate the indigenous development of a nuclear capability rather than as a substitute for it. States derive considerable regional and international leverage from their nuclear programmes and are unlikely to be willing to abandon them in favour of an external supply system that is bound to be unpredictable and unreliable, particularly when every effort is being made internationally to shut it down altogether.[67]

Whether this equates to an increased likelihood of state-sponsored nuclear terrorism is more problematic. The former Director General of MI5 has said that 'Some two dozen governments are currently trying to obtain such technology. A number of these countries sponsor or even practise terrorism, and we cannot rule out the possibility that these weapons could be used for that purpose.'[68] However, sponsoring states would have to be completely certain of plausible deniability in perpetuity for any terrorist attack, since the repercussions from states that have been the victim of an act of nuclear terrorism could be immense. Furthermore, having given a client terrorist group a nuclear weapon, the sponsor state has very little control over the group, and may even be subjected to blackmail by the organisation. This conclusion is emphasised by the experience of East Germany in sponsoring the actions of Illich Ramirez Sanchez (Carlos the Jackal) in the late 1970s and early 1980s. Markus Wolf, who controlled much of East Germany's foreign intelligence network, regarded Carlos as a liability, someone who 'disregarded all the rules of discretion, there-by endangering those who worked with him.' Wolf's main objective was

> getting him out of the country as soon as possible – no simple task. One of the most difficult aspects of liaison with terrorists like Carlos was that the power relationship between us and them had an unfortunate tendency to reverse itself. Originally, Carlos was grateful for assistance in organising his clandestine life. But once he sensed that we were less keen on his presence, his mood turned nasty. He began to make the same threats towards us that he carried out against enemy governments, warning those who tried to dissuade him from a visit that he would seek out East German targets abroad.[69]

Although state-sponsored nuclear terrorism is not impossible, particularly if a state found itself *in extremis,* it makes more sense to suggest that, having obtained fissile material, a state would use its own agencies to exploit the situation. Richard Falkenrath argues that unless a state could guarantee complete control over its client group, it is very unlikely that a state would use a terrorist organisation to deliver a nuclear device because the stakes are too high.[70] This is certainly true for a nuclear-yield weapon, but may not be so for radiological devices since it might be possible to ensure that such a weapon dispersed radiation covertly, minimising the risk of detection. Whether a state would choose to utilise such a capability is another question, but it is not inconceivable, although its effects would almost certainly be long-term, rather than instantaneous, so would be more likely to be a form of extended punishment than a means of leverage for the terrorists. States seek membership of 'the nuclear club' primarily for the security, prestige and the leverage that it conveys on a regional and global level, rather than for the overt intention of imminently using the new capability. It is worth noting, as an analogue, that while there are a number of states that sponsor terrorism and have a chemical or biological weapons capability, there is little evidence that there has been biological or chemical terrorism by sub-state actors as a result.

While state-sponsored groups potentially have many advantages in terms of resources, the real danger from an intelligence and incident aversion perspective comes from groups such as Aum Shinrikyo or loosely affiliated splinters of larger organisations, such as the bombers of the Murrah Building in Oklahoma, because they come from nowhere. Aum 'just weren't on anyone's radar screens'.[71] As yet, there is little evidence that terrorist groups are buyers in their own right,[72] although if the flow of nuclear materials out of Russia continues, it is probably only a matter of time before a well-resourced organisation is able to become a purchaser. Such a group need not be state-sponsored: the Aum Shinrikyo cult had a billion dollars and 40,000 members spread worldwide.[73] John Deutch has stated: 'We currently have no evidence that any terrorist organization has obtained contraband nuclear materials. However, we are concerned because only a small amount of material is necessary to terrorize populated areas.'[74]

It is worth noting though that it would be unwise to assume that cost alone is likely to be the determining factor that precludes terrorist groups from acquiring fissile material. Although Aum were certainly exceptional, in terms of their assets, an increasing number of terrorist organisations are self-funded. This is as a result of two, interrelated trends: first, the amount of state-sponsorship for terrorism has decreased dramatically with the end of the Cold War and the declining necessity for surrogate warfare in other states; and second, to compensate, terrorist groups have become increasingly involved in racketeering and transnational crime. The Revolutionary Armed Forces of Colombia (FARC), has been heavily involved in drug trafficking. A study of Colombian guerrilla finances found that they had doubled between 1991 and 1994, with drugs contributing 34 per cent of the income, extortion and robbery 26 per cent and kidnappings 23 per cent.[75] The IRA has been involved in social clubs, charities, gaming and fraud to supplement its finances.[76] Many of these activities are international: the Liberation Tigers of Tamil Eelam are allegedly involved in fraud, extortion, alien smuggling and drug trafficking in Canada, all to aid their cause in Sri Lanka.[77] It is increasingly obvious that 'the links between war and crime are growing stronger in the 1990s.' The connection between the two types of illegal organisation stems, in part, from the increased accessibility of international crime for terrorists, arising from easier travel, communications and money-laundering in the modern world. Sometimes, terrorism itself has become a source of income: both the IRA and the UDA have construction rackets that largely determine which firms receive the building contracts (in exchange for a kick-back) to reconstruct the areas of Belfast wrecked by the two groups' violence.[78]

Whether this equates to terrorist groups having considerable disposable income, and therefore being potential buyers of fissile material, is questionable. It seems likely that it is the largest, most sophisticated groups that are able to exploit these opportunities. For others, it probably remains that terrorism is an expensive occupation, especially for underground organisations, needing to support members who are unlikely to be able to have another form of income. Rather than building up their assets, most groups seem to lead a relatively hand-to-mouth financial existence, dictated by immediate operational needs, as well as the prerequisite of maintaining the group as a viable organisation.

## NUCLEAR TERRORISM

Prior to 1989, the literature on nuclear terrorism dealt with the subject from two main perspectives: the means by which terrorists might be able to 'go nuclear', and the reasons that might compel them to use or to reject such a possibility. With the end of the Cold War, the dynamics that underpinned the answers to both of these questions have altered considerably. Not only have the means by which sub-state actors could acquire fissile material changed, but the nature and motivations of terrorism itself have also changed. In the 1990s, there has been a growth in terrorism perpetrated by groups that cannot be readily pigeon-holed as nationalist-separatist, left-wing, right-wing, religious or any of the other typologies that were effective in describing varieties of group. In every case, examples of these types still exist, but supplementing these have been other types of organisation, such as Aum Shinrikyo, the bombers of the Murrah Building in Oklahoma City, or the *ad hoc* group, led by Ramzi Yousef, responsible for the attack on the World Trade Center in 1993, that do not easily fit into an existing category. In the past, several terrorist groups talked about resorting to nuclear weapons, but were, in general, conservative in their tactics and in the levels of violence they were willing to use to pursue their goals. The newer groups have not only been more violent, they have also been more innovative, and more willing to use new types of weaponry. Furthermore, they have, in many cases, been unconstrained by considerations of proportionality or the need to appeal to an audience for support, factors that have previously been critical in ensuring that terrorist groups used a measure of self-restraint.[79] It is therefore valid to question not only whether the opportunities for nuclear terrorism have changed, but also whether the desire of terrorist groups to perpetrate such attacks has altered after the Cold War. The question of why terrorists might resort to nuclear weapons, beyond the increased opportunities for doing so, remain to some extent, unaddressed. This book attempts to analyse the nature of terrorism in the post-Cold War world. The issue of nuclear terrorism acts as a catalyst for this study. The book shows that while nuclear terrorism is important and remains a critical threat, even if the increased opportunities for fissile proliferation did not exist, the nature of contemporary terrorism would mean that mass-destructive terrorism would still be a problem. In order to achieve this, the book will, having already discussed the increased opportunities for terrorists to 'go nuclear', concentrate on the desirability, from the terrorist's perspective, of doing so.

By examining the psychology of terrorists and terrorism, both from an individual and an organisational perspective, using the theoretical literature and comparing it to empirical examples, this book draws conclusions about the reasons that people join and remain within terrorist groups, as well as the pressures that are exerted on the group to escalate the levels of violence that they employ. The concept of political violence as the result of some set personality or terrorist type is dismissed, but it is argued that leaders do play an important role in determining the character of the group. The nature of terrorist groups is that they make dissent and exiting extremely difficult, and deflect responsibility for actions onto others, so that it is easier to remain within the organisation and accept its use of violence. Furthermore, violence is the activity that sets the group apart, it gives the organisation its identity, so any attempt to alter that is extremely difficult.

The tactics and targeting decisions of terrorist organisations are then considered, using the psychological insights gained from the previous chapter and comparing them to a rational, instrumental perspective of why groups use the methods they do and the basis for that decision. Although terrorism is not an effective means of achieving strategic political objectives, except in the historical case of colonial campaigns, groups that use it are often unable to resort to alternative strategies, for the reasons that are outlined above. Consequently, as the group begins to fail and face the possibility of defeat, it will often favour escalating the level of violence that it employs, believing it to be the best means of recapturing their advantage.

The book then considers the case of religious terrorism, arguing that it offers a unique legitimising force for violence, one that is increasing in importance as a justification and that is the most probable motivating force for an act of mass-destructive terrorism. It analyses how the divinely ordained aspect of this terrorism makes it more absolutist and less constrained by secular morality than is the case for other types of terrorist group. The two varieties, secular and religious, are compared and some key similarities in their organisational dynamics are discussed. The chapter concludes by considering messianic violence that is especially relevant to mass-destructive terrorism since, in some cases, it may promote the use of extreme levels of violence to hasten the end of the world and the salvation of the messianic adherents.

The study then discusses politically motivated terrorism, from both the right and the left sides of the political spectrum. Right-wing terrorism is subdivided into conservative violence and radical violence, the latter of which is the increasingly prevalent variety. The perpetrators, motivations, and group dynamics of the two types are then compared with the conclusions derived from the previous chapter on psychology and the importance of split delegitimisation, the belief that the government and the undesirable sections of society that they seek to protect are enemies, is noted. The section concludes that, although most right-wing terrorism is instrumental, amongst groups, notably White Supremacists in the United States, where religion is also important to their beliefs, the likelihood of mass-destructive violence is much greater. This is supported by the fact that it is precisely amongst such groups that most attempted cases of non-conventional terrorism have occurred in the United States.

In contrast, although left-wing groups are the least likely to engage in high-level nuclear terrorism, it is anti-nuclear groups that have been responsible for most low-level nuclear acts to date. This phenomenon of single-issue terrorism is examined and is connected to other forms of radical leftist violence. As with each of the other main types of terrorism, the motivations, psychology and dynamics of left-wing groups are discussed. Of particular importance is their self-perception as the just protectors of the people and the environment against the forces of imperialist big business and government. This is key because it means that such groups tend to be self-limiting, making an act of nuclear terrorism from such a group very unlikely, since they emphasise the proportionality and justice of their cause and so would believe that an act of mass terror would be counter-productive and unjust.

The book's final chapter draws together the elements already discussed and considers their implications for nuclear terrorism. It begins by discussing the feasibility of constructing a nuclear-yield device from fissile material and decides that, though not impossible, it still would be a difficult task. Radiological terrorism is then considered as an alternative to a nuclear-yield device, since it would offer many of the same benefits to the terrorists without the same difficulty in acquiring the material and constructing a nuclear-yield bomb. The chapter then discusses the changing nature of modern terrorism, asking whether there are circumstances in which terrorists might want to kill as many people as possible, and whether a nuclear weapon was likely to be the way that this could be achieved. The conservative attitude of many terrorist groups towards weaponry and tactics is noted and contrasted with the increasing lethality of terrorism itself. Previous cases of nuclear terrorism are noted and then chemical and biological weapons are considered as alternatives to nuclear weapons. The conclusion is that while nuclear-yield weapons remain unlikely, radiological ones are more plausible. However, the changing nature of terrorism and in particular, the increased importance of religion as a motivation, makes a full nuclear attack impossible to discount completely. The book's ultimate conclusion is that, although counter-proliferation measures may help the immediate problem and lessen the risk of nuclear terrorism stemming from the collapse of the Soviet Union, the changing nature of terrorism, and the constant escalatory pressures on individuals and groups within terrorist organisations, means that the problem and the threat of mass-destructive violence will remain, even after the present proliferation danger has been mitigated.

# 2 Terrorism: Psychological and Instrumental Approaches

Terrorism is an extraordinary and extreme form of political behaviour; its historical, political, economic, religious and social causes are far from clear, but it does seem apparent that a major influence is the individual psychology of those who perpetrate such acts. However, terrorism is extremely diffuse, making it questionable whether any single psychological theory of the phenomenon could be sufficiently comprehensive so as to include the vast variety. The basis of terrorism extends ideologically from revolution or national self-determination to defence of the status quo; structurally from centralised and hierarchical to a near anarchical model; methods and targeting vary from group to group and even within the same group over time. Moreover, the motivations for terrorism may be quite different across cultures, what drives an individual in Northern Ireland to join the IRA differs from that which drove someone in Germany to join the RAF, so is likely to vary just as significantly from someone in the Middle East joining Abu Nidal's organisation or someone in Peru joining Sendero Luminoso. Crenshaw has argued that political and social context are as important in determining terrorist's actions.[1] While this context is vital, it is the psychological explanation for terrorist actions that this section will focus on, along with the implications of that for acts of mass-destructive terrorism.

It is important to note at the outset that there are considerable differences in the psychological pressures and motivations of initiating a campaign of terrorism and continuing one, and, furthermore, the idea of being a terrorist is not a straightforward one: it is not necessary to have physical interaction with victims to be a terrorist. Most organised groups also consist of individuals involved in finance, logistics, propaganda, or weapons-building, to name only a few of the activities besides violence. There are several categories of member within ETA, each of which has a vital role to play in the preservation and support of the organisation. However, relatively few *etarras* carry weapons and even fewer have been involved in activities that could clearly be defined as 'terrorist'.[2] Such individuals are clearly still terrorists, but does their psychological motivation differ from those that are involved in violent acts? They are terrorists by association, but does that mean that they share the guilt that those terrorists involved in violent acts have to deal with?[3]


## INDIVIDUAL PSYCHOLOGY

Terrorist acts appear unnecessarily violent to the outside observer, because they target seemingly innocent and random victims. Consequently, there is a tendency to seek explanations that set the terrorist apart from other people, to assume that the terrorist is unusual simply because the acts they commit are in that they break the 'rules of engagement'. There is a tendency to give labels to terrorists and their actions: Dominic McGlinchey, former leader of the INLA, was known as the 'Mad Dog';[4] Tim McVeigh, bomber of the Murrah Building in Oklahoma, has been described as a 'monster'.[5] A practical example of the dangers of attempting to dehumanise terrorists is provided by Menachem Begin, Irgun's leader. When British security forces raided his flat, they found two pictures of him, one that bore a fair resemblance to him, the second of which did not. They chose to disseminate the second photograph because the first made him look 'more or less human'. The result was that Begin, unrecognisable from his picture, was able to continue to walk the streets with some degree of impunity.[6] However, it appears that terrorists often do follow rules but not necessarily the ones that might be deemed 'conventional' by most people. Even within the bounds of conventional rules, acts of extreme violence are not invariably regarded as abnormal or unacceptable: the cases of warfare or self-defence are both examples of this and both are frequently used by terrorists as justifications for their acts.[7] The key difference is that in conventional morality, justifications such as self-defence or war require an element of proportionality to be acceptable, the idea of 'reasonable force'. Terrorist morality is more likely to be absolutist and therefore to lack this component, so that the end can be made to justify the means in a way that is not possible, certainly using Judaeo-Christian morality. This emphasis on proportionality means that it would be difficult to justify an act of mass-destructive violence with such conventional constraints. By contrast, the absolutist terrorist's focus on results over methods makes it impossible to completely rule out any action, including nuclear terrorism, no matter how heinous, purely on the basis of morality. This is because, as Bandura argues, by rationalising their actions as warfare, the terrorist is able to ensure that killing is free from self-censoring restraints by 'cognitively restructuring the moral value of killing'.[8] This task is eased if, through the moral sanction of violent means, people are able to see themselves as battling against violent oppressors; non-violent means of opposition have been ineffective; and the suffering caused by these terrorist counter-attacks can be portrayed as less than that inflicted by the enemy. The end is the key; the means secondary. Margolin is right to emphasise 'not so much the normality of terrorism (which it clearly is not) but its susceptibility to the normal rules controlling behaviour'.[9] The psychology governing terrorist behaviour is applicable to other people; terrorist acts however, are still far from conventional behaviour. Terrorism is abnormal, terrorists are not: they conform to psychological rules and can thus be analysed in such terms.

If there is a risk of over generalisation in dealing with psychological explanations for terrorism, there is also the danger of reductionism, of finding mono-casual explanations for the phenomenon. Psychologists who have written on the subject of terrorism are in general agreement that there is no common 'terrorist personality'; and, in fact, terrorism is as much a result of group interaction as of individual choice.[10] Post argues that while there was no set terrorist 'type', a number of personality traits did occur frequently amongst individuals involved in terrorism, notably that of 'splitting'. This is characteristic of people whose personality development has been shaped by psychological damage during childhood, they have a damaged self-image and never wholly reconcile the 'good' and 'bad' aspects of their nature. Instead they split it into what 'is me' and that which is 'not me', projecting all their weaknesses onto others. They seek an external target to blame for all their inadequacies, gaining satisfaction and respite by being able to believe that 'it's not my fault'[11] and this is a trait that is frequently found in the terrorists' own explanations of their actions. Irgun, the group responsible for the bombing of the King David Hotel in Jerusalem, on 22 July 1946, planned to give enough time for the hotel to be evacuated. They issued bomb warnings to the hotel, the Palestine Post and the French Consulate. Furthermore, since the bombers became involved in a gun fight with British forces shortly after planting the device, the British could reasonably have been expected to believe that the threats were genuine. However, the hotel was not evacuated and 91 people were killed and 45 injured.[12] Maria

McGuire, in many respects an IRA moderate, described an attack in 1971 in which there were widespread civilian casualties. The IRA blamed the security forces in Belfast for failing to clear the area quickly enough; the security services blamed the IRA for giving a deliberately ambiguous warning; McGuire believed that the result was due to a misunderstanding, that the IRA's aim was not to deliberately cause casualties in this case. Her description also shows the connection between action and audience and the way that many terrorists assess the success of an operation, in terms of its impact on the audience: 'I did not connect with the people who were killed or injured in such explosions. I always judged such deaths in terms of the effect they would have on our support – and I felt this in turn depended on how many people accepted our explanation.'[13] This is an important aspect of terrorism because, as will be discussed later, it is this awareness of the consequences of such acts on terrorist support that, to some extent, determines the levels of violence that the terrorist is willing to employ. The constraints that mitigate against highly lethal acts of terrorism are therefore not moral, so much as political and instrumental.

Taylor and Quayle state that 'the violence and damage the terrorist inflicts is the result not of a personality trait or disposition, but of an act of some form – a behaviour … responses to circumstances and forces.' It is terrorist actions that are the key defining factor, rather than a psychological profile that is specific to terrorists.[14] They do not have traits that are unique to those who commit acts of political violence, instead, it is necessary to regard such acts as stemming from individuals who are psychologically normal. There is widespread consensus that the overwhelming majority of terrorists are not mentally ill, abnormal, psychopaths or even especially psychologically disposed towards violence. One possible and high-profile exception to this may be Kozo Okamoto, one of the JRA members responsible for the Lod Airport attack in May 1972. While he was declared sane to stand trial for the attack, he exhibited indications of a 'death wish' and 'survival guilt', repeatedly stating that he only wanted to die after his capture. Kozo treated his trial as a propaganda opportunity for the proletarian revolution against the bourgeoisie. His statement ended:

> When I was a child, I was told that when people died they became stars. I didn't really believe it, but I could appreciate it. We three Red Army soldiers wanted to become Orion when we died. And it calms my heart that all the people we killed will also become stars

in the same heavens. As the revolution goes on, how the stars will multiply!

To some extent, this reflects the Japanese Buddhist tradition that an individual's life and death are merely stations in the greater continuum of human existence, that life is only meaningful in its social context, not in the individual's experience. This would have made his sacrifice of life easier to rationalise, it was a by-product of the act rather than being the aim in itself. Although it is possible to partially rationalise Kozo's attitude, his statement, along with the fact that he attempted to circumcise himself with a pair of scissors whilst in prison, must cast serious doubts on his sanity.[15] While an individual must be oriented towards terrorism, to some extent, they are selected by existing members of the group. The covert and illegal nature of terrorism makes it unlikely that such an unstable individual would knowingly be chosen. A mentally ill member of a terrorist group would be a 'loose cannon', a security threat that endangered the entire group. Sam Melville 'played' at being a terrorist, storing dynamite at his home. He consistently broke his own rules on not discussing terrorist activities or using friend's houses as addresses for illegal activities that could have led to the whole group being traced. His violence was impulsive: he unilaterally planted a bomb at the Marine Midland Bank in New York. When Alpert asked him why he had chosen Marine Midland, his response was: 'No particular reason. I just walked around Wall Street until I found a likely-looking place.' He had merely planted the bomb at random. Unsurprisingly, his actions appalled the other members of his group.[16] Therefore, it is logical that most terrorist groups would avoid recruiting such a person; although it is possible that in cell-based organisations with less central control, it would be harder for the group to exercise such a stringent hold over recruitment, making it possible that a psychopath could become a member of the group. A further exception might be Eliahu Giladi, a leader of LEHI, who according to Shamir:

was perhaps the only one of us who was, by nature, an extremist, a fanatic, a man free of the fetters of personal loyalties or ordinary sentiments, who found it difficult to function within any framework or discipline...

He was not a traitor or an informer, but he was irrational. I waited for him to change, for the dreadful fantasies to leave him, but he went on, talking icily about the need to kill... I decided that

we couldn't go on like that; Giladi was too dangerous to the movement. The circumstances being what they were [most members of
the organisation were in prison], there weren't many people I could
talk to freely, but I did speak to two or three of my colleagues and
the next day the decision was made – and carried out.

However, these cases are unusual: Shamir in the same passage
says: 'I tried to find out what happened in other underground groups,
other resistance movements, but never found a parallel.'[17] The
nature of most terrorism is that it involves long periods of inaction
interspersed with bouts of activity. It therefore requires reflective
rather than impulsive violence and the ability to delay gratification
derived from activity through the long and dull planning stages that
characterise the preparation for an attack in most organised terrorist groups. It is doubtful whether such inactivity would appeal greatly,
or satisfy the psychological needs of a psychopath, even were they to
join a terrorist group. Taylor and Quayle distinguish between hostile
and instrumental aggression. The former was a spontaneous upsurge
of emotion and anger whereas the latter referred to aggression as a
means towards some other end, it was calculated and usually a deliberate policy for a specific goal. Most terrorist acts fall into this
second category; they are born not of frustration but of planning.
They argue that aggression, like any behaviour, can be learned, that
it is related to its consequences, and that when it is rewarded, by
media attention for example, then it occurs more frequently.[18] Post
suggests that individuals are drawn to the path of terrorism because
it gives an opportunity to commit acts of violence and they are
psychologically compelled to commit these acts in order to exorcise
the enemy within.[19] Jane Alpert says that her terrorism 'stemmed as
much from a longing for acceptance as from a passion to rebel, as
much from the kinds of relationships I formed in childhood as from
my outrage at the United States government'.[20] Post too believes that
most terrorism is not a result of terrorists being psychopathic or
psychotic, and that most terrorists are 'normal', the factors governing behaviour in most people can still be applied to terrorists.[21]
Taylor notes that:

> [An] important difference between the psychopath and the terror-
> ist is that ... for the psychopath, the purposiveness of the behaviour
> if it exists, is essentially personal. This is clearly not the case for the
> terrorist.[22]

Although most terrorists are 'normal' psychologically, some do display schizoid tendencies: McDonald cites the example of the ETA member, Amaia, who denied being responsible for people's deaths yet in the next sentence said that she was pleased to have killed 'the bastards'.[23] Such examples of 'splitting' do not necessarily reflect mental instability, but the individual's means of dealing with the effects of their actions: by separating its results from the credit for the action, the terrorist is able to derive the necessary satisfaction without having to overcome the guilt associated with it. Such traits certainly do not correspond to any tendency towards psychopathy in the overwhelming majority of terrorists that operate within groups. This is important for nuclear terrorism because it largely dispels the scenario, so beloved of film-makers and novelists, that an act of nuclear terrorism would be the work of some maniacal individual, intent on either dominating the world or holding it to ransom. Terrorism, especially nuclear terrorism, is more likely to be conducted for limited political (rather than purely financial) gains and to require the resources of a group of psychologically normal individuals.

Far from being psychopathic, Knutson found that many terrorists were 'psychologically non-violent'.[24] They spent a great deal of their efforts in attempting to avoid the ultimate responsibility for deaths by transferring the guilt onto an external source and in planning their actions so that while violence was threatened, it was rarely actually used. They saw terrorism as a last resort, an act of personal futility when all other options had been exhausted. However, there is a difficulty here in separating motivation from rationalisation, the idea of 'we had no choice' as a justification for their actions. In seeking to displace responsibility, they sought to view their activities as arising from the dictates of authorities, not from their own volition; they are an instrument, not the cause of the violence, so are freed from self-censorship for it.[25] Begin applied an almost existential aspect to the Irgun's decision to resort to violence:

> ...we steeled our hearts against doubts, and against alternative 'solutions.'
> What use was there in writing memoranda? What value in speeches?...No, there was no other way. If we did not fight we should be destroyed. To fight was the only way to salvation.
> ...There are times when everything in you cries out: your very self-respect as a human being lies in your resistance to evil.
> We fight therefore we are![26]

Knutson's observations apply only to some terrorists: Morf found a fascination with violence amongst members of the FLQ[27] and Bollinger amongst West German groups. Members of the organisations showed unconscious aggressive tendencies and the group provided an outlet for these emotions that stemmed from personal feelings of inadequacy and inferiority.[28] Kaplan suggests that: 'terrorism is a response to a lack of self-esteem'.[29] However, it seems that Sean O'Callaghan is more typical of terrorists. Describing his killing of Detective Inspector Peter Flanagan, of the RUC Special Branch, he said: 'I felt that he had been a legitimate target and that it was a job well done. But I do not think I enjoyed killing.'[30]

Erikson developed a theory linking an individual's psychology to society which helps explain the need of many terrorists to belong to a group, and which would reinforce the idea that being a terrorist is of secondary importance to membership of the organisation.[31] He argued that the concept of identity was the key; that personality developed through a series of childhood turning points that formed developmental stages. These crises could either be resolved or not, but if not, they could come back to dog the individual, especially in adolescence when they were seeking to find a stable identity. The earlier failure to establish trust, autonomy, initiative or industry would be a handicap in their search for a positive identity and could lead to confusion or a negative identity. Identity is rooted in the ethnic, family and national inheritance of an individual, based on collectivity and connected to historical circumstances. Erikson explored the need for 'fidelity', to have faith in something, the key role played by ideology as the guardian of identity.[32]

Erikson argued that the rage felt by individuals at being helpless was projected onto controlling figures and engendered feelings of guilt. Failure to achieve objectives could lead such individuals to suffer feelings of self-doubt, suspicion, shame, inferiority and incompetence that acted as a further handicap on their subsequent activities, leading to their underachieving again. Bollinger suggested that the act of joining a terrorist group represented the last attempt to establish an identity; in doing so, an individual was seeking purpose and identity from the organisation.[33] Often they would abandon their individual responsibilities and assume the collective identity of the group, enabling a feeling of belonging. Both Susan Stern, a member of the Weathermen organisation, and Michael Baumann, founder of the 2nd of June Movement in West Germany during the early 1970s, cite membership of the group as a key factor in their progression into political violence.[34] This is a vital point in an explanation of why individuals join a terrorist group and why they are able to commit terrorist acts: the group enables them to feel valued and omnipotent and express aggressive tendencies whilst neutralising any feelings of guilt through the intellectual and emotional justifications of the group. The individual's justification for terrorism is related at a fundamental psychological level to a sense of purpose and self worth.[35] The fact that belonging to a terrorist organisation may be a final attempt to establish identity by an individual means that it is entirely plausible to suggest that they believe that they have 'nowhere else to go'. This would certainly make the individual more willing to accept the absolutist perspective of the terrorist group and willing to justify the violent consequences of that.

Many terrorists have a 'negative identity', a vindictive rejection of the roles and norms considered desirable and proper by the individual's family and community. Having failed to achieve the objectives set, the individual prefers to be 'a bad person' rather than a nobody. If early steps towards acquisition of a negative identity are treated by society as final, then individuals may be railroaded into conformity with the worst that is expected of them, finding their refuge in radical groups that assure them of a degree of certainty, and forced into their choice by others' interpretation of their behaviour. The same effect can be seen to exist when governments put pressure on terrorist groups; they make the group into 'something' by being forced to recognise its presence, and narrow the choices of the group if it wishes to continue being so acknowledged. Media coverage is also vital, the life blood of terrorist organisations: the group is in constant need of reaffirmation of its existence and importance, and such coverage provides this. When the SLA kidnapped Patty Hearst:

> ... Cinque and his comrades could not hide their delight and illusions of grandeur over the widespread blast of publicity given to them in the press as a result of my kidnapping. I was their passport to fame and popularity ... It would all help spread the word of their revolutionary war against the government, they said, for 'the people' would now know that the oppressors could be engaged in open combat. It proved that they had been right all the time ...[36]

Begin also noted the key role of publicity for the campaign of the Irgun: 'The interest of the newspapers is the measure of the interest of the public. And the public – not only Jews but non-Jews too – were manifestly interested in the blows we were striking in Eretz Israel.' He suggested that this publicity was important not only for publicising the Irgun's cause, but because it precluded excessive measures being used to repress the revolt, the British being sensitive to world opinion.[37] Consequently, it might be possible to argue that in some circumstances, as far as some groups are concerned, adverse publicity is better than no publicity at all to maintain the existence of the group. If true, it would remove a major constraint from the actions of such groups because the consequences would be secondary in importance to the fact of having staged a publicly acknowledged attack. In such a case, the results would matter less than that it was spectacular and newsworthy. Given these criteria, a high level act of terrorism, such as a nuclear attack, would have considerable attractions for the group.

There is little doubt that nationalist-separatist terrorist groups, such as ETA or the IRA, differ considerably in this respect from anarchic-ideologue groups, such as the RAF. They have different degrees of negative identity, since it is quite possible that the former type will not be perceived wholly adversely in their own community, and that joining a terrorist group was an act of solidarity and commitment to the community into which an individual was born, although even in this case, the decision to be a terrorist would be an extreme one.[38] One clear exception to this is that of Armenian groups where the resort to violence is encouraged by embracing the concepts of martyrdom, armed struggle and the legacy of ancestors in pursuing the first two as central to the political and religious culture.[39] Even in this instance, in an Armenian diaspora of around 1.5 million, fewer than 150 people have been active members of the Justice Commandos, Armenian Revolutionary Army or Armenian Secret Army for the Liberation of Armenia (ASALA).[40] Some terrorist groups claiming to act on behalf of a minority community actually have almost no support there: the African-American community in the United States largely rejected the actions of the Black Panthers, even if sometimes in agreement with their grievances.[41] A third category, religious fundamentalist terrorists, is also crucially different since their intended audience of influence is not elite decision-makers, but the deity.[42] As with nationalist-separatist movements, their community may be sympathetic to their cause, even if it condemns their actions. In one sense, although the perception that they have at least some support is important, the actual level of support that a terrorist group enjoys is secondary to the belief that they are in the right and will ultimately be seen to be so. Yalin-Mor, a member of LEHI, provides an example of this:

I admit that in 1944 most Jews were quite satisfied with British rule in Palestine. They did business, they were quite well off. If you had taken a vote, perhaps eighty or ninety per cent would have given a good opinion of the British. But this was not the point. They were the alien power and we had to fight them to gain our freedom, whether they were liberal or inhuman.[43]

Providing that they believe themselves to be right and to be ahead of public opinion, terrorists may be willing to act against the prevailing popular consensus. Support and thus public opinion about a situation is important, and is a major restriction on extremes of terrorism, such as the use of nuclear weaponry, but it is not the sole factor in terrorists' rationalisation of how to conduct their campaign. Consequently, it would be unwise to assume that public opinion or support alone would determine or necessarily constrain the action of a terrorist group.

The anarchic-ideologue group remains most likely to be isolated from society and is far more likely to be seen in purely negative terms. It draws its strength from political ideals which provide both the goals to aim for and the justification for the methods to achieve that goal.[44] Even this represents something of an over generalisation since the degree to which a group exists 'underground' varies. Some, such as the RAF in West Germany, consist largely of professional terrorists who have no other employment and live concealed from the authorities; whilst others, such as the Red Cells, were 'part-time' terrorists. Obviously, the extent to which members of the group remain in touch with the outside world has implications for the amount of cohesion and solidarity that exists within the group. If the organisation is underground or in some other way isolated, then the members of the group will become increasingly dependent on one another for company and a release from the pressure the individual is experiencing in the highly stressful situation they are in. The group and its activities become the individual's life, all-encompassing in a way that is not the case if the individual has an existence beyond the group. In the former case, the individual increasingly focuses on, and identifies with, the group. This difference is also significant for the strategic choices that the group makes. Crenshaw suggests that part-time terrorists are less likely to use actions that require extensive planning whereas the costs of maintaining a professional terrorist group means that the organisation has to spend involved in fund-raising activities such as bank robberies.[45]

Knutson argued that negative identity reflects the values instilled early in life, that it reaffirms ethnic traditions and roots, and that it is unwise to blame all terrorist activity on individual difficulties with a positive identity. Many adolescents with a negative identity rebel socially, in their choice of clothes or music for example, but not politically. This may reflect their inner needs or a lack of opportunity to join a terrorist group, or it may show that there are more factors to be considered than simply whether or not an individual has difficulty with their identity. The resort to terrorism is not one but two decisions, firstly to break with society and secondly to join a group espousing political violence. They are not synonymous because many people achieve the former and not the latter; monks are just one example.[46] An additional trait in a number of terrorists has been their sense of being morally betrayed at a crucial stage in their development that formed the basis for an acute sensibility to perceived injustices by the establishment later. For members of the Baader-Meinhof gang, this betrayal was their parents' Nazi past. The early failure of their parents to prove worthy of the role model that was assigned to them led the members of the gang to violently oppose what their parents had stood for, and by extension, what the establishment stood for.[47] These circumstances are extreme and exceptional; however, the tendency for terrorists to feel that they have been betrayed is a frequent one. As well as occurring in individuals with anarchic-ideologue leanings, it is an aspect of nationalist-separatist terrorism. Leila Khaled argues that no Palestinian should ever forget 'the three historic days of betrayal...: the Balfour Declaration of November 2, 1917; the partition of Palestine, November 29, 1947; and the proclamation of the state of Israel, May 15, 1948.'[48]

Erikson argues that the individual who was unable to violently challenge their parents' authority at the time that they were a child may later try to overcome that fear by attacking external authorities such as the social and political elites.[49] Post suggests that there is a key difference here between anarchic-ideologue terrorists and those involved in nationalist-separatist movements. The latter reflected loyalty to parents who had been disloyal to the established regime, so was an effort to carry on the mission of elders who had been wounded by the regime. For them, terrorist acts represented a rite of passage, enabling them to be widely known in the community and even lionised.[50] It was only anarchic-ideologue terrorism that represented an attack on the parental generation who had been loyal to the regime. Where individuals were loyal to their parents' generation who in turn had been loyal to the regime, then terrorism rarely occurred.[51] Susan Stern, a member of the Weatherman Organisation, became involved in terrorism through the radical student movement of the late 1960s to which she had been introduced by her husband, Robby Stern. In the Autumn of 1965, she taught at a ghetto school in Syracuse which profoundly affected her view of society and its failings. In August 1967, she was introduced to the national organisers of the Students for Democratic Society (SDS), and, by August 1968, was working in their Los Angeles office. She attended the Democratic Convention in Chicago, and was one of those outside the Convention Hall involved in repeated clashes with Mayor Daly's police force. She became increasingly affiliated to the Progressive Labor faction within the SDS, which split from the rest of the SDS, forming the Seattle Weatherman in August 1969. By this time, Stern had participated in the Ave riots in Seattle's University District; and in the Days of Rage in Chicago, where she was arrested for assaulting a police officer. By the end of the year, the Weathermen were attacking university ROTCs; and had decided to go underground. From there, they organised further demonstrations and attacks on establishment targets connected with the Vietnam War.[52]

It is possible that terrorists are 'stress-seekers' who find terrorism attractive because it offers an element of danger.[53] When Susan Stern became a terrorist, she says: 'I knew that that part of my life was over. I would never again know how to be or want to be Susan Stern – student, housewife, potential mother.'[54] This would be significant for the likelihood of nuclear terrorism because it would mean that acts were primarily the result of an individual's internal rather than external imperatives; the factors that are the primary causes of terrorism stem predominantly from psychological motivations, rather than from socio-economic conditions or any other form of outside stimuli. More importantly, it would suggest that terrorism is escalatory, something that obviously would have great significance for the prospects for nuclear terrorism. Terrorists have to do increasingly difficult acts in order to satisfy their need.

Sullwold, a German psychologist, noted two types of terrorist leader: the extrovert who tended to be unstable, uninhibited, inconsiderate, self-interested and unemotional with a high tolerance for stress and a reluctance to accept responsibility for their actions; and the neurotically hostile who tended to be suspicious, defensive, intolerant, aggressive, to reject internal criticism and be hypersensitive to external criticism.[55] Abu Nidal, while a mixture of the two types, clearly displayed more aspects of the latter variety than the former. He is extremely violent and generates great fear, even amongst his own members; yet he is a fantasist who trusts no one and lives a secluded, self-protective life, with few of the trappings of his considerable success in his role. Although not materialistic, he is egotistic; as one acquaintance put it: 'For Abu Nidal, self is everything. When he feels personally threatened, he goes berserk.'[56] Cinque, leader of the SLA, displayed considerably more of the second group of tendencies. Hearst says that:

> He was the leader and never hesitated to remind you of that...he told us on several occasions that our top priority in this or any other action was to protect our leader. [He would say] 'I'm the black leadership of the SLA. Without me, you'd all be nothing. There'd be no revolution.'...To me, he seemed to be a strutting egomaniac, swilling plum wine most of the day...doing whatever he damn well pleased, while all the others struggled mightily to shape up to his fantasy of an elite army of revolutionary cadre.[57]

Not all terrorist leaders are as extreme in their behaviour as Cinque or Abu Nidal. Most of the founders and leaders of the Tupamaros in Uruguay were singularly mainstream. They mostly came from regular families and were recognised and respected members of the community. Although political militants, most of them began their involvement in one of the three major political parties in the country. For these leaders, many of them professionals of high repute that had actively and fully participated in other organisations prior to forming the Tupamaros, the resort to terrorism cannot be simply labelled as a search for identity or belonging. It seems to have been fired primarily by ideology. It was a conscious tactical decision based on the belief that the time for revolution was at hand and mounting frustration at the failure of their previous efforts to achieve their objectives.[58]

However, Weinberg and Eubank, in their study of Italian groups suggest that the notion of the leader as an entity emotionally and psychologically separate from ordinary members of the organisation may be problematic. Terrorist groups may be sufficiently unusual that leadership requires relatively few additional predispositions, in which case the fact of being a leader may reflect a particular situation or interaction that causes individuals to move from being followers. Another possibility is natural evolution: since many terrorist groups have a high turnover with members exiting the group, dying or being captured, it is possible that leadership comes to those who simply remain with the group longest. This hypothesis would particularly apply to organisations that exist over several generations of terrorists, but seems to be largely disproved by groups such as ETA or the IRA where leaders seem to be selected more on the basis of ability than longevity. The idea of leadership in itself is not straightforward: the role a leader has to play in a terrorist organisation depends to a large extent on the type of group. One variety of leadership might entail directing a small band in dangerous violent acts, while another might be to refine the group's political views and to manage its resources. The differences might mean that the psychology of leadership in terrorist groups was dependent more on the type of organisation and therefore the type of role played by the leader, than on simply the fact of being a terrorist leader.[59]

## GROUP PSYCHOLOGY

Terrorism, though, is not the act of individuals; it is committed by groups who reach collective decisions based on commonly held beliefs. While a few individuals do act alone to commit acts of violence with a political end in mind, such as the Unabomber in the United States, most terrorism is not the work of such people, but rather of groups; and it is the psychology of collections of individuals, groups, that is important in assessing the driving forces behind terrorism. It is a political act perpetrated by individuals acting together and trying, together, to justify their behaviour. These justifications reflect prevailing social values and to some extent, social conditions, although the individual's perception of the latter is more important than the reality.[60] Cinque genuinely believed that 'the news media were all owned by fascist multinational corporations... This was a class war: the capitalists and the bourgeoisie against the SLA and the people.'[61] It represents a response to the psychological and social environment as experienced by the individual rather than being a quality inherent within the individual terrorist.[62] There clearly are links between background conditions and the incidence of terrorism; the former undoubtedly affects susceptibility to the attractions of terrorism, ability to overcome moral restraint or fear of the costs, and collective beliefs. Jorde, a former terrorist with Abu Nidal's organisation, was a petty thief, unemployed and very reluctant to work to take care of his mother and sisters. He was attracted to the organisation predominantly because it offered to him a meal a day, and a bed without the necessity of regular work. His former life did not appeal greatly, and he hoped that after his unpleasant training was ended, he would be able to live at the organisation's expense in appealing European cities.[63] Studies of the backgrounds of terrorists from the RAF and Red Brigades show a pattern of incomplete family structure, especially during adolescence. In the German example, 25 per cent had lost a parent by the age of 14; and one third had had juvenile convictions.[64] Their lives were characterised by social isolation and personal failure.

The decision to join a national-separatist group represents less of an extreme break with society, but even there, it often stems from a feeling of alienation. Children of mixed Spanish-Basque heritage are scorned and rejected in the Basque region, they make up only eight per cent of the population yet 40 per cent of the membership of ETA. They attempt to be more nationalistic than the Basques themselves; they attempt to exaggerate their political identity to find a psycho-social identity.[65] Idoia Lopez Riano was one of ETA's most effective assassins until her capture in France in 1994, yet her parents were from Salamanca, not the Basque country. She learnt the language at school, and while not perfect was quite fluent. Her introduction to ETA probably came via a boyfriend; and by the age of twenty she had joined one of the organisation's most lethal cells, led by Juan Manuel Soares. As part of this group, she participated in some of the worst atrocities of ETA's campaign, including the execution at point-blank range of three soldiers; a car bomb that killed nine and the rocketing of the Defence Ministry across a ten-lane motorway. When four of the cell were captured in 1989, they received a total of 9000 years in prison sentences. It appears that Lopez Riano actively sought out danger and was unable to avoid drawing attention to herself, even to the extent that she became known as *La Tigressa* (the tigress) in the Spanish press.[66]

The same tendency to exaggerate a national identity might be said to exist amongst a number of the IRA's members. Sean MacStiofain, leader of the break by the Provisionals from the Official IRA, and first Provisional Chief of Staff, was born John Stephenson in England. His mother was Irish, but it was his service with the Royal Air Force that accentuated his ancestral nationalism. He joined the IRA via various Irish Language movements in the 1950s; served a prison term for his part in the Felstead School armoury raid of 1953; and was a key factor in the Provisional's organisational build up between 1969 and 1971.[67] Undeniably dedicated to the cause of Irish nationalism, he did take his Irish identity to extremes: Maria McGuire states in her autobiography that he refused to speak anything other than Gaelic in his house and expected others to do likewise.[68]

Even if most Western terrorists did come from identifiable categories, such as being young, or middle class rebels of broken homes, it is unhelpful to a general explanation of terrorism since it is largely culturally specific, and more crucially it fails to account for the fact that the vast majority of people of similar backgrounds do not resort to terrorism. Consequently, few analysts of terrorism attribute it exclusively to environment.

Where political culture is important is in bringing meaningful symbols and narratives to the individual's attention. This is particularly the case with national-separatist groups where the community's history and experience may be a key factor.[69] Toloyan has identified several such symbols that are central to an Armenian consciousness and self-identity: that of the Genocide that occurred under Turkish rule in 1915 and 1922, which in the Armenian narrative is closely identified with Christ's Passion, and the victims of which are invariably regarded as martyrs; the story of St Vartan which deals with heroic resistance and the eventual martyrdom of Vartan and his followers in the battle of Avarayr in 450–1 AD; and the betrayal by the Great Powers at the Congress of Berlin in 1878, where Armenian interests where ignored. The Armenian representative at Berlin was the Patriarch of Constantinople, Megerdich Khrimian, who used the metaphor of herisa (an Armenian dish); but whereas the Powers had iron ladles, he had only a paper one, so got no herisa. Until the Armenians got an iron ladle (seen as an image for armed force), the situation would continue because they could never rely on their allies for help. The narrative of St Vartan is also vital because he was prepared to risk all in defence of Armenian Christianity, a crucial component of national identity. Therefore martyrdom is accepted as wholly valid in such cases; and because all Armenians recognise Vartan as an ancestor, they acknowledge his moral and symbolic authority. These three narratives mesh the elements of armed self-reliance, martyrdom and an acute awareness of being persecuted by other powers into the Armenian national identity, and thus do much to engender an environment in which terrorism may be seen as a valid option in pursuit of nationalist objectives.[70] Furthermore, in cases, as with the Armenian one, where the terrorist comes from a community that believes it has been grossly persecuted or wronged, it is easier to morally justify high-level acts of violence as an attempt to gain revenge, acquire justice or otherwise right that wrong.

It is often suggested that violence is self-perpetuating, that if children are socialised into patterns of violence then these acts may become part of the social fabric, the norm in the community, and the Armenian example would certainly appear to support this perspective. However, it is unclear whether this occurs on a wider basis; growing up surrounded by violence might, to some degree, inure the individual to the horror of it, possibly therefore lowering the moral constraints that might otherwise exist. More significant though, is that if such violence exists in an individual's society, it offers an outlet for their emotions that they would be forced to spend elsewhere otherwise. Observational learning also plays a significant role in the development of aggression. Violent cultures, through the provision of role models, may provide many opportunities for the young to be initiated into violence. Groups in themselves can act to facilitate violence by giving opportunity for imitation.[71] It is undeniable that groups also learn through imitation of their predecessors, by studying their publications and deriving lessons from their mistakes. The Irgun under the leadership of Begin, was acutely aware of the Zealot revolt in 73 CE which resulted in a 1,900-year exile from the Jewish homeland. He blamed this on two factors: that the Zealots engaged in fratricidal violence and that the scale of their terrorism was so considerable that it compelled the Romans to crush the rising. Begin was careful to ensure that the Irgun did not retaliate, no matter how extreme the provocation from other Jewish groups, and that they struck against only 'legitimate' targets.[72] Terrorist groups may even receive training from other organisations: the PFLP ran training camps for European radicals in the late 1960s,[73] Kozo Okamoto acquired his weapons expertise there prior to the attack on Lod Airport; and 'Carlos' was recruited by Bassam Abu-Sharif, and later helped to run such camps for foreigners.[74] The resort to terrorism in all but a few cases represents the combination of motivation and opportunity. While it is common sense that terrorist groups have an origin in some way, and may coalesce around a leader, the majority of terrorists become members of existing groups or found their own after membership of another group. A vital element in an individual's progress towards terrorism, therefore, is access to a group that offers, and accepts the individual into, membership.[75] Sean O'Callaghan was able to join the IRA at the start of their campaign because he was known and could be used for low-level work. He recounted that:

> When the Provisional IRA was formed and started seeking support around Tralee, the members knew who I was because of my father [who had been interned by the Irish government as a result of his IRA activities in the 1940s]. It turned out that the owner of a sweetie shop was the man to talk to about joining. He passed me on to the owner of a supermarket up the street, who was in charge.
>
> I was taken to a big farm and into a granary, where there was a group of people. Some of them started digging away grain with wooden shovels, revealing a pile of about 30 to 40 guns. Our job was to clean and package them for shipment up to Northern Ireland.[76]

For most followers, membership of the group is the vital motive. Before engaging in acts of terrorism, usually there is a progression through the ranks of the group or a drift from other organisations. As the individual moves towards those that espouse violence, the groups become increasingly radical. Kellen suggests that there is a long process of alienation, rebellion and experimentation with a variety of social settings and political ideas, and only then a commitment to terrorist action and a clandestine lifestyle.[77] The decision by an individual to use violence is not a sudden one. Participation in riots or demonstrations is often the entry into a life of violence although obviously not all rioters or demonstrators go on to become terrorists.[78] For the Italian Red Brigades, the main recruitment area was groups formed in Milanese factories that functioned primarily as critics of union policy. They used alternative methods of action to strikes such as sabotage or picketing, actions that would damage production without harming the workers in the factories. These movements were gradually infiltrated by the Red Brigades, and with that came a progression towards illegality. In the Red Brigades, people were initially asked to perform 'individual illegal actions' such as distributing propaganda documents around their factory or storing weapons at their home. Later they might be required to spray graffiti on factory walls or leave intimidator messages in the offices or homes of the management. The progression to violence occurred only after the individual had passed a number of tests of their commitment to the group and their willingness to conform within it.[79] In ETA, the process of gaining membership is also a gradual one. Although most members were in their mid to late twenties on joining the organisation, as adolescents, many engaged in 'searching behaviour', seeking solutions to the crises of culture and national-identity that affected them. In most cases, they sought alternatives to armed struggle before they joined ETA. Older *etarras* approach the prospective member, usually on an innocuous occasion. If the young prospective member expresses interest, they are approached again a few months later and invited to participate in a simple, low-security operation, such as spray-painting slogans on a wall. If they perform well, they will be invited to be involved in increasingly complex and risky actions. It may be as much as a year before the new recruit gains full membership of ETA. This time frame can even be considerably longer, because it is quite common for young prospects to resist joining the group for months or even years after the initial approach, presumably until they come to believe that there is no alternative to terrorism.[80]

Crenshaw states that the decision to resort to violence is a result of association with the group. The choice is between participating in violence and leaving the group. The individual who is already a member of the group and has become dependent on the things it could supply, finds it difficult, in psychological terms, to go back.[81] Taylor and Quayle assert that the realisation of this boundary being crossed is a key point in the psychology of a terrorist, but that it is a state of mind rather than a legal or moral point of reference. It might arise as a result of a personal event such as the death of a friend 'in action' or from an incident of significance to the community or party, such as an atrocity committed by the establishment. Whereas before, the individual might be willing to perform small and unimportant tasks for the group, afterwards there is a willingness to act as a fully fledged terrorist.[82] German sources refer to this critical point as *der sprung* (the leap). For Baumann, the event was the shooting of a student by the police during a demonstration; he refers to its impact on him as 'a tremendous flash' and that 'it left an indelible impression.'[83] For Bassam Abu-Sharif, the key moment was when, in the aftermath of the Arab defeat in the 1967 War, a Palestinian girl offered to sleep with him for five dinars. He describes the moment:

> [Palestinian girls] had to sell themselves, dishonour themselves just to survive? Anger took hold of me... I understood now what I had to do. There was no going back. My own fight began here, now. I would not stop until that girl, and the thousands like her, were back in their rightful homes. I would regain our country or die for it.[84]

However, this is not a universal event. Clark found almost no evidence of a single catalytic occurrence that transformed the opinions of ETA recruits. Instead, it was a gradual progression, as a result of discussion and thought, that brought them to membership of the organisation.[85] However, it does seem to be generally true amongst terrorist groups that the qualitative decision to turn to violence is harder to make than the quantitative one on the level of violence to employ and, at a later stage, whether to increase that level. Particularly if the progression is steady, rather than rapid, terrorists evidently find it psychologically easier to escalate their violence than to engage in terrorist acts in the first place. This suggests that even the highest levels of violence differ in quantity, rather than quality from more standard acts of terrorism, and therefore may not be as psychologically troubling for the terrorist as might be otherwise supposed. Furthermore, when the alternative is to leave the group, many individuals appear willing to acquiesce to committing extremely violent acts on behalf of the organisation.

When the existence of the group precedes the decision to turn to terrorism, the decision might be made by the group as a whole or by a faction within the organisation. Alpert's group discussed the issue from the perspectives of its morality, effectiveness and the precedents for terrorism. They argued about targeting and came to the conclusion that 'physical destruction aimed at the enemy [was] the only course left to revolutionaries.' However, they also found that it was impossible to be completely candid, since no one was willing to admit to having second thoughts for fear that they would be accused of cowardice.[86] The individual who has become highly dependent on the group may acquiesce with the decision to use violence even though they may not have made an independent choice.[87] Obviously, this is not always the case: Leila Khaled debated the Arab–Israeli conflict, and the morality of hijacking and the legitimacy of revolutionary violence, before she became deeply involved in illegal activities for the Palestinian campaign, although she had been involved in non-violent actions for the cause for years beforehand. The progression to violence was not natural or automatic.[88] In some groups, the decision to use violence appears not to be controversial: in LEHI, revolutionary terror was the only means of promoting the objective of removing the British from Palestine. The main point of debate was over its efficacy. Yitzhak Shamir says that they undertook no action blindly or automatically or for brutality's sake. Instead, the aim was less to punish than to deter the British and Arabs from taking or damaging Jewish lives.[89]

The terrorist group may become a surrogate family for the terrorist and the leader of the group a mentor for the younger members.
This applies more in ideological terrorism, where terrorism is in part
a reaction against society and an individual's origins, than with
nationalist-separatist terrorism where, to some extent, the individual
is more likely to be acting in accordance with their background and
familial origins. Being underground, cut off from the rest of society is
almost certainly the key determinant in whether the terrorist group
does become a surrogate family for the terrorist. Maria McGuire
stayed in regular contact with her family throughout her association
with the IRA,[90] whereas members of the Irgun were forced into
hiding during the campaign. Begin wrote of the group; 'We were a
family. There was mutual trust. Each was prepared to give his life for
his comrade...It was love, love of the ideal, that infused the fighters
with mutual fraternal affection.'[91] Terrorists are individuals with a
powerful need to belong and this is not satisfied outside the group
which provides the emotional protection and company that other
people find in their family or circle of friends. The group therefore
has a strong hold over the individual and the leader of the group is
likely to be highly influential in determining how new recruits view
the organisation and its goals. Personal contacts are obviously important in an individual's decision to join a group; although in the case of
Armenian groups it appears that the entire political culture has a
radicalising effect, in the same way that individuals do in other organisations. Certainly, this can be seen to be so for Monte Melkonian,
Armenian guerrilla leader in Nagorno-Karabakh until his death in
June 1993.[92] Other terrorists, though, clearly are influenced by individuals: Kozo Okamoto, was introduced to the JRA by his brother,
Takeshi,[93] and the Italian Red Brigades were found to contain a
number of married couples. Sullwold argued that for women terrorists, personal contacts were especially influential in affecting their
degree of participation, although the core motivations remained
intrinsically the same as for male terrorists. It is possible to suggest
that without Sam Melville, Jane Alpert would have been politically
radical, but perhaps not a terrorist: his influence in her decision to
resort to violence was immense. She became involved in radical politics at university. Being vehemently antiwar she felt disenfranchised
during the 1968 Presidential Election, so joined the SDS. She met
Melville, with whom she became besotted and acquiesced in his wild
schemes of violence. She seems to have been a moderating influence
in the group, but was also the one that gave intellectual weight and

some ideological justification to their actions. Once outside Melville's influence, she remained radical and on the run for several years, but did not return to violence.[94]

Galvin disagrees with Sullwold's assessment: she believes that there are appreciable differences between male and female terrorists since the socialisation process and power structure of outside society that impacts on women generally are just as applicable within the terrorist group.[95] MacDonald also believes that important differences exist in the motivations of female terrorists compared to their male counterparts: '[They regard] themselves as victims not only of what their male comrades would call "political oppression" but also of male oppression... The key awareness is of being a double victim, with oppression having to be fought on two fronts.'[96] Galvin did agree with Sullwold that personal contacts were important to female terrorists, citing women in Northern Ireland, witnessing the effects of terrorism at first hand and seeking revenge for injuries to acquaintances and the community. However, this aspect seems very similar for both men and women involved in terrorism.[97]

There is a danger in clustering women terrorists together; clearly they are no more a homogenous group than are terrorists as a whole. However, there do seem to be a number of factors common to many women who become terrorists, but largely these apply to terrorists generally, such as the relatively ordinary lives that they were relieved to leave; or the limitations on their lives once they had joined the terrorist group. Female members of radical terrorist groups, such as Susanna Ronconi or Jane Alpert, began as radical feminists and moved on to join men in a struggle against society's wider injustices.[98]

The main reason why individuals embark on terrorism remains that it is an alternative that offers the terrorist a sense of purpose and control over their own lives and equally importantly, those of other people. It enables them to master their feelings of futility through achieving goals. They become important, people who have to be acknowledged and dealt with by the authorities. At last, they are someone.[99] This tendency applies as much to groups as it does to individuals; recognition of the terrorist group is a form of legitimation, an acknowledgement of their existence. It is for this reason, above all others, that terrorists seek the attention of the media, and through that, publicity. This is a major motivating force in the planning of terrorist 'spectaculars', of which nuclear terrorism would be a prime example. Such acts are therefore a means of pursuing recognition from the authorities, but also from the population at large. Bassam

Abu-Sharif describes the PLO campaign following the 1967 Arab–Israeli War:

> There was no way a relative handful of young men, armed for the most part with antiquated hunting rifles, could take on the Israeli tanks, mines, and machine guns, the well armed and vigilant army patrols. But these raids were a necessary step. They showed the world that the Palestinian spirit was not crushed. They showed the Israelis that the Palestinian people would never give up, that they would fight with whatever came to hand, by whatever means they could, to recover their dignity and their lost lands, to get justice. But the cross-border raids were never practical. Looking back now, they were a joke.[100]

This is an example of Bakunin's 'propaganda by deed', actions aimed at ensuring that both the Israelis and the Palestinian people remained conscious that the PLO was still a force able to continue the fight, even after the defeats of 1967. In 1968, the PFLP began hijacking planes outside the Middle East to prove their point and in September 1970, attempted to simultaneously hijack three planes bound for New York; they were partially successful: the attack led by Leila Khaled was foiled, but they managed to capture another plane in its place. The operation was clearly aimed at displaying the power of the PFLP, as well as forcing Israel and European states holding Palestinian prisoners to negotiate.[101] This desire for widespread recognition and acknowledgement by authorities would be the ideal motivation for an act of low-level nuclear terrorism, since even a minor incident involving nuclear material would be likely to be highly publicised. However, there have been literally dozens of hoaxes involving nuclear material in the United States alone, most of which have gone largely unnoticed by the public and the media, in part because there is a understandable reluctance by the authorities to cause unjustified alarm. This means that, to be effective, a threat would have to be credible and sufficiently severe that it could not be reasonably kept secret by the government concerned. While this does not wholly exclude the possibility, it sets the standard sufficiently high that there are undoubtedly easier ways of attracting attention and publicity, if that is the terrorist's sole objective.

  If the psychological attractions of being a terrorist are important then this has significant implications for group outcomes. The leader cannot moderate without risking being usurped by someone willing to prosecute the campaign more vigorously. In extreme cases, this can actually result in a split within the group, as one faction seeks to increase the level of violence employed. In 1940, the Stern Gang split from their parent organisation, the Irgun, over the best way to pursue the campaign to create a free and independent Jewish homeland. Irgun was motivated partly by an inability to continue the violence and partly by a reluctance to undermine the British position in the Middle East at a critical point in the Second World War. Abraham Stern, the gang's leader, by contrast, was unwilling to accept any cessation of action. In his break from Irgun, he was accompanied by impatient, driven men who distrusted politics and instead required that action be taken.[102] Personality clashes may also act as a catalyst for a split: in 1968 Ahmad Jibril left George Habash's PFLP to form his own group, the Popular Front for the Liberation of Palestine–General Command (PFLP-GC) and in 1969 Nayif Hawatmah formed the Democratic Front for the Liberation of Palestine. Both were, at least in part, reacting against the organisational dominance of Habash within the PFLP.[103]

Terrorists tend to be action-oriented individuals who consequently will find inaction highly stressful, leading to tensions within the group. When Patty Hearst and two other members of the SLA were underground, trapped in a flat together, and unable to go out for fear that they would be recognised and challenged, there was a great deal of fighting between them. Hearst says: 'As time went on in that small apartment, they fought more and more over petty, ridiculous issues... When I quieted them they would usually sulk at opposite ends of the room. But just as often, they would both turn on me.'[104] This willingness to fight within the group seems to apply particularly to underground terrorist organisations. The group has to commit terrorist acts to justify its existence and the leader has to plan such acts to enable the group to release its aggressive tendencies and re-affirm its identity. It is also extremely difficult for the leader to amend this identity in any way: the SLA was ostensibly an organisation that sought to liberate blacks and other oppressed people in the United States. However, Cinque was its only black member. When Teko, the leader of the surviving rump of the group, tried to suggest that Doc Holiday, a black man, should be invited to lead the group so as to maintain the focus of the organisation, he was strongly opposed by those in the organisation who felt that the real aim of the group was simply revolutionary and that colour was an irrelevance. Both factions believed that they were trying to retain the true character of the organisation against encroachment by the other.[105] Group dynamics therefore mitigate towards a maintenance of existing patterns of identity and action: a continuation of violence and the taking of ever greater risks. Janis thought that such organisations become subject to 'group think': illusions of invulnerability leading to over-optimism and excessive risk-taking; a presumption of the group's morality; a one-dimensional perception of the enemy as wholly evil; and an intolerance of internal challenges to shared key beliefs.[106] These characteristics all increase the likelihood that the terrorist group concerned will believe that heightened levels of violence, perhaps including nuclear terrorism, can and should be achieved in the pursuit of their campaign.

Terrorist organisations are likely to contain a combination of people whose need is the group and those who are seeking to change the political or social environment; both, however, need the organisation to satisfy their objectives. The social psychological dynamics of the group help to determine not only why individuals join, but why they stay and why terrorism is chosen as a tactic. Terrorist organisations offer a counterculture with their own norms and values into which new recruits are indoctrinated. They tend to demand complete obedience from their members, and to be largely exclusive, isolated from society. Abu Nidal controlled his members' lives by keeping the rank-and-file members in camps isolated from the outside world. He forbade all socialising amongst his followers except on official business; all passports had to be handed in to him; and phone calls were restricted. As much as anything, it was a means for Abu Nidal to impose his authority on the members of his group.[107] Terrorist organisations strive for uniformity and cohesiveness, the group is built on the political homogeneity of like-minded individuals, their futures, goals and even their lives are bound together. It is essential that members are able to trust one another fully not to betray the group; they stand or fall together and that engenders cohesiveness.

This cohesiveness may be further enhanced by the promise of violence if an individual appears to threaten to leave or in some way betray the group. The Justice Committee of Abu Nidal's organisation regularly pursued purges of the group in its quest to eradicate spies. Prisoners were tortured and revealed their guilt, genuine or not, as a result. They were usually executed to avoid the Committee's methods from emerging although enough did survive for these means to be well known throughout the organisation.[108] This all means that individuals have considerable influence over one another in the group, but also that the group's influence over the individual rises with growing cohesiveness. The element of shared danger increases the group's solidarity, and the motivation for the individual to remain affiliated to the group and therefore not to deviate from its norms because it is only within the group that the individual can receive the reassurance that they require when faced with the external threat of society. There is a lack of alternatives to membership of the group, there can be no going back, partly because the individual has become a pariah by being a terrorist, but more because they abandoned their previous life since it was so unsatisfactory. The main fear of group members is that they will be rejected by other members and abandoned by the group. It is this that is the key element in ensuring conformity within the group, and explains why ideologically antiauthoritarian terrorist groups can be highly authoritarian in their organisational psychology.[109] Members of such groups often feel a responsibility, a duty to their superiors and their peers. Bandura argues that:

> Self-sanctions operate most efficiently in the service of authority when followers assume personal responsibility for being dutiful executors while relinquishing personal responsibility for the harm caused by their behaviour. Followers who disowned responsibility without being bound by a sense of duty would be quite unreliable.[110]

Individuals therefore find it hard to question or criticise the direction that the group is taking, unless it is to urge even greater commitment to violence, without triggering a crisis in their identity. Consequently, particularly in small, cellular organisations, it is possible for such groups to conform to the agenda and concept of just a few of their members or even, in some cases, to acquire a momentum of their own in pursuit of their campaign. There are few mitigating factors or members calling for restraint on the levels of violence being employed. It is not inconceivable to suggest that in extreme cases, high levels of violence are employed by groups, none of whose members, individually, believe it is justified by the situation, but who are unwilling to speak out for fear of endangering their position within the organisation.

The factors that encouraged the individual to become a terrorist in the first place also lessen the opportunities for their re-entry to the society from which they have become isolated. The strong ties between members of the organisation reinforce the pressure to conform; the rewards for membership may be more related to the approval of an individual's peers than task-oriented, and this approval may be linked as much to a willingness to conform as to successful actions. Increasingly, the goal of the group becomes self-maintenance and decreasingly changing the political environment; members' primary objective is to keep the group together. It offers security to members; the group and its survival are paramount. An exception to this is the SLA. The dissent of the group, discussed above, became too much for Teko who said: 'That's it... It's all over... We have to split up and go our own separate ways!' He felt that violence and black leadership were integral to the SLA; others were less certain. While schisms within terrorist organisations are not unusual, the defection of the leadership is more so. However, the lack of willingness of the members of the group to conform made Teko believe they were endangering the group of which he and Yolanda had become the only true guardians.[111] The ease with which an individual is able to exit the group also has considerable correlation with the type of existence they have had within the organisation. Members who continue to live in their communities, such as most IRA or ETA terrorists, who largely have ordinary lives, interspersed with flurries of violent activity, find it easier to simply leave the group, even if the terrorist organisation does threaten reprisals against those to leave the struggle.[112] It tends to be those involved in underground movements, whose whole life is subsumed by the group, that find it especially difficult to exit. However, in any variety of organisation, it seems to be a decision that is seldom taken lightly.

Group cohesiveness encourages the pursuit of violence because as the group becomes increasingly cut off from society most news of the outside world is filtered through the group, leading to increased misperceptions of the external environment, which in turn reinforce the beliefs of the group and make it easier to assume that the enemy is unrelentingly hostile. Obviously, such groups remain in touch with the wider world via newspapers and the media, but if the group is the only form of human contact then the media sources are interpreted solely by the group. Hearst says that the SLA

> ...Sunk into the depths of psychosis. We were cut off from the outside world and lived in an isolated realm of our own...The radio played all day long and most of the night too and Cinque would often hear song lyrics which contained for him special allusions to the revolution...we would all focus on a song's lyrics for a

hint of our revolution. I never doubted that the hidden meaning was there, only that I was not sufficiently knowledgeable to understand what our leader heard.[113]

This process serves an important purpose since the internal group tensions and hostilities can be projected onto an external source. There is also a propensity for individuals to be more willing to take risks when they are part of a group than they would be solely as individuals, encouraging escalation because the terrorist becomes less inhibited by the prospect of the negative consequences of their actions. Peer pressure means that individuals are more willing to perform acts that they would otherwise balk at. This willingness seems to correspond to the extent of relief that the recruit felt on joining the group.[114] The pressure also promotes acts of self-sacrifice: individuals imagine themselves as martyrs or avengers for the wrongs that been committed by the enemy or for former colleagues who have been captured or killed.[115] The fallen comrade then becomes an icon, a symbol that further precludes turning back since it would be a betrayal of their memory and would make their death merely a waste. Joe McCann, a member of the Official IRA, was shot by British soldiers on June 15, 1972. He was given a hero's funeral by the IRA and as McGuire says: '... his life story, and the nature of his death, quickly became one of the myths of Irish Republican history'.[116] This willingness for self-sacrifice is an important means for the terrorist to believe that their actions are not only justified, but also altruistic. Guilt avoidance of this type increases dependency on the group; induces the individual to commit more guilt-ridden acts; and makes exit from the group even more difficult since the individual would encounter social approbation, legal sanctions and remorse.

Terrorist groups seem to regard dissent as a more severe threat than exit; it is equated with treason and is as divisive because it questions the accepted reasoning and leadership of the group. Morucci, a member of the Italian Red Brigades, explained that organisational reasons always prevailed over individual intentions. When influential members of the group attempted to change things the organisation broke up.[117] Even in such cases though, the ideological framework continues to be used as a justification for the actions of the group. It may not necessarily encourage the use of violence directly, but it remains functional to many terrorists who resort to terrorism, being a means of reaffirmation for their beliefs and actions, and a core pillar of the group.[118] What the group, through its interpretation of its ideology, defines as moral becomes moral and the authority for compliant members: if 'they' are responsible for our problems then 'their' destruction can be justified. Stern rationalised her violent actions as part of the Weathermen group:

> I had tried working in the Establishment, first as a teacher, then as a social worker. Then I had tried to be a pacifist, first with the Civil Rights movement, then with the anti-war movement. I had joined SDS and demonstrated and marched for two years. And still the war continued. While the rich were getting richer, the poor were getting poorer. Since the government and the capitalist wouldn't listen to reason, then other means had to be employed.[119]

However, ideology may become increasingly corrupted and 'surrealistic, used to escape a disconcerting reality rather than to guide actions. The extreme abstractness of such beliefs... disconnect their holders from objective reality.'[120] The individual becomes ever more dependent on the group for their existence. Post believes that violence becomes an end in itself and that group ideology is simply a rationale for the acts that terrorists are driven to commit. He argues that individuals join terrorist groups to become terrorists and commit acts of terrorism.[121] If terrorism is instrumental then it ought to cease if the goals it sought were achieved. He cites ETA which continues to use violence even though many of its tactical demands have been met and the use of force may be counter-productive. Its goals are absolutist, it seeks nothing less than total victory. The primary aim of all groups is survival. This is especially the case for terrorist groups and success is a threat because it removes the objectives of the organisation. It has to find a balance between being successful enough to attract members and perpetuate itself, yet not so successful that it puts itself out of business. It solves this dilemma by finding fresh goals to pursue through its use of absolutist rhetoric.[122] The paramount importance placed on the survival of the group means that other, non-terrorist, activity is justifiable in the greater good. Terrorism is expensive: apart from weapons, ammunition and publicity, especially if the group is underground, other items such as food are equally vital. Many organisations have relied on criminal acts such as bank robberies or extortion to finance their terrorist activities. LEHI, especially in the months after its split from Irgun, did little else beyond work towards its own survival by stealing and threatening until sufficient funds were gained. However, the primary objective, group survival, was achieved.[123]

Hirschman notes that organisations attempt to limit the risk of members' departure by imposing 'severe initiation costs', the idea that recruits will be reluctant to leave the group if they have had to invest a great deal to join initially.[124] Jorde, a Kabyle recruit, joined Abu Nidal in Beirut. He was made to write out the story of his life; and was then flown to Libya for training in a camp run by the group. There, the discipline was extremely strict, and every aspect of the recruit's life was controlled. He was imprisoned for months, periodically tortured and led to believe he would be executed. Instead, he was congratulated on having passed the test, and his terrorist training began. After weapons, surveillance and intelligence training, Jorde was sent on trial missions to Athens, Belgrade and Brussels, before he was given his first genuine operation: to steal some passports and set up contacts in various European cities. After that, his role was predominantly to reconnoitre a target prior to an attack, as he did in synagogues in Istanbul. Jorde's experience is certainly exceptional: even within Abu Nidal's organisation few recruits received such a lengthy or tough initiation; the suspicion that he was a spy must in part account for this.[125] By contrast, Shamir's initiation into Irgun was designed to impress the importance of the undertaking into the recruit, but was a ritual, the decision to accept the recruit already having been made. Shamir writes:

> It took place one evening in the darkened classroom of a Tel Aviv school...The only source of light was a gooseneck lamp beamed right at me to ensure that I could not get a good (i.e. an identifying) look at the three members of the admissions committee sitting at a table in front of me. Someone solemnly asked ritual questions: 'Are you prepared to make sacrifices if called upon to do so?' 'Are you prepared to accept military discipline?' 'Are you aware that joining this organization may involve you in great danger?' Equally solemnly I gave ritual answers.[126]

Terrorist organisations often require an illegal act as the cost of admission in order to eliminate the option of exiting for the new member; to test their commitment; and to increase the impetus for them to go underground. This has the added effect of inducing the individual to 'fight harder' because it means that they are reluctant to admit defeat even if they believe that the group has failed in its objectives since they must prove that they were right to pay a high entrance fee to join the organisation. When all but three members of the SLA, including Hearst, were killed in a siege with the police, the group was clearly destroyed as a revolutionary organisation. Teko, the leader of the remaining group, had said that the three of them should go and die with their comrades in the siege. Yolanda, one of the survivors, favoured making the deaths worthwhile and meaningful; Teko wanted them to sacrifice themselves in the name of their cause: both are different elements of the same phenomenon.[127] It may take the individual a considerable time to move beyond this self-deception, in fighting the realisation that the group to which they belong is in the process of deterioration.[128] Adriana Faranda remained with the group long after she had ceased to support it and explained that the individual is extremely insecure and more likely to attribute the fault to themselves than the organisation, so stays within the group until the evidence against the organisation is undeniable. In an underground terrorist group, such as the Red Brigades, the individual has often had a close relationship with other members of the group, and may well be dependant on them in a number of ways, increasing the difficulties of leaving.[129] If there appears to be no alternative to exit, either because dissent is impossible or ineffective, then the individual may seek to lessen the strain of defection by persuading others to leave as well. When the IRA split, in 1969, into what became the Official IRA and the Provisional IRA, Sean MacStiofain made repeated attempts to persuade the IRA leadership in Belfast that they were on the wrong course, hoping that it would be possible to retain a united movement. MacStiofain, then Director of Intelligence, failed to defeat a vote, at the General Army Council meeting in mid December, to allow members of Sinn Fein to sit in the parliaments at Dublin, Westminster or Stormont, if they were elected. MacStiofain left the Army Convention with his allies, reconvened elsewhere, and contacted the units that had either been absent from the meeting or had been reorganised in recent months. A new IRA leadership was elected with MacStiofain as Chief of Staff. At Sinn Fein's annual conference, held on 10 January 1970, in Dublin, MacStiofain rejected a call for a vote of allegiance to the old Army Council; announced that a 'Provisional' Army Council had been established; pledged his allegiance to this; and urged all Republicans to leave the conference with him. About 45 per cent did so.[130] This example is perhaps exceptional in terrorist groups because it was such a formalised and drawn-out exit, reflecting the established nature of the Republican movement. Equally exceptional, but because it did permit its members to leave, was the Irgun, in spite of the potential damage to the underground movement that former, disenchanted, members could do.[131]

Hirschman notes that the actual decision to leave, especially by influential members of the group, is dependent less on an assessment of the suffering that the individual would have to endure in the process than on the impact on the organisation. If members believe that they have a voice, they are more likely to be concerned about whether their departure from the group will result in further deterioration or deviation from the organisation's stated goals. This suggests that full exit from the group is impossible, that even after the individual has formally left, they continue to be concerned about the group's activities.[132] Individuals leave because they are disillusioned with the group, not necessarily with the cause. McGuire left the Provisional IRA because she believed that it had destroyed its best chance of success by restarting the military campaign after the truce of 1972; and she believed that power within the organisation had shifted decisively towards those, like MacStiofain, who favoured the military option, at the expense of more moderate members who had lost their voice in the group.[133] Once they have left, they are likely to be super-critical of the parent organisation, fomenting severe inter-group rivalry. This is more the case with ideologically motivated groups than with nationalist-separatist ones: the IRA's membership reflects a steady turnover of people without there being considerable acrimony in the process, the members simply become steadily less active over a period of time, and in many cases, it is hard to judge precisely when the individual does exit the organisation. In the case of groups such as ETA or the IRA, this also reflects the fact that they have developed strong command and organisational structures that mitigate any tendency towards factionalism.[134] With ideologically motivated groups, the breaks do tend to be more extreme. Faranda and Morucci sought to set up a rival group to the Red Brigades, one where violence was not the 'be all and end all' of the campaign,[135] but in other cases, the creation of a rival organisation may mean that they resort to greater levels of violence to demonstrate the superior ardour of the new group and to provide attractive incentives to new recruits.[136]

Such rivalries can occur as easily intra-group as inter-group if the organisation dissolves into factions all intent on displaying their dedication to the cause. Those responsible for the kidnappings of James Cross, the British Trade Commissioner in Montreal, and Pierre Laporte, the Quebec Minister of Labour and Immigration, were centred on two leaders within the FLQ, Paul Rose and Jacques

Lanctot. While Rose was more systematic, Lanctot became frustrated with the ineffectiveness of the organisation's campaign, so decided on a political kidnapping to increase progress.[137] It was a radical departure from the FLQ's usual tactics and was a change strongly opposed by Rose's group. In September 1970, having lost a vote to determine future strategy, Rose decided to establish a separate group and continue with the long-term strategy. Cross was kidnapped by Lanctot's group on 5 October; the intention was that they would take a British diplomat as a protest against 'cultural imperialism' and then an American diplomat as a protest against 'economic imperialism', but with insufficient resources to deal with a double kidnapping, the group determined on consecutive attacks. Rose's group was unaware of this dual strategy and believed that the kidnapping of Cross had actually undermined the likelihood of a successful outcome (the release of 20 FLQ members held by the Canadian authorities). To attempt to strengthen the kidnappers' position they decided to return to Quebec and stage another kidnapping.[138] The result was the taking of Laporte by the Rose faction on 10 October and his death on 17 October. Although they had initially opposed kidnapping as a tactic, it was the Rose group that proved to be more hard-line and extreme in its use once they had determined to emulate the Lanctot group, spurred on by the belief that they were acting in the best interests of their organisation and Quebec as a whole.[139] Another example is that of ASALA in July 1983 when it split into two factions over the bombing of the Turkish Airlines desk at Orly Airport that resulted in eight deaths and 54 injuries. Monte Melkonian, leader of the break away faction described the attack: 'The people who died at Orly are to us innocent dead [sic]. They are detrimental to our cause.' In the aftermath of the split, ASALA leader Hagop Hagopian executed two of Melkonian's allies within ASALA in retaliation for the assassination of two of Hagopian's closest aides.[140]

Where exit is possible through the defection to another group, increases in violence are less likely to be a result of such factionalism. Baeyer-Kaette, a political psychologist, found that there was a high turnover of terrorists among German groups, largely due to individual doubts about the legitimacy of the organisation that had existed from the outset of the individual's membership and which had never been resolved properly. They increasingly questioned the goals of the group and whether their actions did anything to promote these. The duration of their membership averaged only one year, with 36 per cent staying for less than six months.[141] Amongst Belfast members of the IRA, the average age for entry into the group was 19 years, and the average career length was 29 months.[142] However, in the RAF, most of its members remained with the organisation for several years and exited as a result of being captured, rather than disillusionment with the group. Since the average age for the terrorists in all of the groups surveyed by Baeyer-Kaette was around 22, it might be possible to suggest that entrance to a group reflected the uncertainty of adolescence and youth while their exit showed the resolution of some of these dilemmas. Once the reason for the individual joining the terrorist group became less important, the hold on the individual by the group fell too, making exit increasingly likely.[143]

Zawodny argued that the composition of the group could also increase the likelihood of the organisation to use violence, citing the example of women members. He believed that while they were equal in their membership of the group, they also created internal pressures within it, particularly when the organisation was isolated from the rest of society, since the male membership would be in competition for the women, although possibly unconsciously. This competition might well manifest itself in the form of efforts to outdo the other male members of the group, by use of violence directed against external sources.[144] Zawodny's example of women as catalysts for violence is perhaps questionable, although Kaplan agrees that there is an element of machismo to some terrorist acts.[145] It is supported to some extent by the example of Sam Melville, who became increasingly involved in terrorism as Jane Alpert became more focused on other aspects of her life and less on Melville; although the timing also corresponds with when Melville became increasingly erratic in his behaviour generally. In part at least, Melville's violence was an attempt to re-acquire Alpert's attention.[146] Zawodny's hypothesis does highlight an incentive to escalate: that of competition within the group. Individuals compete for peer approval, and may seek it by proposing greater levels of violence, thereby demonstrating the strength of their adherence to the cause. Interestingly, Galvin also suggests that in some circumstances women may increase the probability of increased violence, that an added insecurity many female terrorists feel is sexual inferiority that they attempt to assuage by 'out-doing' their male counterparts in 'daring, obduracy, and brutality.'[147] For such women, power and approval seem to be even greater motivations than they are for terrorists as a whole. Being extremely adept at their job, they have a means of being at least the equal of men and in many cases, superior to them. Leila Khaled found revolutionary activity to be a way of liberating herself from the traditional expectations of women. However, the sexual element was an added factor, not a replacement for ideological or nationalist motivations that were the ostensible cause of terrorist actions by men. Female terrorists' dedication to the cause was no less than that of their male counterparts.[148]

Membership of the group makes it easier to avoid the guilt associated with even the worst terrorist actions since the norms and values of the group make violence against the enemy not merely acceptable but desirable, even a duty. The gross misdeeds of the enemy are emphasised as a justification for acting against it. The opposition is reduced to an abstraction, it is a structure not a body consisting of individuals. In 1971, the IRA's Army Council set a target to kill 36 British soldiers, which was achieved by November of that year. The number was then raised to 80. Clearly, the soldiers were not treated as individuals; they were merely numbers in a quota to be reached as quickly as possible.[149] In this way, it is possible to attack these people as representatives of the structure. They are dehumanised. Obviously, this is not always possible: Leila Khaled hijacked TWA flight 840 from Rome in August 1969, but experienced severe qualms about doing so when she saw a little girl on the plane wearing a badge on her dress with the message 'Make Friends'. It reminded Leila that the girl had committed no crime against the Palestinian people. Leila overcame her conscience by reminding herself of the fact that she and her people had done nothing to deserve the fate that they had received and therefore: 'The operation must be carried out. There can be no doubt or retreat.' Clearly in this case, Leila's commitment to the cause and her training were of greater significance to her ability to carry out the hijacking than to an ability to dehumanise the passengers on the plane.[150] Terrorists are freed from self-censuring restraints not by altering their personalities, aggressive drives or moral values but by redefining their actions as justifiable.[151] Group decision-making ensures that no one person feels responsible for decisions arrived at collectively. When everyone is responsible then no one is really responsible. Collective action can also be used to diffuse the weakening of self-restraints. Any harm done by the group can always be attributed to the actions of other members, can be largely discounted by laying the blame for mistakes or over-reaction with others. People therefore act more harshly when their actions are obscured by collective instrumentality than when they have to hold themselves personally accountable for their actions.[152]

Disregarding or misrepresenting the consequences of action also makes it easier for terrorists to commit their acts. This is achieved by minimising the damage that they cause and thus avoiding having to face the full implications of their actions. It is also easier if the suffering of the victims is not visible and when casual actions are physically and temporally removed from their effects. When aggressors do not know the harm they inflict on their victims, it becomes depersonalised and therefore much less difficult to overcome any moral inhibitions that might otherwise exist. Furthermore, if the decision-makers and executors of an action are not the same people it is easier for the former to call for higher levels of violence. When the SLA carried out a bank raid in which a female customer had been shot dead, those who had actually committed the robbery were initially shocked. Teko, the leader, who had planned the attack and had not been inside the bank, was positively enthusiastic, believing that it would improve the group's cohesion since they had now committed a capital offence; and joking 'If it hadn't been for good ol' Myrna (the dead woman), one of our comrades would be dead now. Good old Myrna, she took all the buckshot.'[153] This divorce from effect is even more of a factor for intermediaries, since they have neither to make the decision nor carry it out, they are merely the messenger.

An individual's ability to disengage from the moral realities of their actions develops slowly rather than emerging complete as a result of conviction or unconventional moral values. It is an evolution of which the individuals themselves may be unaware. The group often eases the progress by asking the individual to perform unpleasant acts that they can endure without much self-censure. By repeated performance and exposure to aggressive modelling by more experienced associates, the bonds of self-reproof and discomfort are weakened, permitting acts of greater ruthlessness, so that acts formerly regarded as abhorrent can readily be performed by the individual. Sean O'Callaghan, describing his feelings after the mortar attack in which he killed an Ulster Defence Regiment officer, Eva Martin, said:

> Looking back I think it was a stinking, shameful thing to have been involved in. But when you are wrapped up in a cause you do not take much of normal life into account.[154]

Patty Hearst was kidnapped and held against her will for months, yet she also participated in the actions of the SLA, her captors. It would be possible to suggest that she collaborated because the alternative was death, and this is partially true, but she had opportunities to escape in the course of missions, yet did not do so. Instead, she carried out her part in these as a full member of the group which she nonetheless hated. Her own view was that she had:

> acted instinctively, because I had been trained and drilled to do just that, to react to a situation without thinking, just as soldiers are trained and drilled to obey an order under fire instinctively, without questioning it. By the time they had finished with me I was, in fact, a soldier in the Symbionese Liberation Army.[155]

The process will be accelerated if acts of violence are presented as morally vital and the victims are depersonalised. This training, combined with immersion in the group's ideology and value system, instils the moral rectitude and importance of the cause for militant action, as well as creating a sense of eliteness and providing the social rewards of group esteem and solidarity for excelling in terrorist activities.[156] It might reasonably be thought that the ability of individual terrorists to disengage from the realities of their actions would decrease as the consequences of that act increased and that therefore, an act of mass terror would be less likely as a result. However, once the victims cease to be individuals and are reduced to an abstract, and provided the attack can be ideologically justified, the difference between an ordinary act of terrorism and an act of mass destructive terrorism is quantitative, not qualitative. It is indicative that even when directly confronted with the victims of the Murrah Building at his trial, the results of his action, so that he had to recognise the consequences of the attack, Tim McVeigh remained impassive and calm, convinced that he had struck a valid blow against a government he hated.

Over time, violence becomes the norm of the group through a process of desensitisation and brutalisation. Whereas the initial use of violent force may be hotly debated within the group, later it becomes the accepted and required means. McGuire says that she accepted the bombing of Belfast, and when civilians were accidentally blown up dismissed this as one of the unfortunate consequences of urban guerrilla warfare.[157] This is especially the case once a terrorist group acquires a longevity beyond the first generation because then its value system is set and violence is a characteristic of the group; it is internalised in the psychological dynamics of the group and its members so that ends and means become blurred since violence is tied irrevocably to the values that it serves. This has the effect of constraining the possibilities for compromise or innovation within the terrorist group, since group norms become a restricting influence on the leadership. Their position is dependent on their interpretation of group goals and effective direction of terrorist operations and they need to use violence as a means of maintaining group cohesiveness as well as pursuing instrumental objectives. It is rarely possible for them to find a substitute for violence since many recruits rejected other organisations precisely because of their nonviolence. Paxto Unzueta, a former member of ETA, said that:

> Today's ETA has nothing to do with the ETA of the beginning
> ...We were against Franco and saw ourselves as part of an intel-
> lectual movement, influenced by the wider events of 1968. Most of
> us came from middle-class, urban backgrounds. A lot of us were
> students. Now the recruits are the disaffected youth in search of a
> ruck with authority.[158]

It appears that violence may have become the end, not the means, and it is this violence that provides the *raison d'être* of the group. As will be discussed later, an excessive focus on the struggle, rather than the goal, poses immense problems for the terrorist organisation, if it still does have a nominal strategic objective. Cathal Goulding recognised that the IRA were in such a position in the early 1960s:

> The fight for freedom had become an end in itself to us. Instead of
> a means, it become an end. We hadn't planned to achieve the
> freedom of Ireland. We simply planned to *fight* for the freedom of
> Ireland. We could never hope to succeed because we never planned
> to succeed.[159]

Psychology may not explain nuclear terrorism specifically, but it does offer significant explanations of the escalatory pressures on terrorists, both individually and collectively, that would be critical to any act of nuclear terrorism. In some cases, terrorist groups move beyond employing violence as a instrument, and instead become driven to commit violent acts by individual and group pressures. This can be used as both an explanation and a justification since it enables the perpetrators of violence to deflect responsibility onto others. They can argue that 'it's not really my fault', blaming outside author-ities for 'driving' them to terrorism as a last resort, and thus avoiding the guilt that would in other circumstances act as a check on their actions. This shifting of responsibility is important not only in the use of terrorism as a tactic, but in the specific levels of violence employed: escalations of violence, even acts of mass terror, can be justified because the terrorists were left with no choice in order to ensure that their message was heard. The need for publicity is 'the lifeblood of terrorism', at least that committed for political ends, is vital and is intimately connected to the survival of the group, the prime objective of the organisation. It is this that makes it hard for terrorist leaders to de-escalate the level of violence employed, particularly if there is competition either from within or without the group. Violence is also the main identifying aspect of the group, it is what sets it apart from other organisations. To consider reducing the level of violence or stopping it altogether is to strike at the heart of the group's identity. Leaders have a key role, especially in close-knit groups that have gone underground. In such cases, the organisation may come to reflect the personality of the leader, especially when fear and the pressures against dissent or exiting are strong. It is then hard to avoid doing the will of the group, as focused by the leader. However, this is not to suggest that there is a 'terrorist personality', either amongst leaders or followers, and although some traits, such as a negative identity, do appear to be more prevalent amongst terrorists than society as a whole, it does not obviously correspond to a determinant of those who engage in terrorism. It is the act of terrorism that is the link between diffuse terrorists and groups with a wide range of motivations, rather than some initial psychological attribute. Psychology does, though, offer a partial explanation for the way that individuals become involved, and the way that group dynamics determine the development of a terrorist campaign. As will be seen in later sections, although there are marked motivational differences between secular and religious terrorism, and even between left and right-wing terrorism, there are also significant psychological similarities, many of which have been discussed here.

TACTICS AND TARGETING

Psychology and motivation may partially explain how an individual becomes a terrorist; why they remain involved and the pressures that are felt by both the individual and the group as a result of the dynamics of the organisation. However, it is of limited efficacy in establishing why a terrorist group uses a specific method to attempt to achieve its ends, and thus to partially assess the likelihood of a group believing that the use of a weapon of mass destruction is in their interests. Psychology and motivation may explain why terrorism is used at all, but it needs a more instrumental approach to determine why the group uses a bomb over a gun, for example. It may be that, especially in the earlier stages of involvement, there is no separation between the resort to terrorism and the method chosen. There is rarely a single, clear-cut decision to use terrorism. Instead, there is a progression towards violence, a process rather than a definite choice. Therefore, it is likely that the first few terrorist attacks are determined by what is feasible, by those materials and skills that are available to the group. Later, the tactics and targeting of the group will largely hinge on organisational dynamics: their belief system, structure and decision-making process. Tactics employed, and the example set, by other groups may also represent an important influence on terrorist organisations. As groups decline in influence or begin to split, there is an increased tendency to escalate the level of violence employed, a trend that is reflected in a number of cases and which might have important implications for nuclear terrorism. However, overarching all this is the question of terrorist rationality: to what extent is strategic choice purely an instrumental decision of which methods will be most effective for the group?[160] Is it also crucially affected by other factors, such as psychology, which partially determine tactics as well as involvement? It is worth clarifying the concept of rational choice. It does not equate to the 'right' decision of which strategy will be most effective in achieving goals. It means that there is a judgement of how to effectively tie means to ends, the conclusions of which are followed through consistently. The decision needs only to appear to be the optimal one at the given moment, once a cost-benefit assessment has been made by the terrorist.[161] Rationality is important as a basis for terrorists' tactical choices. Even in the case of fundamentalist terrorism, often perceived as one of the least rational forms of political violence, there are clear elements of pragmatism and instrumentality in strategic choices. Hizbollah's move from suicide-bombings to kidnapping foreigners in Lebanon during the mid-1980s was due to a number of factors, external as well as internal. First, their previous tactic had succeeded in dramatically reducing the Western presence in Lebanon, so there were simply fewer obvious targets to bomb. However, the group wanted to continue to pressurise the West over its Middle Eastern policies.

Second, they sought a method that would permit this pressure to be exerted over a prolonged period, enabling their campaign to be tied to external factors such as the release of Shiite prisoners, notably the al Da'wa group in Kuwait. The move from kidnapping, with the release of Terry Anderson in 1991, was a reflection of Hizbollah's altering relationship with Iran and its own role within Lebanon, that made holding Western hostages superfluous.[162]

To some extent, terrorism as a strategy has already been discussed. Terrorism is the resort of the desperate: the defence that 'we had no choice' is not only a justification; within the parameters of group goals, objectives, willingness to compromise, and likelihood of success otherwise, it is the truth. The options for would-be terrorist groups are genuinely limited. Often lacking public support, their ability to alter government policies is fatally restricted. Terrorism is often a strategy of the impatient, those who have cursorily attempted to achieve their goals using the instruments available to them, but who are reluctant to invest the time, in mass organisational work for example, especially if the final success is doubtable. Connected to this is a frequent belief that time is short: either that they are unwilling to wait any longer for justice, or else that the moment for action is now, that the time is ripe, that there is an opportunity to be exploited. Terrorism has a number of potential advantages: it places an issue on the public agenda and it forces authorities to acknowledge the problem. Connected to that is that it creates publicity for the group, it makes them an entity that must be dealt with: they exist. Terrorism may also create the conditions for a wider movement, one with more likelihood of success, if it inspires the group's potential constituency, undermines the government's authority, or forces them to take measures that increase sympathy for the group and its cause.[163] It is important at this point to differentiate between the ultimate goals of terrorist groups, their strategic objectives, and the tactical goals employed to achieve this. It is the difference between long-term political goals, such as the overthrow of a regime, and military goals, the means to obtain that.[164] While the IRA's ultimate goal is a free, united Ireland; their military strategy, as defined in the 'Green Book', is:

1. A war of attrition against enemy personnel which is aimed at causing as many casualties and deaths as possible so as to create a demand from their people at home for their withdrawal.
2. A bombing campaign aimed at making the enemy's financial

interest in our country unprofitable while at the same time curbing long term financial investment in our country.

3. To make the Six Counties as at present and for the past several years ungovernable except by colonial military rule.

4. To sustain the war and gain support for its ends by National and International propaganda and publicity campaigns.

5. By defending the war of liberation by punishing criminals, collaborators and informers.[165]

The scale of terrorist demands is also important because it will certainly, at least in part, determine the lengths to which the group will be willing to go. A group seeking only a change in policy has more interest in maintaining the structure of government than a group intent on revolution. Thus, the first group is less likely to be willing to inflict widespread damage on society than the second group. One of the key differences between various types of terrorist organisation is in how they define their enemies. Nationalist groups may regard the enemy as the nation oppressing them; revolutionaries as the ruling class; and religious groups as apostates or other corrupting influences. Each definition produces radically different targets and thus campaigns.[166] This affects the tactics, strategies and means that a terrorist organisation is prepared to use. The question for this section then is 'how are these strategic goals to be achieved, within the framework of terrorism?' How do these goal-related choices affect the level of violence employed by terrorists, and thus how likely are they to use non-conventional weaponry?

Three premodern terrorist groups: the Assassins, Thugs and Zealot-Sicarii were each more durable and posed a greater threat to their society than any modern terrorist organisation. However, the weapons they employed were primitive; travel was by horse or foot; and communications were limited. Rapoport's contends that: 'The critical variable, therefore, cannot be technology: rather, the purpose and organization of particular groups and the vulnerabilities of particular societies to them are decisive factors.'[167] This supported by the example of the shishi, a terrorist movement that, using only traditional samurai weapons, was able to undermine the power of the Shogun and thus hasten the advent of the Meiji Restoration in mid-ninetenth Century Japan.[168]

Terrorists have proved extremely adept at inventing new methods of attack to circumvent the protective counter-measures imposed by state's security forces. Terrorist groups and security forces are engaged in a constant battle for technological supremacy. However, terrorist organisations are also able to inflict significant damage using low technology weaponry. The Armed Islamic Group (GIA), a radical Algerian Islamic group, between July and October 1995, launched a campaign of nail-bombing in France, using camping gas canisters as their explosive. They succeeded in killing eight people, wounding 180, and caused 32,000 security personnel to be mobilised.[169] Other well-established terrorist organisations have also been periodically willing to use crude but effective home-made weapons in pursuit of their campaigns. The IRA bombings of 20 July 1982, also used nail-bombs, although the explosive used, 25lbs of gelignite in the Hyde Park attack, was not as improvised as that of the GIA. The effects were devastating: seven members of the Royal Greenjackets were killed in Regent's Park and four members of the Household Cavalry and several horses died in Hyde Park.[170] Although the organisation used semtex as early as 1976 and retains a sizeable quantity of the plastic explosive, they still sometimes use agricultural chemicals and fuel as the basis for their devices. Furthermore, the IRA has become increasingly adept at building its own mortars, hand grenades, mechanical and electronic timers, mercury fulminate detonators, radio and command wire bombs, and booby trap devices, to name only a selection.[171]

Does a terrorist group use a particular weapon because it has limited alternatives or because it is the best means of attracting attention to the campaign and forcing revolted governments and publics to reassess their willingness to remain committed to a particular course? The two options are not mutually exclusive, but they do have important reverberations for the issue of nuclear terrorism: if there is no terrorism involving nuclear devices, is it because no groups are able to get the necessary materials to commit such an act, or because no group wants to commit such an act, that conventional means remain sufficient? Is it always a sign of organisational weakness if a terrorist group resorts to low technology for their attacks? This is a critical question because one argument for possible circumstances in which terrorists might resort to non-conventional weaponry is precisely this point at which groups believe themselves to be in decline and decide to escalate their level of violence to ensure organisational survival. The two, desperation due to a perception of the group's weakness, and a desire to escalate, are entirely compatible. Terrorist groups decline for more reasons than simply lack of resources. It may not even follow that low technology terrorism equates to a lack of alternatives due to a paucity of resources. Terrorists appear to be extremely technologically conservative. They resort to a few well tested, and, as they perceive, reliable methods.[172] Many terrorist organisations also appear to be risk-adverse: the emphasis is often on the group's survival and that requires keeping its members alive and free from arrest. White and White suggest that a safe means of escape for the terrorist is the dominant feature in PIRA tactics. They rarely plan high risk attacks and, if in doubt, abort the mission.[173] Obviously, this has the effect of mitigating towards the terrorist group favouring the tactics and weaponry with which it is familiar.

Although Aum Shinrikyo's sarin gas attack in Tokyo represents an obvious exception, even non-traditional terrorist organisations such as the Unabomber, Tim McVeigh or the World Trade Center bombers have continued to use variants of traditional terrorist weapons. Even when terrorists want to be certain of making a success-ful attack or are seeking to cause widespread casualties, they may be able to do so by using multiple conventional weapons. This may be especially so, given the untested and therefore unreliable nature of non-conventional weaponry as a terrorist device. On 29 June 1992, Mohammed Boudiaf, president of the Algerian High Committee of State, was assassinated in the town of Annaba as he gave a speech. A bomb was detonated first as a distraction while a gunman wearing a military uniform walked onto the platform and sprayed automatic fire. Boudiaf was fatally wounded in the back and head and 41 others were injured.[174] On 27 August 1979, the IRA succeeded in killing 18 British soldiers at Warrenpoint in Northern Ireland. They used two bombs, detonated by radio, one in a hay truck that exploded as a lorry filled with soldiers went past; and the second in an abandoned stone building that caught reinforcements arriving in two Land Rovers and a helicopter to assist the first group of soldiers.[175] Although obviously neither group had access to non-conventional weaponry for their attacks, it is almost inconceivable that they would have been used, even if available, conventional means being more effective.

Terrorist tactics vary significantly over time. Aircraft hijackings were, during the late 1960s and early 1970s, a regular high-profile target, but now are rarely attacked since fewer countries are willing to accept the planes; weapon-detection at airports has made it harder; and many countries have special units able to deal with such incidents. All this has meant that terrorists have moved on in search of easier targets that offer better returns.[176] Similarly, until the recent barri-cade and hostage situation in Lima, the embassy siege had been in decline as a tactic since the early 1980s, in contrast to 35 such

incidents in 1979 and 42 in 1980 alone.[177] Obviously, tactics vary
dramatically in intensity and violence over time. Between 1963 and
1967, the FLQ planted about 35, mostly small, bombs and carried out
eight hold-ups. In the three years leading up to the October Crisis,
these figures rose to 50–60 bombings and 25 hold-ups. The level of
violence in these attacks also increased: on 24 June 1970, two were
killed and two wounded in a bomb attack at Defense Headquarters in
Ottawa. In July, police defused 150lbs of dynamite planted in a car
outside the Bank of Montreal.[178]

In recent years, there has been a significant decline in the proportion of bombing incidents, compared to other forms of international
terrorism. Between 1968 and 1969, 44 per cent of all such terrorist
attacks were bombings, it rose to 53 per cent in the 1970s and then fell
slightly to 49 per cent in the 1980s. However, by 1995, this figure had
fallen to just 23 per cent. In its place has been an increase in attacks
designed to directly harm persons. Armed attacks for example
provided 44 per cent of incidents in 1995, compared with an average
of only 19 per cent in the 1980s. This is significant, since it supports
the suggestion that terrorism is not only increasing in lethality, but
that terrorists are selecting tactics that are more likely to cause fatalities, in addition to employing familiar weapons in ways that are
aimed at raising the likelihood of fatalities (e.g. by using bigger
bombs). It is worth noting that, in 1995, although the number of fatal
bombings fell to 21 per cent of all types of fatal incidents, 48 per cent
of all fatalities caused by international terrorism were as a result of
bombings.[179] This is not exceptional. In 1994, the figures for bombings
were 20 per cent of all fatal incidents, but 51 per cent of all fatalities.[180] Furthermore, 1994 and 1995 were 'quiet' years, with few high
fatality incidents apart from the 18 July 1994, Hizbollah attack on the
Argentine-Jewish Mutual Aid Association in which 96 people were
killed. In other years, this proportionate figure would be much higher.
Bombings are the terrorist tactic most likely to cause wide-spread
casualties. A significant development has been the move, in some
cases, away from technical sophistication. In the past, terrorists
tended to increase the complexity of their weaponry: the RAF's
attempt to assassinate General Haig in 1979 used 100lbs of TNT,
detonated by a household switch attached to four nine-volt batteries,
which was connected to 180 yards of wire, laid under grass, leading to
the explosive. The ambush relied on visual control: two motorcyclists
with walkie-talkies would warn of the approach of Haig's car. Their
assassination of Herrhausen, CEO of Deutsche Bank, in 1988 relied

on armour-piercing explosives, in a funnel-shaped charge, hidden inside a bicycle, and directed at the rear, right passenger door, exactly where Herrhausen was sitting. The bomb was detonated when the car broke a beam of light between two poles on opposite sides of the road. A control cable was used to activate the trigger, ensuring that it was Herrhausen's car that broke the beam.[181] However, in some of the most significant cases of terrorism of recent years, such as the bombings of the World Trade Center and the Murrah Building in Oklahoma, the perpetrators appear to have deliberately chosen to remain at a low technological level. Constructing bombs from diesel oil and nitrate fertilisers has a number of advantages, not least that it is virtually impossible to prevent terrorists obtaining such materials; but also that, given the amateur nature of those responsible for the bombings, crude home-made devices were almost certainly the most practicable to build.

Sometimes, the tactics employed by a group may have to change. The RAF's strategy until 1977 predominantly relied on kidnappings of leading political, economic and industrial figures, in order to place the authorities under pressure and compel them to release the RAF prisoners from German prisons. With the high profile failures of 1977, the murders of Ponto, Buback and Schleyer, with their attendant adverse and counter-productive reaction from the German public, the RAF abandoned the strategy. They turned instead to killing members of the Military-Industrial Complex and of the 'apparatus of repression'. This was the strategy they would continue to use until their renunciation of violence in 1992.[182] However, most terrorist groups have a repertoire of favoured tactics which they are reluctant to deviate from and which they adapt over time. These are not necessarily the same for all other groups. While almost all terrorist organisations use bombings as part of their tactics, relatively few rely on airline hijackings.[183] To some extent this may be a result of the fact that some activities clearly require less expertise, resources and risk than others. In that sense, at their most simplistic, bombings and shootings are among the most 'accessible' of terrorist activities, and are certainly more so than more complex tactics such as kidnapping. The tactic chosen depends on a number of factors, of which targeting and resources, both human and material, are the most important. If a group has amongst its members a skilled bombmaker, then the likelihood is that they will favour bombing campaigns over other methods. Equally, members with formal military training might be able to effectively use highly technical weaponry in a way that others could not.

However, the bigger determinant is the availability of material: terrorists have repeatedly shown a willingness and an ability to learn new techniques, to adapt favoured tactics, but if the weaponry or the means are absent, then it is obviously a largely hypothetical issue. The four shipments of arms from Libya to the IRA in 1985 and 1986 included a tonne of semtex explosive, 12 SAM-7 ground-to-air missiles, rocket-propelled grenade launchers, and nearly 120 tonnes of explosives, ammunition and guns. This arsenal continued to fuel the IRA's campaign for years: by 1990, British security forces had accounted for only a minute fraction of the weapons shipped into Ireland.[184] It would be inaccurate to suggest that IRA military strategy was determined by the shipment, but the availability of the arms did increase the options and directions that that strategy could take. The issue of resources is, at least in part, connected to the stage that the terrorist group is at. In 1968, the arsenal of the Belfast unit of the IRA consisted of two Thompson submachine guns, one Sten gun, one rifle and nine pistols.[185] Similarly, the FLQ's campaigns from 1967 benefited greatly from the ready availability of detonators and dynamite, as a result of the construction of the Montreal Metro, Expo '67 and the Laurentian Autoroute, and from a number of quarries around Quebec. At all these sites, security was poor and the explosives were available in such large quantities that it took some time for the losses to be recognised.[186] Such weaponry obviously limited the first few actions of the unit, until a wider range of arms was available. This may be related to the reason that there often appears to be a time-lag between the decision to resort to form a quasi-military organisation and the first attacks they carry out. Other factors in this include the need for training in techniques and the time needed to construct an organisational structure. Clearly, this varies according to the size, complexity and sophistication of the group and the acts it intends to perpetrate. The Tupamaros carried out their first operations in 1967, but the underground military group from which they stemmed, the MLN, was created in mid-1963.[187]

The subject of targeting is vast in itself, but it is worth considering one particular aspect in this context: the intended audience. Some attacks clearly have an international viewer as their prime object. They hope to bring international coverage to their cause and possibly increase the likelihood of international interference on the terrorist's behalf. It is not a coincidence that the Tupac Amaru rebels chose to stage a take-over of the Japanese Ambassador's residence in Lima during a reception that so many of the diplomatic corps attended.

Not only did the rebels succeed in refuting President Fujimori's claim to have finally defeated terrorism in Peru, they also gained world-wide publicity for their ailing campaign.[188] The ability of terrorists to attract this sort of coverage hinges on two aspects: either they must involve victims of interest to the world's media, which probably means citizens of Western countries, or else the implications or scale of the attack needs to be so immense that it is covered for its own sake. This is increasingly hard to achieve: on 31 January 1996, a suicide truck bomber drove into the Central Bank in the heart of Colombo's business district. The 500kgs of high explosive killed nearly 100 people, injured 1,400 others and caused millions of dollars worth of damage, and possibly cost billions of dollars in loss of business confidence. In spite of this, the coverage of the incident was modest in the Western press, certainly compared to an incident such as the World Trade Center bombing, or even the Peru siege.[189] In view of these circumstances, a terrorist group might be willing to consider a non-conventional attack, since that would increase the likelihood of widespread press coverage. However, it obviously poses considerable problems in other respects for the organisation.

This problem of receiving publicity and acknowledgement is not a new one for terrorists. The Stern Gang, when they broke from Irgun in 1940, were badly equipped and funded and had few members. Consequently, they adopted their tactics to accommodate this weakness. Revolutionary violence was only to be one part of the strategy, but it rapidly came to dominate all the others. Initially, due to their belief that the Irgun would never take part in an armed revolt, the LEHI decided to act alone. Their basic tactic was to strike at the British in whatever way would hurt. This had the effect of encouraging sporadic and ill-directed violence.[190]

By 1944, LEHI sought a victim that would 'change history', rather than the police constables and inspectors who had been their main targets to date. Just as crucial was Irgun's return to prominence (with their revolt of February 1944) which was utterly eclipsing the efforts of LEHI. The group had to find a new tactic to reclaim the limelight. They chose, as their next target, High Commissioner Sir Harold MacMichael because he was the highest representative of the British in Palestine; and because they wanted to educate the British to the follies of their policy in the region and their fellow Jews to the benefits of armed resistance. Throughout the summer of 1944, five assassination attempts had to be aborted for various reasons before LEHI were able to ambush MacMichael's car between Jerusalem and

Jaffa on 8 August. A petrol bomb was thrown, covering the road in flames and then the car was raked with machine gun fire. MacMichael himself suffered only minor injuries and, since he returned to Britain shortly afterwards, had to be abandoned as a target. LEHI again sought a significant victim and found one in Lord Moyne, British Minister of State in Cairo and the highest ranking British official in the Middle East. Yalin-Mor, a member of LEHI, explained:

> What was important to us was that he symbolized the British Empire in Cairo. We weren't yet in a position to try to hit Churchill in London, so the logical second best was to hit Lord Moyne in Cairo.[191]

Moyne was an attractive victim: a cabinet minister, titled, a friend of the Prime Minister, his death would be noticed. It would force Britain to regard Palestine as an international problem, not an isolated and internal one as they would have liked to believe. A less important reason was that, as the Irgun also sought to do, LEHI hoped that it would draw Arab attention to the frailty of the British position, perhaps encouraging resistance there too, easing their task in Palestine. Two young members of the group were selected, Eliahu Hakim and Eliahu Bet-Zouri. Hakim spent the autumn of 1944 watching Moyne's movements and was joined at the end of October by Bet-Zouri. On 6 November, as Moyne, in his car, pulled up outside the ministerial residence for lunch, Hakim and Bet-Zouri approached on foot. Bet-Zouri shot Moyne's driver as he stood by the car and then Hakim, opening the rear door of the car, fatally shot Moyne. They left Moyne's ADC, Captain Hughes-Onslow, and his secretary, Dorothy Osmond, entirely unharmed. The two assassins then tried to escape on rented bicycles they had left on the street, but were caught by a member of the Ministerial Protection Squad, El-Amin Mahomed Abdullah, whom they also refused to shoot at because it would have alienated Arab support, potential allies, to do so. It was an example of the rationality and instrumentality of a group renowned for its bloody use of violence. It also offered LEHI two more martyrs, as Hakim and Bet-Zouri were tried, and then executed on 23 March 1945.[192]

Terrorists may also be able to gain publicity for their cause by using tactics that are fresh, that set them apart from previous groups or tactics. One of the main reasons that 1968 is widely acknowledged as the beginning of the modern age of terrorism is that that was when the first airline hijackings occurred. Had the hijackers instead chosen to pursue a campaign of bombing and shooting, it is questionable whether they would have been perceived to be such a break from the numerous anti-colonial groups that had gone before. Of course, most terrorist organisations will not seek to achieve such 'spectaculars' and will continue with variations on their previous campaigns; but for those that do crave international recognition that sets them apart from other terrorists, the challenge is to find a 'new' method of violence. It is here that a group might consider using non-conventional weaponry to achieve this objective.

Selecting a weakness in a victim's defence need not necessarily preclude employing non-conventional means. The Russian Mafiya allegedly killed a Moscow businessman in 1993, using gamma-ray-emitting pellets, placed in his office.[193] In 1995, they killed Ivan Kivelidi, chairman of Rosbiznesbank using a nerve toxin. Although there was undoubted symbolic significance to the choice of weapon, part of the rationale may also have been that it offered a means to strike at the otherwise heavily protected target, to circumvent his defences.[194]

There are historical precedents for terrorists deciding to make a technological leap in their weaponry. In the second half of the nineteenth century, three groups, Narodnaya Volya in Russia, the Fenians in Ireland and Anarchists across Europe and the United States, relied heavily on the new invention of dynamite to promote their campaigns. The most spectacular example of its use was in the assassination of Tsar Alexander II in 1881. Although using a gun would have been easier and more reliable, dynamite was selected for the attack because, according to Mikhail Frolenko, a member of the executive committee of Narodnaya Volya, using a gun would have meant that 'this assassination would not have created the same impression; it would have been interpreted as an ordinary murder, and would not have expressed a new stage in the revolutionary movement.'[195] Dynamite, as a terrorist weapon, was accorded vast, almost mythical, powers until its limitations became clear. The parallels with terrorist use of non-conventional weaponry today are striking. Both appeared to offer the instrument for enormous destruction and millennial redemption, to annihilate the state, to expose its foundations in a way not possible with other weapons.[196] The dynamite campaigns ended, not as a result of government measures to prevent access to dynamite, but because leaders such as Peter Kropotkin, a founding figure in the Anarchist movement, eventually concluded that it was not possible to destroy historical structures built over thousands of years with a few sticks of explosive.[197] This again suggests that it is the target that matters, more than the weapon selected to attack it with.

One of the main weak spots of advanced industrial societies today may be their reliance on the electronic storage, retrieval, analysis and transmission of information. Vast areas of modern life are affected by computers and are thus vulnerable to sabotage by hackers. Most Western states have communications, medical, transportation, and financial infrastructures that are all heavily dependent on computers. Dedicated hackers, even armed with the most ordinary computer, can cause chaos, as well as access the most sensitive information. The US Department of Defense estimates that it receives around 250,000 computer attacks each year.[198] A concerted effort could, theoretically, render a country unable to function. Laqueur suggests the switch at Culpeper, Virginia, headquarters of the Federal Reserve's electronic network, handling all federal funds and transactions, would be a possible place in the US at which to strike.[199] Although the specific concern of a society vulnerable to attack through its computer system is comparatively new, the concept of states being technologically vulnerable is not. Into the 1980s, there was concern that a single terrorist bomb placed in the right place in the US power grid could disrupt lines to major cities, blacking out huge swathes of the country and causing massive disruption. It was also feared that a potential adversary might attempt to detonate a nuclear device that would create an electro-magnetic pulse over the Midwest, burning out the electronic controls for refineries, gas-processing plants and powerplants, to name only a few. With the difficulty of obtaining parts and the need for highly skilled labour to replace them, the disruption and economic cost would be potentially vast over a protracted period.[200] A similar attack was planned by the IRA in the summer of 1996. They intended to use multiple bombs to destroy six electric substations that link London and the South East of England to the National Grid. Despite the National Grid's contingency plans to deal with a cataclysmic power failure, the destruction of the transformers would have threatened to disrupt power to Britain's capital for months.[201] The economic, and therefore political, consequences of a successful attack would have been immense. However, it also raises the question, which will be returned to later, whether, given the potential effect of such a conventional attack, it would be necessary for any terrorist to resort to non-conventional weaponry.

It is relatively rare for the tactic of terrorism to have the desired effect. Some former terrorists have become leaders of their respective countries, Menachem Begin, Yassir Arafat and Yitzhak Shamir are all examples, but this has always occurred once they have renounced violence in favour of the political process.[202] Most of the marked successes of terrorism have come against colonial powers. Begin's strategy was largely to make the British withdraw from Palestine by making it economically impossible for them to remain. He suggests that the Irgun made a particular attempt to undermine the British government's prestige in Palestine. However, he believed that this arose as much from the existence of the group, as from specific tactics or targeting. While on the one hand, they hit at British prestige 'deliberately, tirelessly and unceasingly', the very fact of their presence, undefeated by repressive measures, was enough to deny 'the legend of its omnipotence'. Begin's point almost certainly applies more widely to most groups fighting governments: 'Even if the attack does not succeed, it makes a dent in that prestige, and that dent widens into a crack which is extended with every succeeding attack.'[203] The targeting of Irgun and LEHI represents a major difference between the groups. Begin said: 'We never attacked individuals, not even policemen or soldiers...Our opinion was that if you killed an individual, there will be another individual. So we did not use this method.'[204] By contrast, LEHI believed that when Irgun focused entirely on attacking buildings, it permitted the British to rebuild them, using money levied in Palestine. Shamir thought that the Irgun's strategy was less humane than LEHI's personal-terror tactic, since Irgun's bombing of buildings risked causing casualties at random, whereas LEHI's victims were all selected individually, for a specific reason.[205] Clearly, it is possible for groups to have a similar objective, to both use terrorism, and still to have significantly different tactics from one another. The most effective strategy to achieve a particular goal is not self-evident; there is no one terrorist tactic that is certain to bring the desired results. Consequently, terrorists have to be willing to alter their targeting and tactics. It also means that it is possible for terrorists to be unsuccessful in achieving their goal, yet believe that it is not the fact of using terrorism that is the problem, so much as the variety of violence they are using. This conclusion would obviously encourage experimentation with other types of terrorism, and, quite possibly, with an escalation of the level of violence being used, conceivably even to the level of non-conventional weaponry.

The attempt to expose the authorities as repressive and provoke them to over-react is a common objective of many terrorist campaigns, since it is hoped that it will lead to increased support, resources, members and thus ultimately to victory. In the 1950s and 1960s, Algeria was governed on the premise that it was not a separate nation, but rather an integral part of France. The FLN sought to drive the French government to react in a way that would show comprehensively to Algerians that the French regarded them as a separate entity. The FLN planted bombs in market places and other crowded locations. The French treated all non-Europeans as potential suspects, and in the mid-1950s, transferred all Algerian Muslim military units to mainland France and replaced them in Africa with European troops. The reality of an *Algérie Française* was thus hopelessly undermined.[206] Terrorism poses severe problems for any regime that is concerned to maintain a state governed by the rule of law and that preserves individual liberties. If the target is unable to protect its people, then it is failing in one of the most fundamental objectives of a state and the regime could be argued to lose some legitimacy as a result. The target's power is, to some extent, deflated. The nature of terrorism, seemingly random hit-and-run attacks, makes it extremely difficult to prevent altogether, and can therefore lend the terrorist organisation an air of superiority in the face of authority impotence. If unable to deal with the terrorist threat directly, a regime must try to minimise support for it. This can pose an awkward choice: do nothing and seem to be helpless; implement security measures that risk restricting the rights of uninvolved people as well as limiting the scope of terrorist actions; or make concessions to moderates, which although it may bleed off support for the terrorist group, can also be perceived as making concessions to the terrorist's cause, possibly encouraging more attacks and groups in the long run.[207] In each case, the results can be diametrically opposed to those intended and further undermine the regime's legitimacy. However, with the exception of anti-colonial struggles, it is still the case that, as Paul Wilkinson has argued: 'There is ample historical evidence that terror alone is not generally an effective weapon in bringing about the overthrow of dictatorships or democracies.' Furthermore, even in those cases where terrorism was successful in achieving major political change, it was almost invariably in the context of other factors, such as overwhelming support for the group in the population at large; or an internecine conflict that precluded a political or negotiated solution.[208] The absolutist nature of many insurgents and their organisations are precisely the factors that undermine their ultimate chances of success. Eamon de Valera, during the Irish Civil War, wrote that: 'What guerrilla warfare leads to is a desire on our opponent's part to come to terms with us, provided that these terms do not mean complete surrender by him to us, which is unfortunately what we require.'[209]

Many terrorist groups have been inefficient in recognising the effectiveness of their campaigns. They frequently delude themselves as to the results they are able to achieve. However, once they do appreciate the true situation, the group is faced with a number of critical choices, all of which threaten potential decline: to carry on regardless, diversifying their tactics, to join another organisation or to escalate the level of violence that they employ. In the mid 1970s, the IRA, bewildered by the lack of success from their campaigns, concluded not that the premise of their strategy had been flawed, but that they simply had not applied enough pressure. Consequently, they escalated the level of violence that they employed. The results were the series of devastating attacks on the British mainland, starting with the Birmingham pub bombings on 21 November 1974, in which 21 people died.[210] Although the IRA themselves are extremely unlikely to resort to nuclear terrorism, their logic, that more violence rather than less was needed, could conceivably be used by other groups to justify acts of mass-destructive terror. This is more plausible if the organisation is on the brink of collapse and failure, since, as has already been discussed, survival of the group can become the dominant motivation in determining a group's strategy.

The reasons for terrorist groups' decline are far from clear and are almost certainly a different combination of factors in each individual case. One instrumental approach might be that terrorism ends when it is no longer viewed by its practitioners as effective or legitimate, is no longer justifiable in terms of the ends it serves.[211] Certainly, the strategic choices of groups are key, but so are their organisational resources and the government's response. The effect of an action or response in ending terrorism is also tremendously variable.[212] While the *pentiti* system in Italy is widely credited with having contributed to the decline of the Red Brigades, the Supergrass system, applied in Northern Ireland, was an abject failure.

Poor strategic choices by the Red Brigades, such as the kidnap and murder of Italian Prime Minister Aldo Moro in 1978, 'initiated its fragmentation and defeat.'[213] As in the Moro case, the kidnapping and murder of Laporte by the FLQ forced the population at large to make the choice between terror and more mainstream methods of pressure. In both cases they chose the peaceable option. When the Tupamaros kidnapped American police advisor, Dan Mitrione, in

August 1970, the Uruguayan government declined to accommodate the terrorist's demands for the release of fellow group members. The Tupamaros felt obliged to execute their hostage, believing the government to be bluffing, but unwilling to risk losing bargaining power and the utility of political kidnapping (the group's main tactic at that point). As with the Red Brigades and the FLQ, their decision was the catalyst that permitted the government to impose heightened security measures that contributed to the ultimate defeat of the organisation.[214]

In the Canadian example, there were other factors at work too. As legitimate Quebec nationalist political parties gained an effective voice, the need for terrorism appeared less pressing. This decline in public support corresponded with increasingly efficient anti-terrorism techniques by the Canadian police and military, widespread short-term imprisonments, and a high incidence of individual burnout amongst members of the FLQ, who increasingly came to believe that their terrorism was no longer an effective weapon.[215] Certainly, this seems compatible with Ross and Gurr's assessment of why terrorism subsides: the authorities make it impossible for the group to act and increase the costs of their trying to do so. At the same time, there may be a decline in popular support for the group and increased disillusionment, causing members to exit the organisation.[216] Crenshaw adds the possibility of physical defeat, a strategic shift, as well as internal disintegration to the possible reasons that terrorism might subside.[217] Reilly believes that the considerations affecting both the initiation and the decline of political violence in a given situation are centred around attitudes and approval levels towards violence in a society, on its utility and on the likelihood of the group achieving their goals. The acceptability of violence in a society is key in whether terrorism is perceived to be a valid form of protest and thus may be closely linked to the level of support a group can hope to receive from their society at large. These perceptions may vary over time and are situationally determined, depending on the possibilities for a non-violent solution and the importance assigned to the issue in question. However, it does seem connected to the role of violence in a society's history, whether constitutional or unconstitutional traditions are dominant and whether violence succeeds in achieving goals for its users.[218] The role of this support is an especially central issue in the rise and decline of groups with nationalist-separatist objectives, where popular support does have some correlation to success. However, this can also apply to other types of terrorist group. The

Tupamaros failed for a number of reasons, but vitally, their inability to attract new members and supporters to their cause. They sought to provide the urban workers with access to a well-organised revolutionary group, 'in order to channel their revolutionary potential'. They emphasised revolutionary actions above rhetoric, believed relative depravation theory, and thought that terrorism would be the spark that would turn mass discontent over falling real wages into revolutionary zeal. However, the group could offer only long-term ethereal gains to the workers, who believed in reform elections anyway. Consequently, the overwhelming majority of people remained loyal to the party political system that already existed. Every use of terrorism by the Tupamaros thus served only to widen the gap between them and their potential constituents who now accepted elective politics as the norm.[219]

The correlation between support for terrorist groups and their decline is far from a straightforward one. Some organisations are clearly less reliant than others on popular support as a prop. Nationalist-separatist organisations seem, in most cases, to have a far higher 'natural rate' of support amongst their constituency than is generally so for anarchic-ideologue groups, although both may perceive their level of popular support to be significantly higher than it really is. Furthermore, support for such nationalist-separatist groups seems much less sensitive to decline as a result of terrorist actions, provided that the actions can be justified within the context of being part of a patriotic struggle and do not endanger fellow ethnics.[220] This is important because the fear of losing popular support is often cited as a reason why terrorists seldom resort to high-level violence. However, provided it is within the accepted traditions of a nationalist struggle, higher levels of terrorism may not jeopardise support for nationalist-separatist groups to the extent that it might for anarchic-ideologue organisations. In this context, acts of mass destructive terrorism are not as inconceivable as was once thought. However, since the idea of acceptable traditions is likely to convey a degree of proportionality, an act of non-conventional terrorism on this basis is singularly unlikely.

This does not necessarily suggest that, if support is lacking, terrorists will renounce violence because it is counter-productive. Part of their problem is that terrorist organisations often have grave difficulties in moving from violence. In part, this is as a result of psychological pressures and a determination to preserve the group's *raison d'être*. However, many terrorist organisations are genuinely slow to recognise when there are gains to be made through non-violent activity. In

1972, the IRA missed the opportunity for effective dialogue with the British government, after the latter had been driven into talks by Republican violence. Then, and in common with many other terrorist groups, they showed an inability to link their political demands to their military strength. This failure may have owed as much to the difficulty of persuading key members of the organisation to temporarily renounce violence, as to a deliberate, strategic choice.[221] Even sophisticated organisations, such as the IRA, that have well-established political wings, appear to have difficulty in pursuing an effective dual-track strategy. Despite a reorganisation, after the failures of the 1970s, and the apparent success of Sinn Fein in the British elections of 1982–3 had suggested that a new 'total strategy', incorporating the military as simply one tool in a wider campaign, might be more fruitful, the IRA retained primacy within the Republican movement and continued to use violence, irrespective of the political repercussions or popular reaction. Instead, compelled by a reluctance to compromise and a fear that any interim progress may become permanent, the campaign remained dominated by the military option.[222] Danny Morrison observed in 1989 that: 'when it is politically costly for the British to remain in Ireland, they'll go ... it won't be triggered until a large number of British soldiers are killed and that's what's going to happen.'[223] Martin McGuiness put it more succinctly in 1977: to keep 'blattering on until the Brits leave'.[224] This inflexibility does not universally apply to terrorist groups: the Tupamaros never used it as their sole strategy, relying on exposing corruption and other mild tactics too. Their initial resort to terrorism stemmed from an assessment of the conditions of Uruguayan society that the time was 'ripe' for more revolutionary actions. It was not until the group neared its end that terrorism as a tactic gained a momentum of its own. Originally it was an experimental, and limited, method that could be abandoned, should it prove unproductive. However, after the kidnapping and murder of Dan Mitrione in 1970, the group, wrought with disagreement, faced with an increasingly repressive regime and unable to admit that they had made a mistake, were driven to pursue the tactic of terrorism more thoroughly. It became the group norm for a time, but the organisation's leaders were also aware that their strategy would ultimately end in failure. Consequently, they abandoned terrorism altogether and instead sought to move to rural guerrilla warfare and more open confrontation with the Uruguayan military. This too, would finish in failure, and finally end the group.[225]

The strategic inflexibility of a movement at a given time does not necessarily preclude that they later learn to use a twin-track approach. The two arms of Republicanism in Northern Ireland, the IRA and Sinn Fein, had competing strategies: coercive military pressure against a desire to be included in any discussions about a solution to the situation in the province. By the 1990s, the movement had become more adept at alternating between the two to put pressure on the British. This can be seen in the use of ceasefires from 1993 onwards that placed the onus on the British government to find a means of maintaining the progress towards a settlement.[226] However, the strategy of the IRA has remained, in essence, unchanged: the British must withdraw, otherwise violence will ensue. The breakdown of the August 1994 ceasefire, after over a year, reflected the growing frustration of the organisation at the perceived failure of the political process. The evolution of the splinter groups, the Red IRA and the Continuity IRA, reflected a similar frustration with the July 1997 ceasefire. Although affiliated to a wider movement, the IRA itself remained a military organisation. As part of the Republican movement, it obviously had other options than the purely military one, but despite being a highly sophisticated organisation, sections of the IRA remained as bound by the organisational dynamics described earlier as any other terrorist group and therefore as dedicated to the military option as ever.

Having made such a choice, terrorist groups are limited in the available possibilities to increase pressure on their target. Escalating the level of that violence is an obvious choice, one that, given the additional psychological and organisational pressures already discussed, can be irresistible. Potentially, this could lead terrorists to consider the ultimate increase in violence, to non-conventional means.

In their 20 April 1998 letter announcing their disbandment, the RAF wrote that: 'It was a strategic error not to build up a socio-political organisation alongside the illegal, armed one.'[227] The German government took action that effectively denied the group's ability to attract new members. Imprisoned members of the RAF were vital to the group's strategy for recruitment. It was evident from the testimonies of former members of the organisation that many second and third generation terrorists joined the RAF because of the alleged inhuman conditions of imprisonment and for the goal of liberating the prisoners. Consequently, from November 1991 to September 1992, led by Justice Minister Klaus Kinkel, the German government released four members of the RAF after they had served the minimum time required by their sentences. The government made it clear that future prisoners would be released early, in accordance with the penal code, provided that the RAF cease-fire of April 1992 held.[228] Denied much of its *raison d'être,* terrorism, as well as the release of the prisoners, the group lost most of its direction and disbanded in 1998. This was more to do with the group's difficulties of recruitment than that the government action *per se* forced them into premature retirement. These problems could also be attributed to the irrelevance of the RAF's ideology in the post-Cold War world and the consequent preference of potential German terrorists for more local, non-underground and issue-specific groups, such as the Revolutionary Cells and Autonomen.[229] LEHI also feared the effects that prison would have on the group. Yalin-Mor said: 'Our slogan was, "Kill or be killed, but don't be arrested." Prison could have destroyed our movement. Conditions in the detention camps were not bad and many people inside were broken. They became neutral.'[230]

Terrorist groups base their tactical and targeting decisions on what is feasible, the availability both of resources and of potential victims, and on what they believe will be effective in promoting the objectives of their campaign. However, the inability of many terrorist groups to see beyond a military option means those organisations, faced with their failure to obtain key objectives, may be more likely to interpret that as being due to insufficient levels of violence being employed, rather than an indication of the instrumental paucity of violence as a strategy. If that is so, the obvious conclusion of such an interpretation would be that an escalation of terrorism should be the preferred option. Given that the feasibility of high-level attacks has risen with the increased availability of new resources, such as fissile material, some groups might even extend that, if they could, to non-conventional weaponry and to nuclear terrorism. The next two sections analyse the two broad types of terrorist organisation that have come closest to resorting to mass-destructive terrorism: those motivated by political extremism, and right-wing beliefs in particular, and those driven by religious ideologies.

# 3 Religious Terror

## RELIGIOUS TERRORISM

Until now, this discussion has focused predominantly on anarchic-ideologue and nationalist-separatist groups, but in the past fifteen years there has been a rising tide of terrorist violence from outside of these categories. In that time there has been a renaissance of religiously motivated actions, and more recently, a resurgence of violence stemming from right-wing organisations. Between them, these types of groups have been responsible for many of the worst terrorist incidents of recent times, and therefore clearly merit exploration in any assessment of possible perpetrators of nuclear terrorism.

Perhaps the easiest method to distinguish religious terrorism from other types is that in the former case, the group will make use of, and require, scripture or a clerical authority to justify, sanction and approve the violence they employ. It is worth noting that nationalism and ethnicism remain the main motivations for domestic terrorism. However, in 1995, 25 of 58, or 42 per cent of, known, active international terrorist groups had a predominantly religious component or motivation. These figures exclude organisations, such as the IRA, ETA or Armenian groups, that clearly have a religious element but whose main impetus is nationalist.[1] It is Rubenstein's contention that even fundamentalist terrorism is clearly nationalist.[2] This is obviously so in some cases, Sikh militarism for example, but other movements do seem more religious than secular and more international than nationalist. Hizbollah is a pan-Islamic movement, that seeks to create a single Islamic community and rejects the concepts of Arab or Persian nationalism.[3] However, even in these cases, terrorism comes from volatile extremist groups on the fringes of nationalist coalitions; this applies equally to Middle Eastern Muslim and to American Christian white supremacist fundamentalism. The decision to remain on that fringe or to break away is largely determined by political issues such as doctrinal differences within the broader movement, tactical and local matters, and the degree of threat posed to their cause by secularisation.[4] Religion is the way that they express political ideals, including hatred of foreign domination, dreams of national redemption and their social conservatism. They seek power to defend the faith, defeat their enemies and establish a regional dominance.

The upsurge in religious terrorism, especially since 1988, can in part be attributed to the widespread belief that the group's respective religions lie at a vital historical point. This stems from increased globalisation, and the perceived erosion of traditional values, along with widespread economic and political upheaval and inequality, leading to heightened feelings of fragility, instability and uncertainty about the future. Terrorists feel the need to preserve their religious identity, but also believe that there is the opportunity to fundamentally alter their futures. Religion is a refuge, familiar, and reflecting constant values, in an age of change. It is also an instrument for political action. However, it remains defensive and reactive in the eyes of its perpetrators. This is often combined with an upsurge in militant clerical leaders. These more activist ideologues increase support, strengthen the group and act as a legitimating force for the use of violence through their theological justifications for terrorism.[5]

Since the quest for power is quintessential to politics and international relations, it is impossible to regard religious terrorists as apolitical.[6] Juergensmeyer suggests that by using a religious justification for violence, terrorists become overtly political: they break the state's monopoly on morally justifiable killing, and therefore make a claim of political independence.[7] While driven by religion, religious terrorists undoubtedly make day-to-day practical political judgements as a result of their particular situation.[8] However, this is not to deny that religious terrorism is significantly different from its secular counterpart, that it clearly has an added component that is lacking from nationalist-separatist or anarchic-ideologue violence.

Religious terror is not new: Rapoport argues that until the nineteenth century religion was the only justification for terrorism,[9] but as a major motivation of modern international terrorism it is comparatively recent; in 1968 none of the 11 identifiable active terrorist groups could be classed as religious.[10] The importance of religion in enhancing the likelihood of violence being employed by some groups is that it has the ability to inspire total loyalty and commitment, and, as has been seen in the case of secular terrorism, such an uncompromisingly holistic attitude is a prime factor in the utilisation of force as a valid means. The intensity of feeling that religion engenders also mitigates against ready resolutions to religious disputes and encourages more violent solutions than might otherwise have been the case.[11] The struggle is often perceived as an all-out fight between good and evil, believer and unbeliever, justice and injustice, order and chaos. This totalism is critical in justifying violence generally, but as with secular terrorism, can also be the legitimation for greater acts of terror than would otherwise be tolerable. The intensity and importance of the battle can be used to justify the levels of violence employed in its name.[12] Also relevant is that, as a result of group fragmentation or the imprisonment or killing of older members, many religious terrorist groups have an extremely young, educated and newly urbanised membership that hold intolerant, radical worldviews. Such terrorists are more likely than their older counterparts to resort to higher levels of violence,[13] and maybe, in some cases, to the very highest levels, acts of nuclear terrorism.

Furthermore, the language of religion often deals explicitly with violence because it reflects the ultimate tension between order and disorder, the latter of which is inherently violent. That language can readily be adopted by terrorists to reinforce their message.[14] This has two purposes: because religious images and metaphors tend to be widely and rapidly recognised by the population as a whole, they enable the terrorist group to easily portray their message, and also have the effect of giving that message a heightened legitimacy through assuming a divine purpose. Many Armenian groups, for instance, identify their struggle with Christ's Passion, an ideal metaphor for revolution since it encompasses violence followed by rebirth. In messianic movements, it is the renewal and revival aspects of the religion that are key, a return to the vital core, and in many cases this means a resort to violence. In both Islam and Judaism, the founding period was defined by force: Mohammed and the early Caliphs were great warriors and in Israel, Gush Emunim members emphasise the ruthless conquest of Canaan and the partnership between God and Israel for taking the Promised Land, revealed in the Sinai Covenant. By contrast, the early Christian church was pacifist in nature, but even here, messianic movements can find support for their cause, emphasising a vengeful Christ, returning to exact retribution for his wronged people and cleansing the world ready for Judgement.[15] Girard argues that religion and violence are inextricably linked, that its prime purpose is to direct violence outside the religious community, to avoid fratricide within the group. He believes that violence is necessary to conquer violence within the group, so that the states of violence and non-violence are not unconnected conditions. He argues that sacrifice is the primary sacred act because it channels their aggressive and violent activities away from their community, ensuring that it is not endangered by such sentiments. Girard attributes violence to 'mimetic desire.' In this, one identifies with an idealised image of another person; but this can also lead to hatred and competition, so it is necessary to have symbols of the rival that can be conquered and thus assimilated, hence the centrality of the rite of sacrifice: it is a scapegoat of the rival.[16] This leads to the conclusion that religious terrorism might be a result of the failure of religious ritual to function correctly, creating a 'sacrificial crisis' in Girard's phraseology. Girard's theory might be successfully applied to all the major world religions with the exception of Buddhism, which differs from the others in at least one key way: whereas other religions attach importance to a cosmic struggle enacted in the terrestrial world (there are numerous examples of this in both the Old and New Testaments and the Hindu Mahabharata, for instance), Buddhism's spiritual clash is internalised in the mind of the believer between the perception that this imperfect and illusory world is real and a higher consciousness that surpasses worldly perception completely. Buddhism is a tradition almost devoid of religious-sanctioned violence, so may offer an exception that proves the rule.[17]

## SACRIFICE AND MARTYRDOM

Some religious terrorism clearly does encompass the idea of sacrifice, sometimes expressed in the form of martyrdom, but much of it seems more akin to warfare than to sacrifice in a meaningful sense. However, there do seem to be Girardian elements in the use and selection of martyrs by Shiite groups in Lebanon during the 1980s. They had to be male; old enough to be deemed individually responsible for their actions, yet young enough that they were not married so there would be no dependants left behind; the martyrs could have no ties to anyone who might consider it their duty to avenge the death against its sponsors; those selected for self-sacrifice also had to have a minimal measure of pious intent and no traits that might be interpreted in the surrounding society, the audience, as a sign of emotional disorder because it is important that only the purest of motives can be attached to the action.[18] It was crucial to Girard that these people lacked a key social link because then they could be exposed to violence without fear of reprisal. Their death would not automatically entail an act of vengeance. Israeli security services drew up a profile of the 'average' Hamas or Islamic Jihad suicide-terrorist. They tended to be single; aged between 18 and 27; from a family of limited means; either unemployed or with a meagre income; and have little education. Of those that lived in the Gaza Strip, most came from Gaza City itself; and from outside the region, most were from around Ramallah or the Jenin/Kalkilya region. In both localities, the terrorists had often been taught at religious educational institutions administered and funded by Hamas. All the terrorists studied by the security services were extreme in their nationalism and religious adherence; and were mentally distressed after specific incidents at the hands of Israeli soldiers or civilians. There were other important secondary motivations too: the desire to imitate other suicides which had been successful in their mission and earned great prestige in the Palestinian community; the desire to avenge attacks by Israeli terrorists such as that by Baruch Goldstein on the Cave of the Patriarchs in Hebron in February 1994, or other past injustices; or the desire to cleanse the individual's name from a charge of collaboration, whether just or unjust, although this motivation appears rare in the case of suicide-terrorists.[19] Bombers also believe that they are assured a place in heaven as a result of their actions.[20]

The voluntary acceptance of death in order to demonstrate the truth to man is a vital method of message-giving religions to dispel the doubts of believers and to aid evangelical efforts. The role of the early saints in Christianity offers an excellent example of this. In Islam, martyrdom is also widely admired, especially if it is achieved attempting to defeat Islam's enemies. Hizbollah described the 1983 embassy bombers in Beirut as: 'two martyr mujahidin [who] set out to inflict on the US Administration an utter defeat not experienced since Vietnam, and a similar one upon the French Administration'.[21] However, as Taylor points out, it is not only religion that incites martyrdom amongst adherents: he cites the example of the IRA hunger strikers in the early 1980s. Although they did not die committing a terrorist action, their deliberate, preplanned deaths clearly were a form of suicide in the pursuit of the cause. Roman Catholicism does play a significant role in Irish Nationalism, but it is not the primary motivation of the IRA. This suggests that religion *per se* is not the critical factor in suicidal terrorism; rather, it is an environmental context that allows and supports martyrdom that is key, and religion is one of the possible environmental facilitators. However, in many cases, it is impossible to separate religion from other forces, such as nationalism. June Leavitt, a neighbour of Goldstein's, and someone who had known him for over ten years, described his motivation for the Hebron attack as follows:

[T]his coldness of character went together with a flaming feeling
for God and the Jewish people, not as individuals who could be
hurt by his severe manner but as a nation. He adored his family, yet
his inner life was larger and more allegorical. He came to Israel
because he believed the biblical prophecy that Jews would return to
the land. He believed that this was the time of the redemption. He
was back in the Bible when God spoke to people... He saw the
ancient Philistines before his eyes. Heard the Jewish nation crying.
The night before he committed his act of revenge, as he tried to
listen to the Book of Esther for Purim in the Cave of the Fathers,
he heard the chants of the modern Arabs '*Itbach el Yehud*' ('Kill the
Jews'). How long he planned to rise up like an ancient Samson and
slay the ancient enemy, no one knows... If there was a God and if
he came to people and made them do earth-shattering things, then
he would come to a man like Baruch. Cold and hard like ice, with a
fiery devotion to things higher and deeper than this world. God
would choose a man who could unblinkingly sit with his son and
listen to the Book of Esther in the night, and in the morning put on
his Army uniform, take his rifle and much ammunition, creep out
of the house, knowing the chances were he'd never see his sleeping
wife or children again.[22]

Martyrdom is important for the likelihood of nuclear terrorism in
two respects. Firstly, it shows that there are individuals who might be
willing to sacrifice themselves to ensure that a nuclear attack was
executed effectively. Given the potential effect of such an attack, if
the terrorist had to have the chance to escape, it would require more
time than is the case with a conventional attack, increasing the possibility that the device might be discovered in the meantime. Secondly,
it is clear that martyrdom is not solely the province of extremely
committed religious adherents. Although religion remains the chief
motivation of suicide-terrorists, individuals willing to sacrifice themselves for such an attack could also come from a much wider, secular,
background.

There are several examples of mass-suicides, usually in a religious
or cult context, from Masada in 73 CE through Jim Jones Peoples
Temple in 1977 to the Branch Davidians at Waco in 1993. While the
religious aspect is obviously important, peer pressure seems to have
been as vital in the decisions of people to voluntarily take their own
lives.[23] The threat to commit suicide remains as a potent weapon to
groups: in April 1982 Rabbi Kahane's followers in Kach barricaded

themselves underground in Yamit, as a protest at the Israeli withdraw
from Sinai. The event achieved widespread coverage and Kahane was
rushed from New York by the Israeli government to negotiate a resolution to the situation. The action was unsuccessful in achieving a
cessation of the withdrawal, but it did raise the profile of the group
and their cause.[24] However, the opportunity to commit mass suicide
does not appear to be an obvious motivation for an act of nuclear
terrorism. There have been groups, such as Aum Shinrikyo, that
attempted to cause massive casualties to hasten Armageddon, as well
as organisations in which everyone killed themselves, but there is
little evidence, as yet, of terrorists that combine both elements,
seeking, Samson-like, to destroy their enemies along with themselves.


## THE OBJECTIVE OF RELIGIOUS TERRORISM

The primary concern of most religious radical movements is to save
their own culture from the dangers of apostates *within* the community,
rather than from the influence of infidels without it. Juergensmeyer
cites the example of Sikh extremists, who find that: 'secularism is as
much a threat as Hinduism, and like fundamentalist movements in
many other parts of the world, Sikh traditionalists have seen the
secular government as the perpetrator of a dangerous anti-religious
ideology that threatens the existence of such traditional religious
communities as their own.'[25] External enemies are of secondary
importance to internal ones, and violence can easily become fratricidal; hence the need in Girard's view for external sacrifices.[26] The
Shiite case provides evidence for this: when in the late 1980s it became
clear that self-sacrifices were not achieving their military objectives,
they were banned by Islamic clerics because they had lost their value
as acts of war and become merely wasteful of life. In January 1989,
several hundred Hizbollah fighters entered villages in southern
Lebanon and slaughtered the followers of the rival Amal movement in
their sleep. The two groups were contesting the ground that the
Israelis left as they withdrew from southern Lebanon, and the conflict
between the Shiite organisations threatened to destroy the community. Clerics appealed for an end to violence and banned the killing of
a Muslim by a Muslim, but it had little effect: passions were deep-
running and the self-sacrificing operations had suggested that one
Muslim might legitimately kill another in the name of Islam. Girard
argues that 'the eroding of the sacrificial system seems to result in the

emergence of reciprocal violence. Neighbours who have previously discharged their mutual aggressions on a third party, joining together in the sacrifice of an "outside" victim, now turn to sacrificing one another.'[27] Another aspect of the same phenomenon is the way that individuals seeking to exit the organisation are treated. Some of the reasons for this are those that apply to secular terrorist groups: exit offers an increased risk of discovery and persecution by the enemies of the cause. As an additional factor though, as well as rejecting the group, the exiting individual may also be perceived to be rejecting the beliefs of the organisation. Effectively, they become apostates of the worst kind. An extreme example is that of the Aum Shinrikyo cult which kept its ordinary members subdued through a poor diet, drugs, little sleep and other various bizarre methods such as the 'Perfect Salvation Initiation (PSI)', an electrified skull cap that administered shocks to the member to harmonise their thought waves with that of cult leader Shoko Asahara. The cult became increasingly violent in dealing with dissent, attempts to leave or members who became excessively weak or mentally unbalanced by their experience within Aum. They were murdered, or made to 'disappear'.[28]

Although the primary concern might be religious purity within a religion, this does not preclude an outward focus too. The reason may reflect a Girardian desire to shift violent conflict onto an external body; but it is more likely that it stems from a belief that it is necessary to attack the cause of godlessness, corrupting parts of the religion, at its root. Such an attitude would seem to be supported by statements such as that contained in the letter given to the hostage, John McCarthy, on his release, to pass on to the UN Secretary General:

> This is a message for mankind, that they may thereby be warned, that they may know that there is but one God, and that men of understanding may ponder it.
>
>    The United Nations... has become a plaything in the hands of the Superpowers, particularly America, the Great Satan, since your organisation has become merely a cover to protect the interests of world imperialism, and suppress the movement of the oppressed peoples yearning for the achievement of their independence...
>
>    We appeal to you... and to the world as a whole, to adopt Islam as an ideology, a code of law, and a system and to follow the teachings of the great Imam Khomeini.[29]

By demonising Islam's enemies, such statements increase the legitimacy, and thus the acceptability, of attacking them. Ramzi Yousef justified attacks on the US because of Western support of Israel against the Palestinians and Lebanese and because it was of the '"utmost importance" for the world to know that Muslims would never agree to give up Jerusalem.'[30] As with secular terrorism, religious terrorists need to use instruments of guilt avoidance: reducing the opponent to an abstraction; transposing blame onto the victims and the enemy; and self-justification and restatement of the validity of the cause. Religious violence offers its perpetrator a greater opportunity for vengeance on their enemy than they would otherwise have. As with all terrorism, it gives them an influence and impact that is out of proportion to their size or voice in the political process. Furthermore, although it is unlikely that terrorists would resort to such indiscriminate methods against members of their own community, for fear of injuring the just, it is entirely plausible to suggest that acts of mass-destructive terrorism could be used in an attempt to destroy as much of a corrupting infidel as possible.

In some cases, violence is given a cleansing, redemptive property by religious groups. Rabbi Meir Kahane argued that the Holocaust was a natural product of anti-Semitism that could occur in any 'normal' society and therefore could recur; it left almost irreparable damage in the Israeli nation's collective psyche that could only be redressed by concrete revenge, a physical humiliation of the Gentiles. For this reason, Kahane attempted to put his teachings into practice by creating a violent order that made anti-Gentile violence and terror the norm; this was reflected in his involvement with groups such as the JDL and Kach.[31] Unlike Fanon, who also espoused violence as a therapeutic recompense for years of oppression and mistreatment,[32] Kahane's theory of violence is almost cosmic, a metahistorical and insatiable desire for revenge. An example of this approach is:

> The bitter battle some 2500 years ago was between those Jews who sought to create a truly Jewish culture and society as opposed to those who sought to be Greek in form and idea. The latter came to be known as the Hellenists and the real battle of the Maccabees was against them, against the perversion and corruption of the Jewish people into a hideous, Hebrew caricature of foreign, gentilized, culture. That is precisely what the struggle is today in the Jewish state.[33]

By contrast, Fanon's theory is wholly rooted in a specific situation: the anti-colonial struggle in Africa. Kahane's violence is not political; it stems from the belief that anti-Semitism will continue even after the foundation of the Israeli state. Gentiles will continue to wish to dese-crate the name of God through the humiliation and persecution of His people until the arrival of the Messiah and the redemption of the world. This means that Jews should fight Gentiles wherever they are and since such violence is always legitimate, there is no need to worry about legality or restraints.[34]

## A COMPARISON OF RELIGIOUS AND SECULAR TERRORISM

There are, however, some clear similarities in motivations between these religiously-motivated terrorists and their secular counterparts: both experience a key event that altered their perspective and will-ingness to take action (*der sprung*); the need for recognition and praise in their community; the use of role models and imitation of them; and aspects of 'survivor guilt', manifested in the need to avenge fallen colleagues or coreligionists. A variant of survivor guilt is provided by several religions' historical traditions, and this may be instrumental in the resort to violence in some cases. Shiite Muslims bear communal guilt for failing to defend one of the founders of their tradition, Husain, when he was killed by the evil Yazid. By attacking subsequent enemies of Shiism as Yazids returned, Shiites might hope to right an ancient wrong. The denial and betrayal of Christ by early Christians, and the individual responsibility for that which is an aspect of subsequent Christianity has led some Christians to violent anti-Semitism, believing that it was to the Jews that Christ was delivered by such negligence.[35]

Religious terrorists can be seen to be similar to nationalist-separ-atist terrorists in their use of violence as a means of attacking authority whilst reinforcing their place in their community and there-fore it might be possible to argue that religious terrorism is as motivated by the need to establish identity as is secular terrorism. The role of the group in the move to violence is also key in the case of Palestinian suicide-terrorists. The group takes the bomber to a secret place where they are isolated with their trainers and instructed in the use of the explosive device and on how to react in various possible situations; and at the same time the suicide bomber undergoes a process of indoctrination and purification, climaxing on the day of the action.[36] Some of the trainees also undergo an initiation to test their nerve: two 17-year olds, captured before they could go on a Hamas suicide mission, told of being taken to a graveyard at night and then buried alive until dawn with just a small breathing hole. The role of secrecy and mutual trust is vital too, and often arises from personal and family connections: for example, one trio of bombers in March 1996 were two cousins and their neighbour.[37] Clearly the group plays a central role in directing and focusing the actions of the prospective terrorist towards their violent objective. In some cases, the group may also prey on the weaknesses of potential members. An Australian Federal Police psychologist, asked to profile members of the Aum cult, wrote that there was:

[N]o specific psychological profile that would predict a person's susceptibility for recruitment to the sect, although many sect members would have their personal, emotional, social and intellectual needs satisfied.

The recruitment of members could target people experiencing an existential or personal crisis which would provide an illusion of support, meaning, value or power.[38]

The rules are obviously different, but psychologically there is relatively little difference between a religious terrorist and a 'normal' person, constrained by the rules and norms that govern everyday life. The former's behaviour is closely controlled by a set of rules that are tightly interrelated and relatively limited in scope.[39] Religious violence also has the same degree of opportunism on both an individual and institutional level that applies to secular political violence. This reflects that in many cases, individuals wait until there is a movement to join, a ground swell, before acting because it is easier, both psychologically and instrumentally, to challenge the existing order as a member of a group than as an individual. Until that exists, even if they are severely discontented, it is certainly safer to conform to societal norms and avoid such violence.[40] It is obvious that terrorism is situationally dependent: the extreme right in Israel grew greatly in strength after the 1967 Six Day War because it offered fresh hope to territorial maximalists and enabled the principle of an undivided *Eretz Yisrael* to become a central tenet of modern Zionism.[41] For the extreme right, the victories of 1967 were nothing less than the hand of God assisting His people to reclaim another portion of land lost, by the pragmatism of Ben-Gurion and the betrayals of the UN, to the Arabs. Gush Emunim, founded in 1974, was able to exploit the idea of a Greater Israel to make political capital from the 1978 Camp David Accords that seemed to pose a threat to the gains of 1967. However, Gush Emunim and Kach form only a small part of those committed to Greater *Eretz Yisrael*. It also incorporates the radical leaders of the political parties Tehiya, Moledet and Tzomet, as well as elements within Likud, all of whom support the cause for reasons not related to religious extremism.[42] Radical organisations such as Gush Emunim can, in such circumstances, be viewed as beneficiaries of a more widespread movement.

Religious terror is significantly different from its secular counterpart in a number of key aspects. In secular terrorism, violence usually begins as an instrument and may become an end in itself; in religious terrorism, violence is predominantly a sacramental act or divine duty carried out in response to a theological imperative.[43] It is the deity that has a decisive impact on the determination of means and ends, in contrast to the modern secular-motivated terrorist for whom political ends are the objective and are to be achieved wholly through human efforts.[44] Fromm noted that religion can have such an influence that it can even impel a parent to injure their child; one Biblical example would be that of Abraham and Isaac. Fromm argued that this reflected complete devotion to, and operation within, the parameters of a religious system.[45] There is an absence of conflict for true believers whose actions are reaffirmed by clerical authority as being consistent with the word of God and His mission.[46] This characteristic means that religious-motivated terrorists may be less constrained by the moral, political or practical obstacles that impede other terrorists. Religion is a legitimising force; it can morally justify and may even require the sort of indiscriminate or mass-destructive violence that most secular terrorists would regard as immoral and counterproductive. This is because the constituencies of the two varieties of terrorism differ so greatly. Secular terrorists attempt to appeal to their actual or potential sympathisers, the people they claim to defend or speak for; in almost all cases, it is assumed that perpetrators mean only to harm their victims incidentally. It is the public that is the primary object of the action.[47] Religious terrorists, however, are simultaneously both the perpetrator and the audience; they comprise the constituents themselves. Post believes that for religious terrorists, the intended audience is the deity.[48] This is important because, whereas usually the symbolic and the audience-oriented aspects of terrorism are separate, in the case of religious-inspired violence, the two are synonymous. The need to gear action to what the terrorist believes the audience considers appropriate is therefore removed as a constraining influence in the case of religious terror. This clearly increases the possibility that religion could be used as a justification for nuclear terrorism. The level of symbolism in much religiously motivated terrorism is high. For groups such as Kach or Gush Emunim, the Land of Israel is key. The symbols of force and power are harnessed to intense symbolic nostalgia for the past, represented by the land. The messianic Jews believe that it is only through the land that redemption will come.[49] Other examples include striking at the heart of enemy territory, at the root of the perceived evil: an Islamic group attacking the World Trade Center in 1992 is a good case of this. The timing of an attack may also be highly symbolic: the upsurge in Hamas violence in February 1996 coincided with the second anniversary of the massacre in Hebron.[50]

Furthermore, in some extreme cases, the act of terrorism may satisfy no political, but only religious, purpose. The Thugs would be such an example. This is not to suggest that no religious terrorism has a secular audience: in contrast to the Thugs, the Assassins and the Zealot-Sicariis had a human audience of importance. To some extent, this reflects the difference between terrorist sects based on the Hindu religion, where there is no ground for believing that the world can be changed so the Thugs were convinced their role was simply to maintain the world in balance, and Islam or Judaism where the possibilities for radical attacks are intrinsic to the concept of unfulfilled divine promises. Since the promises are known to every member of the religious community, the Islamic and Jewish terrorist has a human audience not present for their Hindu counterparts.[51] This human audience may have an important impact on the tactics or targeting employed, in the same way that it does for secular terrorism: Islamic Jihad, unlike Hamas, does distinguish in its attacks between civilians and soldiers or settlers, trying to avoid victims from the former type. This may reflect that the relatively small group is keen to avoid incurring the condemnation of the Palestinian majority who reject the indiscriminate killing of women and children.[52] Even here though, it remains that the prime object is not the secular audience as it is with non-religious terrorism. However, such considerations do play a role, and would make it much less likely that a group such as Islamic Jihad would resort to the sort of widespread and wholly indiscriminate attack that is necessarily implied in an act of mass-destructive terrorism.

One key similarity between religious and secular terrorism is that they both operate within the bounds of perceived rationality: the 'mad bomber' is no more an aspect of the former than it is of the latter. Instead, as has been demonstrated, they represent a differing value system from that considered conventional. An example would be Yehuda Etzion, ideologist of Kach, who, when asked whether he respected the legitimacy of the government, replied that he recognised its legitimacy as the sovereign, but not the legitimacy of every law it passed, each of which had to be analysed separately to see if it was compatible with the Law of the Torah. When the government disobeys the Law, it disobeys God and brings anarchy. If it did so, it lost any legal or moral right to the obedience of the people who wished to live according to the Law, and who therefore had a duty to oppose such a government by whatever means necessary.[53]

On an individual level, some of the motivations for religious involvement are similar to those that impel activity in secular terrorist organisations. Erikson's hypothesis of the need by some (mostly young) people for identity applies equally in the case of religions organisations and may offer a partial explanation of the recruitment of individuals into such groups.[54] Individuals may be able to relieve their feelings of fragmented identity by adhering to an idealised self-image and by projecting weaknesses and faults onto scapegoats selected by the group's world view. The amount of relief and belonging that adherents feel on joining a religious group seems to be related to the extent of their societal alienation. They rapidly become dependent on the group for support and psychologically dependent on their enemies who symbolise evil to provide a focus and *raison d'être* for the adherent's group.[55] By 1989, Aum had brilliant, highly qualified chemists, biologists, doctors and computer programmers amongst their members. Many of these recruits were attracted to the cult by the alternative that it offered to Japanese society; it appealed to those lost and alienated by the system. However, Aum also targeted potential recruits: those who were young, lonely, financially needy, dropouts or otherwise detached from the norms of Japanese society were encouraged to join the cult, and then found it exceptionally difficult to leave.[56] As with secular terrorists, this has the effect of making individual terrorists far more willing to accept acts of violence that they might otherwise question.

Another significant similarity between religious and secular terrorism is the existence of inter-group rivalries; as in secular terrorism, they have the effect of increasing the frequency and level of violence

employed. Amal and Hizbollah competed with each other for dominance in sponsoring suicide assaults. They sought to outdo the other in
demonstrating their capacity for mobilising the necessary forces for
the operation. Amal and Hizbollah are fraternal movements: alle-
giances divided families, villages and neighbourhoods. Balance was
crucial to maintaining peace between them and when Hizbollah initiated self-martyring operations, Amal had to follow suit. As the
military advantages of these became less significant, self-martyrdom
was presented as having its own rewards. Therefore, the practical
yield of such operations diminished as Hizbollah and Amal sought to
outdo the other in the frequency of their operations.[57] This is important because it suggests that other inter and intra-group pressures that
exist in secular groups might be just as prevalent within terrorist
organisations with predominantly religious motives. It might be that
the vital driving forces behind religious terrorism are psychological
and organisational, just as they are with secular groups. This may
mean that, as rival groups seek to outdo each other in exhibiting their
piety and fervour, they will resort to ever increasing levels of action,
to attract support and new adherents. What could better display
commitment to, and a dedication to the pursuit of, the cause than an
unsurpassed attack against the enemies of one's religion? In his study
of the structure of Hizbollah, Ranstorp has shown that such rivalry
certainly applies with that group, and therefore it is almost impossible
to regard it as an unitary actor. Rather, it is a loose coalition of
Lebanese Shiite clerics, all with their own views and followings and all
engaged in almost continuous factionalism amongst themselves.[58]
The example of Muhyiden Sharif suggests that dissent or attempted
moderation within a group are just as unacceptable within religious
terrorist organisations as secular ones. Sharif, Hamas's chief bomb
maker, was killed in March 1998, allegedly by his own group, reflecting 'differences within Hamas over whether to compromise with the
Palestinian Authority' and cease terrorist attacks on Israel.[59]

Many underground terrorist organisations are similar to religious
cults in their redemptive nature: dividing the world into those who are
damned (them) and those who are to be saved (us); being authoritarian in nature; rejecting society; and offering solidarity and identity for
their members.[60] LEHI contained this element of salvation for its
members. Bell wrote:

Everyone who came to LEHI entered into a mystical bond. All
were dedicated to the destruction of the alien occupier and the

creation of a Jewish state ... [T]hey answered an ecstatic call within themselves to participate in a violent redemption. Not only power and the state would come from the barrel of a gun, but also their own salvation.[61]

In one sense, religious terrorists are quite limited in their objectives: they seek simply the maximum benefit for themselves and their co-religionists; whereas secular terrorists seek the maximum benefit for the greatest number possible. However, the reality of this is that secular terrorists (unless anarchists) tend to regard themselves as part of a system that they operate within and attempt to alter to their advantage; religious terrorists are more inclined to reject the system as a whole and seek to replace it with another, based on theological grounds. This self-perception of themselves as 'outsiders' makes it easier for them to contemplate more deadly and extreme forms of political violence against a more widely defined enemy than is the case with secular terrorists.[62]

## MESSIANISM AND MILLENARIANISM

It is worth differentiating at this point between those religions which believe that the promised future will occur only when all humanity hears their message and messianic religions which are more prepared to emphasise the role of man in hastening the coming of a prophesied messiah. Messianic belief means that the end of the world is coming because God has promised that it is; and at that time, He will inter- vene to save only those who deserve to be saved. This is called millenarianism or millennialism. Whereas most religions are prepared to take a passive role in this respect, waiting in expectation, for some of the fundamentalist religions, it is possible to facilitate redemption, 'to force the end'. An example of the former, Hinduism, has a messianic figure in the universal god, Vishnu, who will reappear at the time of worst distress. However, because this appearance is not predicted until 32899 CE, and not even Vishnu can break the endless cosmic cycle and bring eternal redemption, the idea of a messiah figure is not significant in Hinduism. Likewise, in orthodox Buddhism, there is little need for a messiah because the emphasis is on the religious transformation of the individual and any change would occur only when a majority of people were inwardly reformed, an event that might not happen for ages to come, if ever. This is not to deny that Hinduism and, to a lesser extent, Buddhism can and have been used to justify religious violence: for example, Hindu rulers have rights and duties under sacred law, which if breached, justify their subjects in revolting against the ruler.[63] However, millenarianism does not form a major part of either religion.

By contrast, Jewish Messianism, the belief in the heavenly ordained redemption of the Jewish people and the whole of mankind, is central to Judaism. Yahweh, as experienced by Israel in the Exodus, is a God of action who expresses his power and purpose through historical events. There is a strong belief that God is working out his prime objective through human history for the good of his chosen people. Yahweh is completely distinct from the world and completely supreme, and uses King-Messiah figures (David is the most important of these) as political and spiritual heads, whilst Yahweh remains the redeemer. The 'Day of Yahweh' (Amos 5:18) speaks of God executing judgement and on that day the messianic era will become a fact.[64] The traditional concept of it, especially following the failure of the Zealot's rising, involved a passive and apolitical attitude, while Jews awaited the coming of the Messiah, supported by texts such as the Book of Lamentations (3:26) which says 'it is good to wait quietly for the salvation of the Lord'. However, religious Zionism, as expounded by groups such as Gush Emunim, introduced a political element into that tradition by insisting on the religious right and duty of Jews in the post-emancipation period to actively participate in the God-ordained national redemption process, to be achieved by political, economic and other means to resettle Jews in the land of Israel, and regain their national independence.[65] Rabbi Kahane argued that although the redemption was inevitable, Jews had a choice how and when it would occur: if they repented, then it would come quickly and painlessly, otherwise it would be preceded by a period of great troubles and strife.[66]

As with Judaism, Christianity has a rich tradition of divinely inspired radical movements, dating back to the earliest church. The synoptic Gospels predict the early realisation of the heavenly kingdom, as Christ returned and consummated the messianic vision. Likewise, Paul assured the Thessalonians that the Second Coming was near and that he and many of them would live to see the day (1 Thessalonians 4:13–17). Just as much of the Old Testament deals with the tribulations of the Jewish nation; so too do the persecutions of the early Christians inspire apocalyptic writing, the best known of which is the Book of Revelation, written to comfort Christians

suffering for their faith. It contains multiple references to the impend-
ing Second Coming: 'The Lord, the God of the spirits of the prophets,
sent his angel to show his servants the things that must soon take
place' (22:6); 'The time is near' (22:10); or 'Behold, I am coming
soon!' (22:12). Christ will defeat Satan and establish his kingdom on
earth for 1,000 years. After that will be the Last Judgement and then
the new heaven and earth predicted in Isaiah 65:17. Mainstream
Christianity also espouses a passive waiting for the Coming, of salvation through faith alone. Christians must stand firm and continue to
follow the teachings of Christ, until He comes again (2 Thessalonians
2:15). Neither are Christians to resist the established authorities
(Romans 13:1–2), but they do have a higher loyalty to the principles of
Christianity, so must 'obey God rather than men' (Acts 5:29).[67] None
of this calls for a proactive stance, to speed the Coming, but it is a
constant theme throughout the New Testament to be ready, to 'keep
watch, because you do not know the day or the hour' (Matthew 25:13).

Islamic millenarian movements are predominantly associated with
Shia Muslims who believe that eventually a Mahdi (Messiah or
Rightly Guided One) will emerge to lead a cleansing holy war against
the Islamic orthodox establishment. This jihad (armed revolutionary
struggle) is essential in Mahdist theory as the method to achieve a
perfected social order.[68] One method of doing this is to remove or
eliminate those who interfere with the propagation of the Truth.[69]
There is no mention of a Mahdi in either the Koran or in the collections of the Prophet's teachings. Lewy suggests this may be because in
orthodox Islam, the faithful are saved by their membership of the
Islamic community. The first Mahdi was Mohammed, the son of Ali
(the Prophet Mohammed's son-in-law). This Mohammed was the first
of a line of infallible leaders or Imams. The twelfth of these is
expected to return to earth, from heaven, as the Mahdi, to establish
an era of righteousness. Eventually, messianic traditions established
themselves in the beliefs of many Sunni Muslims too, and the role of
the Mahdi developed from merely a just and righteous sovereign into
a redeemer of the faithful.[70]

Not all messianic beliefs result in terrorism.[71] They are not essentially or inherently violent; most of their adherents must be pushed
before resorting to such extremes of action. However, such beliefs do
create a background conducive to violence by polarising society and
thereby exacerbating existing tensions.[72] Messianism appeals because
although many established religions preach that the timing of the
Messiah's coming is preordained, they also encourage the belief that

the righteous and the wicked have different fates. Logically then, an individual's actions do count, and this makes it impossible for some who believe that the Coming is imminent to wait passively, because the risks of being mistaken are so momentous. There is a need to 'prove' faith to God through acts that display moral worthiness. However, it is possible to prove faith with God by inaction too: Jesus' disciples were explicitly told not to take up arms, but to await the justice of God.[73] Rapoport suggests that Messianic followers, believing that the time was near, tend to resort to one of two methods for 'seeing the process in': pacifism or violence. The two responses are not as diametrically opposed as might at first seem to be the case since both reflect a rejection of conventional actions. Which is chosen at any given point is, to some extent, a matter of timing. The major revealed religions all contain doctrinal images of both 'the suffering servant' and 'the avenging angel', the latter usually being reserved for the final days and the former appropriate only while waiting for the messianic activity to begin. Therefore, a choice between the two is dependent on the stage that the group believes the messianic process is at; and it is possible for such organisations to move between the two, based on the belief that they were formerly mistaken about the stage.[74] Kaplan points out that this is an aspect of millenarian groups within White Supremacist movements in the United States. By the 1980s, they were bitterly split, due to differing interpretations of inerrant texts. Overall, they tend towards a quietist position, withdrawing to the greatest possible degree from a society that is inherently contaminating. Occasionally, they appear as activists or even as violent centres of revolutionary activism, before retiring back into withdrawal.[75] Rosenfeld suggests that millenarian movements may still incite violence by withdrawing, if they proclaim allegiance to a higher law, effectively rejecting society and declaring their own theocracy.[76]

Both Islam and Judaism contain examples of pacifist and violent groups. Members of Gush Emunim believe that it is possible to shape the messianic process and are zealous in promoting the messianic convictions of the order, to the extent of organising the 'Jewish Underground' and the 'Temple Mount Plot', terrorist activities directed against the Palestinians. The Haredi tend towards the other extreme, believing it presumptuous for humans to attempt to alter the messianic process, so they withdraw from a Jewish state they do not recognise, usually only acting to prevent Jews around them from breaching sacred laws. In Islam, the entire Shia community moves at irregular intervals between passive and active phases, the latter usually accompanied by violence. Some Sunni millenarian sects follow a similar pattern.[77] Most messianic visions associate the destruction of the old order and the birth of the new with a series of cataclysmic disasters: a sign of deliverance is therefore a period of unsurpassed woe. This encourages people to commission and commit atrocities because if the fulfilment of the Promise is dependent on life being as terrible as possible, violence has no limits because it cannot be associated with principles that demand cession or moderation of action. If disasters do not bring forth the Promise, it may be that life is not yet terrible enough; more suffering and violence are required. However, the failure of messianic activity to occur can also lead to great disappointment amongst the believers, and with it, a search for explanations. Commonly, there is a belief that traitors were responsible, possibly with severe consequences for those who have been seen to have betrayed the cause. There is a tendency to perceive the enemy as wholly evil, always dangerous and thus to be ruthlessly destroyed since there is a belief by the group in the righteousness of themselves and their cause.[78] In such circumstances, it is vital to remove these people that are delaying or possibly even threatening redemption. Since their destruction is committed in the pursuit of a higher good, any means to achieve this is likely to be viewed as justified. The overt rationale for many of Aum's actions was also redemptive: drawing on apocalyptic aspects of Shiva, the Hindu god of destruction, Nostradamus, the Book of Revelation, and the science fiction of Isaac Asimov's Foundation books, Aum saw their mission as saving mankind after Armageddon. When a vast earthquake struck the city of Kobe on 17 January 1995, it served only to confirm Aum in their beliefs that the end was near. By that time, after their defeats in elections for the Diet of February 1990, Asahara and Aum, feeling rejected and bent on revenge, had already decided that the world as a whole was irredeemable, and therefore needed to be destroyed.[79]

As the end of the century approaches, the amount of millennial terrorism is likely to increase, a trend that is already occurring. Messianism is closely associated with 'signs': for example, 'The Last Days' in the Christian, Jewish and Islamic religions tend to be perceived as consisting predominantly of world catastrophe, of Armageddon, a possibility that has seemed much more real in the last fifty years in a nuclear world than at any time in the past. Another common theme in both Christian and Jewish apocalyptic prophecies is the restoration of a state of Israel, which has again occurred within the last fifty years.[80] Finally, the impact of a new millennium is likely to be viewed by some groups as significant and a key date in the coming redemption, possibly a further impetus for action.[81] Important dates are often a spur to messianic action: in Islam, it is prophesied that a Mahdi will come at the start of a century, according to the Islamic calendar. The 1979 attack on the Grand Mosque in Mecca corresponded with the first hour of the year 1400 in the Islamic calendar and had clear messianic connotations.[82] Messianism may mean that, as Aum did, some groups attempt to 'hasten the end', to speed Armageddon. The destructive force of nuclear weapons makes them an attractive potential instrument for groups that hold such aims, once they believe that the time has come.

Religion gives a unique character to the violence perpetrated in its name because although religious terrorists are influenced by factors such as politics or nationalism, the justification and purpose of their violence is clearly qualitatively different from its secular equivalents. Religion offers a sanctuary of tradition and certainty, a refuge from an increasingly changing and unpredictable world, but religion itself must be defended against the apostasy and different cultures that are parts of this process. It is in this defence that religious terrorism occurs. The nature of religion, an all-out struggle for order and good against the corrupting forces of evil, means that it may inspire total loyalty, commitment and an uncompromising position. Consequently, not only is violence valid in defence of religion, but also it is possible to use the images and language of the religion to reinforce and justify terror against a much broader-defined foe than is the case with secular terrorism. Whereas secular terrorism is, in most cases, instrumental and goal-oriented, religious terrorism is more focused on the divine for inspiration and as a determinant of objectives and therefore can justify high levels of violence, unfettered by the need for proportionality or support from an audience within the wider population because religious terrorists regard themselves to be outsiders in the world system.

This trend appears to be especially prevalent in the case of messianic groups, which form a part of Islam, Judaism and Christianity, in particular. By believing that the role of Man is critical to the timing of the coming messiah, end of the world and salvation, they increase the importance of destroying those elements in the world that threaten the process. Since the individual must prove their faith at a time when the stakes are so high, when their eternal life is directly involved, it is unsurprising that there should be a willingness to resort to whatever means are necessary to achieve the required objective.

While religious factors are central to the pursuit of terrorism perpetrated in the name of religion, it is also the case that individual and organisational aspects have important influences as well, just as they do with secular terrorist groups. On an individual level, they encompass the need to establish identity, to follow the example of others, gain widespread acceptance and commendation, as well as for personnel spiritual gain. Religious groups are no less in competition with other religious organisations for adherents and support, than is so for secular groups. While support is not critical to religious terrorist groups for approbation and approval of their actions, it is central in determining their influence within the community and their survival. Continued terrorism not only displays commitment to the cause, but ensures that the group's voice remains heard, vital since the organisation is likely to be certain of the ultimate truth of their interpretation and pursuit of the correct path. It is for this reason that, as with secular groups, there is little toleration for dissent or exiting the organisation, since both are a betrayal not only of the group, but of their faith as well.

It is with the White Supremacist movement in the United States that it is hardest to separate religious and right-wing terrorism, but the two have some similarities. Both are rooted in a defensive reaction to a corrupting threat that endangers traditional-bound values and both offer the heightened opportunity for exacting vengeance on that debasing influence. If Girard's theory is accepted, violence is central to religion as a whole, but it certainly has a redemptive value for some millenarian groups, a role not dissimilar to some right-wing terrorist groups. Violence in that context may be justified as promoting the true way. This is especially likely to occur in the case of millenarian groups that believe they have a role to play in speeding the Last Days, the end of the world and redemption. It is such a group, Aum, that carried out the only major terrorist attack using non-conventional weaponry; and it is such a group that is still the most likely contender for any further incident. However, those motivated by right-wing beliefs should not be discounted either, as the next chapter will argue.

# 4 Ideological Terrorism

## RIGHT-WING TERRORISM

Right-wing terrorism is extemely hard to define because it covers a vast spectrum of groups. An important division in strictly secular right-wing terrorism is between that perpetrated by the 'old right', that is, reactionary terrorism, and the 'new right', which is the subject of much of this discussion. The former is mainly perpetrated by those who have lost political power or fear that they are in imminent danger of doing so. It is their quest for power and determination to preserve or restore the status quo that characterises them, rather than their ideology (although this is not to deny the importance of a belief system to such groups). This is 'pro-state' violence, of the sort used by the Ulster loyalist paramilitaries. 'Pro-state' terrorism is illegal violence employed in the defence of the state from its enemies.[1] Although in this particular case, the term 'right-wing' is probably not a useful one, the loyalist paramilitaries clearly fit the mould of reactionary terrorists. They began as 'defensive' organisations against the onslaught of republican attacks on the loyalist community in Northern Ireland. However, from the Spring of 1972, the loyalist paramilitaries began attacks on the Catholic community at large, killing 102 people by the end of the year. Believing all Catholics to be potential rebels, the predominantly Protestant paramilitaries targeted members of the Catholic community, irrespective of whether they were affiliated to Republican movements. One of the effects of this was, as the attacks continued and escalated and the IRA responded in kind, that it became increasing difficult for the British, in their role of peacekeepers between the communities, to withdraw from Northern Ireland. This withdrawal is something the loyalists were determined to prevent.[2] In Algeria, the Secret Army Organisation (OAS) sought to prevent equal rights for Algerians in the late 1950s and then, in the 1960s, when it became clear that the French government would pull out of the country, assumed a secondary campaign aimed at the French government in France. Although 85 per cent of the OAS's victims were Algerian Muslims, the group also attacked police officers who sought to curtail the group's activities and European liberals who seemed overly sympathetic to the cause of an independent Algeria;

they even attempted to assassinate French President Charles de Gaulle, who, they believed, had 'sold out' French Algeria.[3] This targeting is a vital aspect of 'pro-state' or reactionary terrorism. Groups that use it rarely regard themselves as enemies of the state they purport to support, but, rather, they are in competition with it, seeking to protect their constituents from the erosion of their power within society.[4]

Vigilante violence is used by groups and individuals who believe that they and their rights are not being adequately defended by the government from 'dangerous' sections of society. Consequently, they choose to protect themselves. They also rarely see themselves in conflict with the established authorities. Rather, they are simply enforcing justice and the law in self-defence. Faced by threats that the justice system was unable to control, police and military officers took the law into their own hands. Many of the actions taken in these cases appear to have been with the tacit co-operation of the police and governments involved, and the objective was to free the officers from the constraints of due process.[5] Rubenstein observes that even if they seek to undermine the established government, rightist terrorists often have allies in the armed forces and security services, as well as amongst ultraconservative businessmen and landowners. They may even have support from secret organisations within the army, and covert aid from wealthy backers of large political parties. Such groups are effectively state terrorists if they represent either an authoritarian regime in power or dissident elements within the ruling class or armed forces. Examples such as the death squads of El Salvador or Guatemala, or the Greek terrorists of the 1960s typically specialised in assassination and violence directed against liberal politicians, labour organisers, Communists, Jews, foreigners, and others that were seen as alien influences or enemies of the state. Their membership was largely drawn from the lower classes while their leaders tended to be of the higher echelons of society.[6] It would be a mistake to see such right-wing terrorism as limited to Central American groups or the past: it exists as an element in Western terrorism, from the failed putsch of Colonel Tejero in Spain in February 1981,[7] to the activities of groups closely associated with legitimate political parties such as the MSI in Italy or the Front National in France.[8] Extreme rightists have been characterised, ideologically, by a desire for authoritarian leadership, antipathy towards liberalism, communism and socialism, and by a belief that they alone are the true guardians of the nation's future and identity. The 'old right' have tended to be authoritarian, monarchist and reactionary without sharing the Fascist or neo-Nazi ideals of the 'new', radical right extremists.[9] It is anti-revolutionary or counter-revolutionary in contrast to the 'new' right which clearly does contain revolutionary elements.[10]

Within the armies of the West too, there are clearly extreme right-wing factions, although increasingly, these are of the 'new right'. The perpetrators of the bombing of the Murrah Building, Oklahoma, Tim McVeigh and Terry Nichols, met in the 1st Infantry Division, United States Army;[11] and there was outrage when, in 1993, it was discovered that Aryan Nation's supporters were amongst those serving with the Canadian Airborne Regiment in Somalia.[12] Rubenstein's argument that far-right terrorists are seldom complete outsiders, even in the West, is probably decreasingly the case in North American Supremacist movements, but it does retain an element of the truth when examining European movements and groups, especially when compared to their left-wing counterparts.[13]

Sprinzak argues that one of the key defining aspects of right-wing terror is that it is particularist in contrast to most other forms that are universalist. That is, they are fighting private wars against particular groups in the community: ethnic, 'illegitimate' religious groups, classes of undesirable people or 'inferior races'.[14] This leads to another key difference between right-wing terrorists and other groups: whereas left-wing and nationalist-separatist organisations are in direct conflict with the government of a state, right-wing groups conflict directly with 'antisocial' groups in the community and only indirectly with the government, if they attempt to intervene to protect these groups or fail to be sufficiently sympathetic towards the right-wing group. If the government responds to these cases of private violence by prosecuting the right wingers responsible, then sections of the group will transform the government into the primary enemy and begin acting accordingly.[15] This leads to 'a process of delegitimization' where the terrorist group becomes willing to use violence against the agents of the government. However, the reality of many right-wing groups is one of 'split delegitimization' because they are initially unwilling to risk confrontation with the authorities and instead direct most of their actions at the non-ruling group. This implies an uneven radicalisation of the extremists developing against the two different entities. Most particularist groups begin with a conflict of legitimacy because, as a result of usually long-held beliefs, the object of their antipathy is regarded as illegitimate in the first place. They do not belong in the same society and should not be accorded the same status as the extremists. This is an important difference from other secular forms of terrorism, since, whereas others assume non-violence to be the norm, and that the resort to violence is a temporary but necessary aberration, for particularist terrorists, violence is directed against certain sections of the community that are inferior and do not belong anyway, and who can be therefore treated accordingly. It is a control mechanism, so is reasonable and natural, and certainly does not require a justification. Consequently, it is not inconceivable that an attack, even one that used non-conventional means, that destroyed a large part of that 'illegitimate' section of society could also be defended as valid if it removed that unwanted and unnecessary part of the community.

Some right-wing ideologies, notably Fascism, positively glorify the use of violence and regard it as an essential aspect of government. Traditionally though, even Fascist and neo-Nazi organisations have exercised 'split delegitimization', avoiding conflict with the government and concentrating on targeted groups such as Jews or leftists. This has begun to change and many European and North American rightist organisations have become violently confrontational with governmental authorities that are increasingly seen as Jewish dominated and irretrievably corrupted.[16] Given a desire to attack the government and its agents, but a reluctance to inflict harm on other, innocent, members of society, it is plausible to suggest that terrorists might resort to limited non-conventional attacks, as a high profile alternative to major bombings using conventional explosives. Radiological terrorism and some types of biological or chemical terrorism could all be used in this way. However, although NEST, the Nuclear Emergency Search Team, has dealt with numerous hoaxes, many of them directed against governmental facilities, there has yet to be an unequivocal non-conventional assault of this type.

The most startling aspect of the 'new right' has been the growth of youth counterculture terrorism and the rise of millenarian terrorism. Sprinzak argues that millenarian terrorists rarely resort to violence as a direct result of their views. Instead, it is due either to a violence-prone leader, such as Shoko Asahara, or to having been forced into a corner by society; that is, they are unable to sufficiently seclude themselves from the wider community.[17] However, violence is just as likely to be directed against the millenarians themselves as against the outside world. The youth counterculture, which in this case mainly means Skinheads, does not consist of systematic terrorists and their violence is an extension of their non-political glorification of brutality. Of the 17 Skinhead-caused fatalities in Germany in 1992, 6 were German homeless men; 2 were Germans who got in political arguments with a gang; 2 Germans died for no obvious reason; one was a Romanian asylum seeker; 2 were immigrants, one of which was killed in a discotheque, possibly over a girl; one was a Vietnamese knifed in a Berlin street; and the last 3 were Turkish women living in Mölln. As well as these targets, other, non-fatal, objects of violence included the elderly, gays and lesbians, handicapped people, patrons at restaurants, passers-by, motorists, police, several proprietors of liquor stores, opposing fans at soccer games, and political opponents. Clearly, for such groups, arbitrary violence was the norm, determined by whim, not by political agenda.[18]

However, in the past decade, Skinheads have taken part in numerous murderous assaults and arson attacks. Alcohol seems to play a central part in these attacks: they are particularly prevalent after Skinhead concerts at which there is heavy drinking as well as music extolling violence. Although not politically organised in their own right, there is increasing evidence that Skinhead groups are being used by other more experienced groups and right-wing extremists as foot soldiers in their campaigns. Neo-fascist and neo-Nazi organisations exploit the social marginality, youth and socio-economic alienation of the Skinheads to recruit them to the cause. Most of the Skinhead groups in the USA are affiliated to neo-Nazi organisations or the Aryan Nation, who use them to commit many of their acts of extreme violence. The leaders of these other groups prefer to let others take the legal and political risks. The American Anti-Defamation League believes Skinheads to be the most violent of White Supremacist groups. Almost all of this violence has been directed against minority groups: Blacks, Hispanics, Asians, homosexuals and the homeless.[19] Part of the reason for the recruitment of Skinheads by neo-Nazi groups in North America is that while they are extremely active, the neo-Nazis are also highly fratricidal and small in number, and thus use outside help.[20] Merkl suggests that, in the European case, much of Skinhead violence can be attributed to negative identity, and vicious self-hatred; they turn onto groups that they perceive as weaker and even more contemptible than themselves. While they attempt to attract community support by attacking refugee hostels, to make 'them' go away, the first reason is the more significant: they are displaced and alienated youths that seek a soft target at which to strike out and on which to displace the blame for their own inadequacies.[21] Skinhead violence can also occur within the group: in August 1987 a California group nailed its former leader to a plank. Violence is not only a norm, it is a requirement and pre-requisite of membership. One of the California gang, explaining their action said: 'To be a skinhead, none of the other skinheads are going to respect you unless you go out and mess somebody up, and if you don't, you get messed up.'[22]

A further problem for right-wing groups that emphasise violence so much is that they attract 'mentally unstable people, psychopaths, neurotics...whose hearts do not belong to our good cause'. The issue of uncontrollable, fringe members of terrorist organisations is as much a facet of right wing as left-wing violence. Some Swedish groups try to deal with this difficulty by allowing membership of their organisation only to those who have already 'proved' themselves with their actions. This has the effect of making the group an elite and therefore making membership in it even more desirable to potential recruits since it carries a heightened status.[23] However, whereas left-wing and religiously-motivated terrorists appear not to conform to any psychological profile of abnormality, there is some evidence for believing that many right-wingers are exceptional. Psychiatric studies of imprisoned neo-Fascist terrorists in Italy found that many exhib-ited 'free-floating feelings of aggression and hostility'. They were disturbed in a way that other types of terrorist rarely are. However, the evidence for this is relatively limited, so the implications to be drawn from it are at best fragmentary.[24]

Membership of the Skinheads, along with millenarian sects and very extreme neo-Nazi groups, and unlike other right-wing groups, tends to be a full-time occupation. Their members have a high degree of alienation from society and reject many of its political and economic norms. Many members of other groups lead an almost normal life, maintain families and may regard themselves as pillars of the community. Their terrorism is not a full-time exercise. It is a side-line, a means of dealing with socio-political pressures and concerns and of promoting their beliefs.[25]

The fact that most right-wing terrorists are not complete outsiders is significant. Ross suggests that membership of right-wing groups is flexible: an individual may simultaneously belong to several different radical groups; and others may periodically adhere to the agenda of the group to which they belong, whilst at other times act indepen-dently of these organisations.[26] There are also lone actors who, although rare, occasionally decide to strike a blow for the cause through a random murder. Kaplan cites the murder of the Goldmark family on Christmas Eve, 1985, by a single gunman who mistakenly believed the couple were Jewish.[27] That right-wingers may belong to several groups or to no groups at all suggests that the close-knit, insular organisation that engenders a feeling of identity, of belonging, is less an aspect of right-wing terrorism than that of the left. Therefore, membership in the group, with its attendant pressures and dynamics may be less significant as a reason why right-wingers become and remain terrorists. This makes sense if one considers that such individuals are closer, situationally, to nationalists than to left-wing terrorists, since, if their beliefs are widespread in their community, they have a ready-made constituency from which to gain support. However, this accounts for only some right-wing terrorism: obviously, there are groups and individuals that do not enjoy such support, real or perceived, and the role of the group in such cases is presumably more important. Individuals who joined the Ku Klux Klan appeared to share a number of traits: aimlessness, personal failure, lack of status, low self-esteem, alienation and poor adaptation to the requirements of reality, which, in combination, led them to seek a group that offered support and permitted them to engage in regressive behaviour in some instances. Social groups are used by some adults as a defence against anxiety, because the group is able to organise itself as a defence against the common threat. The Klan is such a group and bolsters the part of society that is positive from a white racist perspective, emphasising a white supremacist social order that evokes the Old South and a supportive bond among the members that excludes the rest of society. It makes its members feel part of a chosen group, an elite; and harks back to an idealised period when society was less threatening.[28] The motivations behind group membership and the progression to violence are similar to that for long-standing terrorist groups of other varieties: the Klan has a tradition of violence, it is a norm of the organisation, so those who elect to join it do so in that knowledge and therefore precisely because it is so.

There clearly are appreciable differences between left and right wing terrorism. Weinberg and Eubank examined these as they appeared in the leaders and ordinary members of Italian groups. The rightist leaders tended to be older than their left-wing counterparts but the age difference between leaders and followers in groups of the right was more exaggerated than was the case with those on the left. Whereas groups from the left were inclined to have both male and female leaders, the right-wing groups, apart from Skinheads which have always had some female leaders, were almost wholly male-dominated, although amongst the followers, women composed about eight per cent of the numbers.[29] There were not significant geograph-ical, religious, or parental occupational differences between left and right leaders. Weinberg and Eubank found no crossover between the two ideologies amongst the leadership, so clearly early political experience is significant, since it served to accentuate their polarisa-tion. Occupation was another key difference: both groups had white collar leaders, but while teachers, students, manual workers and a few sub-proletarians played prominent roles in the left-wing groups, they were largely lacking in the right-wing organisations, where business-men, policemen and soldiers were more dominant, although they were represented amongst the followers.[30] Italian right-wing terror-ism is not representative of the type in a number of ways though. It is more characteristic of the violence of the 'old right'. While there has been some violence directed against minorities, most Italian right-wing terrorism has been anti-Communist and has continued for four decades, since shortly after the Second World War. While Italian right-wing terrorists follow a pattern of split delegitimisation in that they unleashed campaigns of mass violence and sought to attack and replace the government, they do not conform in a number of key aspects. Italian right-wing terrorism was not particularlist. Instead, it was guided by universal neo-Fascist principles. Far from the Italian government and state becoming delegitimised, they were always regarded with the utmost contempt by leaders of the Italian groups. Rather than the transition between stages of disenchantment and alienation from the state, Italian right-wingers sustained violent activ-ity over the course of four decades. There was not a process of delegitimisation.[31]

The difference between terrorists from the left and right does apply beyond the Italian example however. Handler's socio-economic profile of American terrorists of the 1960s and 1970s reiterates many of the same points. Women, while heavily represented at all levels in left-wing groups, were almost an irrelevance in right-wing groups. The pattern of leadership between terrorist groups appears to have been influenced by their political ideology. Whereas leftist groups seem more liberal, more egalitarian, right-wing groups, are reac-tionary by definition, pro-family and against anything that disrupted the pattern of the nuclear family. This view of the limited role for women meant that such groups were not very attractive or welcoming to women. The chasm between leaders and ordinary members was clear in right-wing organisations: the former were mostly educated to college level and many held white-collar jobs; the latter had usually only completed high school and were overwhelmingly blue-collar. This difference may have important implications for the group dynamics of such organisations since it suggests a lack of uniformity between the two that might lead to difficulties in acting concertedly and in policy formulation and implementation.[32] Only the geographical origin of right-wing terrorists appears to be altering radically in recent years: as militias and other non-specifically White Supremacist movements grow in importance, areas such as the Northwest have risen in prominence alongside the Bible Belt.

In Sweden, in a study of the 165 arrested perpetrators of racist crime between 1990 and 1993, the majority of suspected or convicted perpetrators were between 16 and 20 years old at the time of their crime. Over half (52 per cent) had previous convictions; almost all (98 per cent) came from the town or village where the crime was committed or from the surrounding region. Very few of them can be traced to a nationalist or racist organisation and only slightly over half of them were intoxicated at the time of their crime. It is the last two points that are unusual: the lack of affiliation to a group and the role of drinking.[33] Otherwise, the Swedish example does seem to correspond to the wider model of the perpetrators of hate violence. The lack of affiliation can perhaps be explained by suggesting that those caught had yet to 'prove' themselves, a precondition of membership in some Swedish extreme right groups. Drinking is a central part of Skinhead violence, but is less so with other extreme right movements whose violence is more instrumental. This suggests that, in Sweden, right-wing violence is caused both by Skinhead and by more politically focused organisations. Willems found some similarities in his study of right-wing youth violence in Germany between 1990 and 1993. Over 90 per cent of crimes were committed by groups and especially by those connected with the Skinhead subculture (about 30 per cent of all cases). There were relatively few examples of preplanned, instrumental violence. Instead, it was more likely to be spontaneous, encouraged by large quantities of alcohol. Around 10 per cent of the perpetrators already had convictions for politically-motivated crimes and over 35 per cent for other crimes. Over 95 per cent of xenophobic crimes were committed by men; over 75 per cent by men under 20 years old; and 35 per cent by men under 18 years old. There was some correlation between such violence and lower levels of education, social problems, deficient family structures and lower social class. Once the perpetrators were subdivided into four types, though, considerable differences emerged in their socio-economic profiles. Politically-motivated right-wing extremists were mostly well-educated, had successfully undergone training and held jobs. They generally exhibited an ideologically validated, disciplined and instrumentally oriented attitude to violence against specific 'ungerman' groups. It was such extremists who directed many of the other youths ideologically and, to some extent, strategically to commit their acts. Xenophobe or ethnocentric youths were more likely to have left school earlier and to have been sociologically disadvantaged than the right-wing extremists. Their motivation was primarily one of feeling threatened by 'foreigners' and refugees in particular who competed with them for jobs, housing and financial assistance. Their violence, although directed against specific groups, was more expressive than instrumental. Criminal and marginalised youths tended to be slightly older, to be unsuccessful at their careers and to have more likelihood of criminal records. They tended to be action and violence-oriented. Violence was a norm, not a political means, and was directed much more widely than simply against foreigners or refugees. The final type, fellow travellers, were better educated and often came from functional middle-class families. They rarely had prior convictions and were found in both skinhead and fascist groups. Their motivation for participation was group pressure and dynamics, rather than ideology or xenophobia. Although they did little to prevent violence, they were rarely violent themselves.[34]

The example of Ingo Hasselbach indicates that, on an individual level too, there may be motivational similarities between left and right wing terrorists. Hasselbach, an East German, was one of the leading neo-Nazis in the reunified Germany until his defection in 1993. His father was a supporter of the East German state and despised the Nazis. Hasselbach said: 'The state that oppressed us all was the same. It was literally the extension of the will of our parents, whose generation had strived to establish the first German "anti-Fascist" state... My father's voice *was* the state, and I directed all my rage at it, rather than at him. He barely existed for me.' As it was for RAF members, Hasselbach's terrorism represented a rebellion against parental authority, transposed onto the state. He began by being a fringe member of a hippie commune, but progressed through being a punk and then a skinhead and neo-Nazi, all increasingly extreme means of reacting against the state. Imprisoned for anti-state activities, he was exposed to unrepentant Nazis and it was here that his hatred of anti-Fascism grew:

[In prison] the German anti-Fascist state carried on with the trappings of the German Fascist state... The hypocrisy of it bothered
me more than anything: If you're going to worship power, why not
admit it? At least the Nazis had been straightforward in their
brutality. These people insisted that they were beating you and
locking you up for your own edification and for the sake of universal brotherhood... For me, protest became ever more closely
associated with the forbidden Nazi past. I'd reached a point where
I thought, I've always rejected Communism and the idea of the
anti-Fascist state: now I would fight the anti-Fascists by being a
Fascist.[35]

A vital point of Hasselbach's decision to be a neo-Nazi was when he
encountered West German members who gave him literature
'proving' that Auschwitz and other Nazi atrocities had not occurred.
He describes the moment:

It was a revelation beyond words. No gas chambers! No mass
murder of the Jews! It had all been Communist lies, like so much
else... And in this moment of relief and joy for me and other new
recruits I think we passed from being simply rebels against the
GDR to being true neo-Nazis. Even as citizens of the GDR, we'd
grown up with German Guilt. Now this guilt was lifted.[36]

This suggests that *der sprung* is as applicable to far-right terrorist
groups as to other organisations. Loow cites a Swedish member of the
extreme right who had a similar moment of revelation when he went
to hear a former Nazi speak: 'At first I thought the Nazis were just
shit, I hated Germans, everything German, but I was interested in the
Second World War... I and my friends went to a meeting where an
old nationalist socialist spoke. He spoke about democracy, the
hypocrisy, the double standard, the lies, it was like something fell
from my eyes. I woke up.'[37] This is also significant because it shows
the importance of the older generation of right wingers in motivating
and politicising some of the modern activists.

Like other terrorists, Hasselbach developed the ability to distance
himself from everything except his group:

I never thought about the safety or well-being of the people in the
house [that was being attacked]. They didn't exist for me. Only my
friends and I existed. And the Cause, the Party. The foreigners

were far away from me somehow, even though I was acting as
though they were so much in my way and pasting things on the walls
of their house.[38]

It is common for activists to live together, and for the group to
become a surrogate family for them. Even those with families of their
own tend to steadily break their ties with the outside world as they
become more and more centred on the group. Loyalty towards the
group is of central importance for members. They are bound not only
to the immediate cell, but also to the wider community of the extreme
right who are regarded as brothers-in-arms.[39]

Hasselbach's movement was decentralised to enable its members to
deny responsibility for violent actions and ease the process of justifying membership of the group. He states:

> This deniability helps keep its members both morally and legally in
> the clear. Though I trained young people to hate, I could still
> express shock that any of them would go out and actually commit
> murder. Our racist propaganda always put hate in a positive light –
> it expressed racism as racial pride – and removed from the reader
> any responsibility for its bloody consequences. All responsibility
> rested with the victim, who was biologically inferior and brought
> trouble on himself by mixing with the master race, or so the think-
> ing went.[40]

The legitimacy of a target was also important. Hasselbach says that
he never enjoyed attacking foreigners; they were a problem that had
to be solved politically. The only violence he considered legitimate
was that directed against the Anarchist Anti-Fascists who attacked
the neo-Nazis with equal fervour.[41] After the Mölln killings of
November 1992, he felt that a boundary had been crossed and that the
act was reprehensible, cowardly and deadly.[42] However, by this point,
he was seeking to exit the group: he had begun to doubt whether the
Cause was worth risking his life for.[43] The attack sickened him and
made him question the group's tactics, especially since anti-immi-
grant feeling was so widespread amongst the German population as a
whole that Hasselbach believed violence was now redundant.[44] He
quit publicly in March 1993, burning a picture of Hitler on national
television, and has continued to campaign against his former
colleagues, a common response by terrorists who succeed in exiting
from their group. This was perceived as the ultimate betrayal, and

Hasselbach was targeted by his former comrades who sought to kill him and his relatives.[45]

Right-wing groups, like those engaged in other forms of terrorism, have contacts with similar, like-minded organisations, and learn from their experiences. Combat 18, a British neo-Nazi group, has clear links with groups in Denmark, Belgium, France, the Netherlands, Austria and eastern Europe. Previously limited to arson, Combat 18's links enabled it to escalate its level of violence and plan to send letter bombs from Sweden to targets in London.[46] Likewise, the German neo-Nazis feel an affinity with right-wingers in the United States, based on a hatred of government, a belief that their freedoms as white men are being infringed by a multi-cultural society, and a general anti-Semitism. Hasselbach states that virtually all of his group's literature came from extremist organisations in the United States, where it is easier to publish such material. The neo-Nazis did a lot of weapons training, and read a great deal on terrorist tactics and on how to destroy bridges, cars, and train tracks. This was based on handbooks such as 'A Movement in Arms' that were sent to the group from Nebraska via the Internet. Hasselbach says the inter-national neo-Nazis movement was highly dependent on Gary Rex Lauck in Lincoln, Nebraska, who was the publisher and distributor of most of their propaganda. His 'was also the center of a worldwide umbrella organization, with which practically every serious neo-Nazi had contact'.[47]

European radical rightists are rarely admirers of American society. They particularly despise the ethnic and racial diversity of the United States, with all its attendant problems. This is an attitude that is shared by many on the American right. As the social and economic impact of migration to European states continues, right-wingers there see a society reminiscent of the American one developing. The result is the feelings of hatred and being dispossessed by immigrants that are indicative of much of European extreme right action. The link with American extremists is further cemented by the martyrology and extraordinary views that they hold in common and which bind them to each other: of Holocaust revisionism, Identity theology and Odinism.[48] This heightens the perception within the group that there is also some wider community of right-wingers.

Although the American White Supremacist movement is extremely diverse, there are a number of common factors to all of them: a myth of a lost and bygone world of innocence and purity; a culture that has been stolen by influxes of immigrants into the United States; an ideology based on scriptural texts; a Manichaean world view; a conspiratorial view of history; the view of themselves as a persecuted elite; and a millenarian view centred on an imminent apocalypse. The Christian Identity Church, part of the United States White Supremacist movement, is premillennialist (they believe that Jesus will return before the thousand-year period of total bliss on earth begins); but they do not believe that the Chosen will be spared the seven-year Tribulation period of war, turmoil and suffering. This means that adherents are encouraged to act decisively to ensure their place amongst God's elect, and to survive the Tribulation period.[49] They see the existing order as irredeemably evil and destined for destruction, and attribute the fulfilment of the millenarian to divine forces; yet they do occasionally resort to violence, believing that their actions do have some bearing on events. They seek the violent overthrow of the government and believe it is possible, basing their campaign on that laid out in *The Turner Diaries*, an apocalyptic novel, written under a pseudonym by William Pierce, leader of the National Alliance. It culminates with supremacists gaining control of the US nuclear arsenal and using it to obliterate their foes, and is one of the reasons that some white supremacists seem to positively welcome the prospect of nuclear war as a means to achieve their objective of creating a new world order consisting exclusively of the white race. Supremacists believe that there has to be a battle, a day of reckoning, between the children of darkness (Jews) and those of light (the Aryan race), not only to usher in the millennium of saintly rule, but also to ensure that the usurping Jews are thrown out as the chosen people return to their roots and their 'special destiny'. Since the government of the United States is currently in the hands of the 'Zionist Occupation Government' (ZOG), the country has been corrupted beyond reform; the political process is therefore a closed avenue and bringing down ZOG as quickly as possible is the only solution, enabling an Aryan state to be declared prior to the Tribulation.[50]

The role of martyrdom is of importance to many right-wing groups, and has assumed a central role in the mythology of some, notably those American organisations that emphasise events such as the Weaver siege in August 1993. Randy Weaver, a Christian Identity member, failed to appear at his trial for selling a sawn-off shotgun, and fled to a cabin in Idaho, where federal agents kept him and his family under surveillance for 20 months. When the Weaver dog was killed attacking a federal agent, this precipitated a gunfight in which Federal Marshal William Degan and Weaver's 14-year-old son,

Samuel, were killed. The siege then went on another 11 days, until
Weaver's wife, Vicki, was also killed, as she sat at the kitchen table
holding their ten month old baby. At the subsequent trial, the jury,
conscious of the recent apocalyptic end to the Waco siege, in which
85 people died, and persuaded by Weaver's lawyer that the government could do this to anyone, acquitted Weaver and his co-defendant
of all charges, including the original firearms offence. This suggests
that Sprinzak's theory of split delegitimization may not be wholly
accurate with regard to these North American groups that have come
to believe the government and the 'other' are inextricably linked.
Increasingly, it is the government that is seen as the main threat and
is targeted.[51] Tim McVeigh was profoundly affected by Waco and
timed his attack in Oklahoma to correspond with the second anniversary of the siege's end.[52]

Closely connected with right-wing terrorism in the United States in
recent years has been the growth of the militia movement, of which
there are about 270 in 48 states, at least 66 of which have links to the
White Supremacist Movement.[53] They reject all forms of government
above the local level and deny the legitimacy of the means, such as
taxes and the judiciary, that state and federal authorities use to
reinforce their role. However, militias are more than simply anti-
government movements. They embrace a wide variety of beliefs,
connected to a religious veneer and racial intolerance. They combine
a traditional right-wing fear of an elitist cabal with a millenarian view
of history.[54] They tend to be strongly anti-communist, believe in the
Protestant work ethic and distributive justice, and be based in rural
areas.[55] They are obsessed with achieving religious and racial purity in
the United States and with overthrowing the all-pervasive ZOG.
Believing that the final victory of this cabal is imminent, they call for
immediate action in the ultimate battle between good and evil.[56] They
are convinced that there is a world-wide conspiracy to create a New
World Order, using the UN and other international forces, which will
ultimately lead to the subjugation of the American people. Such
conspiracy theorists have no difficulty pointing to suspicious government activities and agencies, such as the Federal Emergency
Management Agency (FEMA), that are acting to bring this disaster to
reality[57] and to other agencies that are committed to eradicating anti-
government violence and therefore have increasingly focused on the
activities of such organisations.[58] The connecting theme of many of
these groups is the Christian Identity movement. The beliefs within
the movement are diverse, depending to a large degree on which of

the pastors within the movement is followed, but they almost all include that Christ was an Aryan rather than a Jew, as were the Lost Tribes of Israel; that the USA is the Promised Land; and that Anglo-Saxons are God's Chosen People. In the Last Days, the Chosen will fight against their foes until racial victory and the Kingdom of God is won.[59]

At the centre of the Christian Identity movement is the Aryan Nations, an anti-Semitic, neo-Nazi group founded in 1974 by Richard Butler. The organisation forms a liaison between like-minded groups and helps co-ordinate their efforts. There is little doubt that the militias and their connected organisations have an intimate link with much of the domestic terrorism occurring in the United States today, including the bombing of the Murrah Building in Oklahoma. These groups, like others that are inspired by religious extremism, seem unconstrained by the norms of proportionality, instrumentality and societal acceptability that govern the action of most other terrorists. It is for this reason that their potential for acts of mass-destructive terrorism cannot be discounted.[60] However, confusingly, some of the militias clearly are not racist and may therefore simply be Patriot movements, dedicated to the rigorous upholding of the Constitution. However, this is possibly irrelevant, given the role militias play in the right-wing movement in America.[61] They are an important link between other far-right organisations and the wider population. Militias espouse a number of core American values, such as patriotism and constitutional fidelity, that make them more attractive to people within the mainstream and introduce them to other, more radical ideas.[62] Even where the militia leader is not a white supremacist, it is impossible to go to a militia meeting, read their literature or join a newsgroup on the Internet without being exposed to white supremacist views.[63]

In the early 1980s, there were a string of right-wing terrorist attacks, such as at Bologna train station or the Munich Oktoberfest, that seemed to herald a new period of highly violent and relatively indiscriminate incidents, of a variety rarely observed in secular political terrorism until then. These attacks have subsequently proved to be exceptional: the 1980s did not see a period of heightened right-wing violence in Europe, and, apart from the attack on the Naples–Milan express train in December 1984, in which 15 people died, there were relatively few indiscriminate bombings. Between 1969 and 1987, there were 359 attacks that caused death or injury in Italy, of which only 7.6 per cent were perpetrated by the right-wing, compared to 74 per cent by left-wing groups and 7 per cent by foreign groups. However, of these attacks, the right-wing ones resulted in 193 deaths, compared to 148 in left wing-attacks. Even if the Bologna attack, in which 85 people died, is discounted as abnormal, the right-wing can be seen to be considerably more lethal per attack than their left-wing contemporaries.[64] With a few exceptions, right-wing terrorism in Europe was not indiscriminate: instead, it was mostly targeted against immigrants, Jews or Arabs in France and Germany and against left-wing targets in Italy.[65] The targets of such attacks were carefully chosen, but since these targets were often entire sections of the community, the intended victims were merely representatives of that group, rather than individual targets. In that sense, the violence is not so different from sectarian killings, purely on the basis of religion, that have been so much an aspect of terrorism in Northern Ireland, or indeed from any other terrorism that is waged on communal grounds.[66]

Providing that such an attack could be limited to members of that alien community, so that it is indiscriminate within only that group, a widespread attack, possibly even using mass-destructive weaponry, seems initially plausible. However, when applied to purely secular right-wing terrorism, Hoffman's analysis, written in 1989, is still completely relevant:

> Right-wing terrorism is based not on some pathological obsession to kill as many innocent people as possible... The right-wing terrorists see themselves... as a catalyst of events that will lead to an authoritarian form of government. Thus, they tailor their violence to appeal to their perceived constituency... and, with the exception of a few indiscriminate bombings, they seek to keep it within the bounds of what the ruling government will tolerate without undertaking massive repressive actions against the terrorists themselves.[67]

Thus, terrorism is an instrument to further a particular outcome, be it governmental policy or the driving of an ethnic or religious group out of a state. That seems to utterly preclude extreme levels of violence, especially in view of the certain governmental reaction to such an attack. However, in some groups, notably Skinhead organisations, violence is a norm, a prerequisite for membership, and assumes an almost therapeutic quality. This violence can be directed, but it probably has relatively little impact on high-level terrorism because such groups seem to relish a type of violence that is intensely personal and low-tech, involving brutal contact with the victim. Much of their violence is committed without the long-term planning or rigorous preparations that would characterise most acts of nuclear terrorism. However, when discussing the effect of the combination of religion and right-wing violence, as occurs amongst white supremacists in North America or in Jewish groups such as Kach, it can be seen that the results are more dangerous. There are several examples of North American right-wingers using or threatening to use non-conventional weaponry. In March 1995, two members of the Minnesota Patriots Council, a militia-type organisation, were convicted of attempting to kill federal officials by mixing ricin with a solvent which would be absorbed through the skin. They rubbed the mixture onto the door-knobs of federal buildings and onto the doorhandles and steering wheels of cars.[68] The possibility that they might move from chemical to nuclear weaponry is a real one that cannot be discounted.

## LEFT-WING AND ANTI-NUCLEAR TERRORISM

Left-wing terrorism is probably the least likely type to cause a high level act of nuclear terrorism. However, it is conversely the variety that has been responsible for most of the low level acts to date. Connected with radicalism, especially since the growth of nuclear power as an alternative to fossil fuels in the 1970s, has been the rise of specifically anti-nuclear groups.

Violence by anti-nuclear groups is an example of single-issue terrorism. It has theoretical similarities with other violent single-cause organisations, such as animal rights activists that attack laboratories or radical environmentalists that 'spike' trees to be logged or vandalise 'destructive technology'. One common feature of their respective campaigns has been a reluctance to attack people rather than property. This may be because such tactics are sufficient for their purpose and are the least likely to alienate potential supporters. Consequently, many militant single-issue groups set their bombs and incendiary devices to go off in the middle of the night, and threaten to escalate to peak-time attacks unless their demands are accommodated.[69] One exception to environmental terrorists' preference of targeting property over people was Theodore Kaczynski, the Unabomber. He was arrested in April 1996 following a 17 year bombing campaign directed predominantly against workers involved with technology in the airline industry and in universities. Kaczynski's hatred of technology appears to have stemmed, in part, from the combination of political radicalism and environmentalism that he developed whilst at the University of California in the 1960s. However, he is exceptional in that he acted alone and, until the New York Times and Washington Post published his 35,000-word Manifesto, shortly before his arrest, Kaczynski made little effort to publicise either his campaign or his beliefs and demands. Consequently, it is doubtful whether he is representative of other violent environmental groups.

Another tactic, this time fairly generally applicable to such organisations, is a strategy of intimidation directed at those who work in such research facilities. In Britain during the 1980s, the Animal Liberation Front (ALF) sprayed paint stripper on workers' cars, and used petrol bombs to start fires. In 1982, they posted letterbombs to four leading politicians, and in 1986 placed magnetic bombs under the cars of research scientists. Their strategy also encompassed intimidating the public at large, hoping that they would pressure the government into meeting their demands. Consequently, in November 1984, they embarked on a campaign of product contamination against the confectionery manufacturer, Mars. The threats were largely hoaxes, but they led to widespread concern amongst the public and to Mars withdrawing and destroying some £3 million of its products.[70] Such intimidation is an aspect of anti-nuclear violence as well. In March 1981, ETA sent death threats to 33 technicians working in the Lemoniz plant. The letter explained that the group would target all specialised personnel 'because of [their] participation in the illegal Lemoniz project'. The threats had little impact: the technicians continued working at the nuclear power plant, even in the wake of the assassinations of the chief engineer and, later, of the project manager.[71]

Anti-nuclear terrorism grows out of a wider, semi-organised movement that, while legal in itself, engages occasionally in illegal acts. This movement is also the umbrella for more radical and violent organisations that favour more illicit action. The objective tends to be 'demonstration' actions that increase public anxiety about nuclear safety and 'co-opt anti-nuclear sentiment or environmental concerns for their own radical agenda' by exposing the lack of security, control and protection provided for nuclear programmes by either the nuclear industry or the government. Such groups rarely resort to high-level terrorist actions. Since the primary aim of anti-nuclear action is to win over public opinion, as well as to halt the construction or operation of nuclear facilities, they favour methods that, while disruptive, are also proportional and unlikely to injure people. Equally, they are usually careful to use tactics that are unlikely to compromise so utterly the safety of a nuclear operation that it might result in the very danger to the surrounding environment that the anti-nuclear protesters most fear. Consequently, most anti-nuclear protests tend to be 'nuisance actions', such as illegal entry into facilities, rather than anything more severe. Trespass actions at reactors are also fairly common and perceived to be a legitimate tactic of anti-nuclear protesters. The activists at Greenham Common in Britain in the early 1980s made frequent attempts to cut through the fence and enter the USAF base, as a demonstration against the deployment of cruise missiles there. However, nuclear facilities, as high-profile targets, even attract actions by adversaries with no obvious anti-nuclear agenda. In February 1993, a man drove through the main gate at the Three Mile Island nuclear plant, and crashed through two closely spaced chain-linked fences into the 'protected area' of the plant, where he hid for four hours, but caused no damage. The assailant, Pierce Hye, had recently been released from the mental ward of a community hospital in Ephrata, Pennsylvania, and had no clear motive.[72]

Where the objective is to be more disruptive, activists have favoured actions such as destroying power lines to nuclear facilities, which has the advantages of being easier for the group, harder for the authorities to defend, and serving as a temporary means of effectively halting work at the facility, without the attendant risks, to workers or the activists, that an attack on the facility itself might entail.[73] Actions such as the bomb placed outside the Lawrence Livermore Laboratory on 28 November 1987, may be fairly representative of violence by anti-nuclear activists. The bomb detonated just after midnight and destroyed dozens of windows and a car, damaged three other cars, and scattered debris over a wide area. However, the bombing, which was claimed by the Nuclear Liberation Front, injured no one.[74] Anti-nuclear protesters have also targeted the system used to transport nuclear materials to and from facilities. Examples of this type of action include the November 1994 sabotage of power lines on a railway line near Hanover, used in the transport of material to the storage site at Gorleben, and the 1996 destruction of this same piece of track.[75] However, it is risky to generalise too much about anti-nuclear activity because it has varied so greatly from one state to another and over time. It was much less prevalent or violent in the United States than outside it between 1970 and 1984 and there was a much greater willingness to target people over property in these protests in other states.[76] There have also been more violent attacks on reactors themselves. An extreme example was the 1982 use of five antitank rockets against the Creys-Malville Superphoenix full-scale breeder reactor, near Lyon. The reactor was still under construction and, apart from damaging the outer shell of the building, little damage was done by the rockets. A previously unknown group, called the Pacifist and Ecologist Committee, claimed responsibility for the attack.[77] However, it is worth trying to differentiate between violence by specifically anti-nuclear groups and attacks by wider organisations that merely have anti-nuclear activities as one of several aspects of their campaign. The most violent groups have, in many cases, fallen into the latter category, so it may still be possible to suggest that the majority of single-issue anti-nuclear groups are not interested in higher level attacks or in attacks directed primarily at people rather than property. Although they are connected, there is a difference between anti-nuclear terrorism and the wider anti-nuclear movement. Increases in the former do not necessarily correspond with the peaks of activity in the latter. The height of peaceful anti-nuclear action was in the late 1970s and early 1980s, when there were widespread attempts, in many states, to affect the decision-making process at a critical time, when the fate of nuclear power was uncertain.[78] There has been significant anti-nuclear terrorism both before and after this period.

Jasper and Poulsen found that US anti-nuclear activists tended to have been first involved in a range of other political protest movements. These ranged from anti-war activities, environmentalism, feminism and the women's movement, nuclear disarmament and civil rights to animal rights. The protesters were mostly young (the median age was 32); well educated (95 per cent were high school graduates and 88 per cent had at least started college); had lower than average incomes; and overwhelmingly described themselves as politically left of centre. Although factors such as friends and family, previous activism and news coverage were important in the recruitment of anti-nuclear protesters, Jasper and Poulsen found that the key factor was specific events or moral shock arising from a series of these events.[79] This would explain rises in anti-nuclear protest in the wake of highly publicised incidents such as Three Mile Island in 1979 or Chernobyl in 1986. However, it seems that such events acted as a multiplier for existing protest, rather than as a catalyst for support where none had previously existed.[80] Although Jasper and Poulsen studied activists, rather than anti-nuclear terrorists specifically, this aspect of the recruitment process is similar to the moment of *der sprung*, described by Baumann and other terrorists. Another key similarity was the depersonalisation and stereotyping of the enemy in general and of governmental authorities in particular. For both, activists and terrorists, this serves as a recruitment aid and a justification for their actions. There is a clear anti-instrumental theme running through the anti-nuclear literature. Technology is depicted as out of control, the natural world as being destroyed and the government complicitous. The main enemy is technocracy: large bureaucracies, driven by money and careerism, uncaring about human needs. The literature calls for moral standards and political control over the instrumental techniques and rationalities of the nuclear industry.[81] In their view, nuclear energy is not only unsafe, uneconomical and unnecessary, it is also socially undesirable. It reinforces commercial growth at the expense of environmental quality, the power of large corporations over individuals, and an undue emphasis on materialistic consumption.[82] Activists feel that they had been alienated. They feel victimised by public authorities that are perceived to be inflexible, secretive, and undemocratic in their decision-making process.[83]

   In the United States, anti-nuclear violence formed a major component of the attacks of the extreme environmentalist group, the Evan Mecham Eco-Terrorist International Conspiracy (EMETIC). This group grew out of the most radical elements of Earth First!, another environmental group. Angered by Earth First!'s increased dedication to civil disobedience as a tactic, its leader, Dave Forman and four others formed EMETIC in October 1987.[84] By then, members of the nascent organisation had probably already been responsible for the May 1986 attack on power lines at Palo Verde Nuclear Generating Station, although they never claimed responsibility. The organisation was formed to conduct sabotage against nuclear power plants in the south-western USA. On 26 September 1988, the group destroyed power lines feeding uranium mines around the Grand Canyon. Thirty-four power poles were damaged, restricting power supplies to two mines owned by Energy Fuels Nuclear. Two days later, EMETIC claimed responsibility for the attack. On 30 May 1989, three members of the group were arrested near Wendon, Arizona, attempting to cut through a support tower that delivered power to a local substation. The attack was intended as a dry-run before simultaneously attacking the electricity transmission cables at three nuclear facilities in Colorado, California and Arizona. They were subsequently sentenced to terms ranging from one month to six years.[85]

Anti-nuclear violence, while it can be single-issue terrorism, can also be part of wider actions. Wieviorka suggests that in both France and the Basque homeland, what began as a campaign against nuclear power, came to be subsumed into a wider revolutionary struggle in France and in ETA's nationalist fight in Spain. The French anti-nuclear campaign moved from being simply a struggle against a particular type of power into a battle between the people and the regions versus a faceless, centralised, state-run entity, the power company, EDF.[86] Nationalism also played a role in some anti-nuclear violence within France. On 15 August 1975, two bombs exploded at the Mt D'Arree Nuclear Power Plant in Brennilis, Brittany, causing minor damage. The chief suspects were Breton separatists.[87] In 1972–3, the Spanish government announced four new nuclear projects (later two: the Ea and Lemoniz facilities). Initially, resistance to these was localised and was driven specifically by fear and doubts. By 1976, the driving force behind the increasingly broad-based anti-nuclear movement had become anger at the highhandedness of the Spanish government and Iberduero SA (the electricity company), and the lack of democratic procedures in arriving at the decisions. The protest was gradually absorbed by the wider Basque nationalist movement. From 1977, it was ETA that spearheaded the campaign, launching a number of attacks on the reactors and their personnel. Activists who were purely anti-nuclear were undoubtedly dismayed at the hijacking of their campaign. Generally, their sphere of operations was oriented towards Spain and even Europe as a whole. However, simultaneously, theirs were uniquely Basque organisations, which emphasised that character until it became their defining aspect.[88]

One group that combined the wider left-wing concerns of the need to fight against an exploitive corporate-dominated state with the focus on environmental and specifically anti-nuclear issues, was the Canadian organisation, Direct Action, which was responsible for a number of attacks in the early 1980s. The five members of the group came from a variety of familial and educational backgrounds, although all were young, and had already shown a level of commitment to radical causes. They showed a number of characteristics, held in common with other terrorist groups: Juliet Belmas, the youngest of the group, 19 at the time of the attacks, was insecure and clearly greatly admired and respected the leaders of the group, Ann Brit Hansen and Brent Taylor. The other 'soldier' of the group, Gerald Hannah, was a reluctant member, and refused to be involved in the bombings that the organisation perpetrated. This strongly hints that the organisational dynamics that make exit from, and dissension within, a group extremely difficult were present in Direct Action. The fifth member of the organisation, Douglas Stewart, was the technical expert and chief bomb-maker. His ability was evident in the 31 May 1982 bombing of the (non-nuclear) Dunsmuir, British Columbia Hydro substation on Vancouver Island, and the 14 October 1982 attack on the Litton Systems of Canada Limited factory in Toronto which were later described by investigating authorities as 'the work of experts'. The group also firebombed three of the pornographic Red Hot Video stores in the Vancouver area on 22 November 1982 and subsequently plotted to attack Canadian Forces jets, and a federal government icebreaker, and rehearsed an armed robbery of a Brink's guard. Their various assaults caused around $10 million of damage and injured ten people. They chose their targets based on 'a moral obligation to do all that is humanly possible to prevent the destruction of the earth'. Even at their trials, the members of the group showed little remorse, declaring that they were not terrorists. Rather, it was 'Businesses such as Litton (which manufactured Cruise missile guidance systems), BC Hydro and Red Hot Video [that] are the real terrorists. They are guilty of crimes against humanity and the earth.' The attack on the Dunsmuir substation was an attempt to halt the building of a power line from Cheekeye that would provide enough electricity for heightened industrial activity on Vancouver Island.[89] Direct Action, claiming responsibility for the attack, said that they:

> reject ecological destruction and human oppression whether they be caused by the corporate machines of the West or the Communist machine of the East ... We must make this an insecure and inhabitable place for the capitalists and their projects. This is the best contribution we can make towards protecting the earth and struggling for a liberated society.[90]

While the attack on the substation was largely environmental and anti-developmental, the bombing of the Litton Systems plant was overtly anti-nuclear. Nuclear war was 'beyond question the ultimate expression of the negative characteristics of Western civilisation'. They explained:

> We believe that people must actively fight the nuclear war system in whatever forms they exist and wherever they exist. Although, in total, the nuclear militarization of the world is a vast and seemingly

unfathomable and omnipotent network, it can be understood and effectively resisted when we recognise that it is designed, built and operated in thousands of separate facilities and industries spread throughout the world. By analysing the interests and institutions in our own regions that are contributing to the nuclear build-up we find the smaller component pieces of the nuclear network that are realistic targets for direct confrontation and sabotage. Our opposition to the insanity of nuclear war must be transformed into militant resistance and direct action on a local and regional basis.[91]

A preoccupation with defending 'the people' against technology and detrimental foreign influences is common to many left-wing movements. It is even possible to see this in groups that have no obvious anti-nuclear agenda. Anti-American sentiment was especially prevalent amongst the European left-wing terrorists that conducted a series of joint operations in the mid 1980s, groups such as the Cellules Communistes Combattants of Belgium that, until 1984, committed attacks which were unlikely to cause fatalities, but after that date, sought to kill the 'Yankee military and their accomplices'.[92] Although there are no nuclear reactors in Peru, this anti-technology strategy can be seen to have been part of the Sendero Luminoso's (Shining Path) campaign against the Peruvian government. They launched their first armed action on 16 June 1980, attacking the town hall of San Martin de Porres with Molotov cocktails. By May, 1983, the group had attacked Lima's Bayer plant and succeeded in blacking out the city. Their objective was the destruction of the state and the creation of a new democracy based on the peasants and the urban workers. By 1988, the focus of their actions had moved from a rural-based insurrection to an urban revolution, and they had attacked factories, power plants and communication and transport systems. They also directed their violence against foreign representatives, attacking the embassies of China, India, West Germany and Spain. These attacks seem to have sought to undermine the Peruvian government rather than to draw the world's attention to their case. Sendero Luminoso differed considerably in objectives from its bitter rival, Tupac Amaru, which, in January and February 1991, as a protest against the Gulf War, attacked the US embassy with rocket propelled grenades and dynamited Lima's Pizza Hut, Kentucky Fried Chicken, Mormon churches and the US Peruvian Institute. Clearly, as with the group's siege at the Japanese Ambassador's residence from December 1996 to April 1997, these actions were intended to have an impact on a foreign audience, not just one in Peru.[93] In contrast, the Tupamaros of Uruguay made little effort to acquire foreign audiences or to attack foreign targets. This was because they had little hope of attracting assistance from other governments as their left-wing cause met with little sympathy amongst the increasingly reactionary regimes of Latin America; the importance of foreign influence was limited in Uruguay, so the assistance or pressure they could bring to bear was minimal; and there was a negligible Uruguayan diaspora, so there were few potential constituents to be won over.[94]

Left-wing terrorism, like religious-inspired violence, is based heavily in textual references. These give both a philosophical and a practical basis for terrorism. Obviously, writers such as Marx, Lenin and Mao were tremendously influential, and all justified violence as a necessary condition of revolution. The Red Brigades read and, to some extent, followed the teachings of Mao and Carlos Marighella. Marighella was admired because he had successfully implemented the techniques he advocated in his 'Mini-Manual of the Urban Guerrilla', which was the first practical text on how to effectively wage a guerrilla war. However, Mao was especially significant to the Red Brigades, possibly in part because a defining experience in the radicalisation of group members was opposition to the Vietnam War, and support for the supposedly Maoist Hanoi regime. However, Mao's real importance came from his guiding framework for revolution, rather than from the teachings themselves. The group especially favoured a teaching that fostered self-belief and patience for ultimate victory: the revolutionary process 'cannot be other than protracted and ruthless...It is wrong to think that...revolution can triumph overnight.' The Red Brigades were also able to use Mao's teachings to justify not only their own potential death, but also their need to kill others in the process of revolution. As Mao himself argued:

> All men must die, but death can vary in its significance. The ancient Chinese writer, Szuma Chien said, 'Though death befalls all men alike, it may be heavier than Mount Tai or lighter than a feather.' To die for the people is heavier than Mount Tai, but to work for the fascists and die for the exploiters and oppressors is lighter than a feather.

Mao therefore glorified dying a 'heavy death', and absolved the murderer that perpetrated a 'light death' of moral responsibility or guilt.[95]

The importance of ideology, in its strict theoretical sense, varies significantly from one group to another. While they would still be classified as anarchic-ideologue, organisations such as Action Direct or the Cellules Communistes Combattantes, in stark contrast to organisations such as the Red Brigades or RAF, both of whom discussed their ideas in depth and produced manifestos, were evidently unimpressed by theoretical discussions, and instead favoured action, as is suggested by statements such as *'les documents qui proposent DOCOM, sont des documents de combats, non des analyses de salon...'*[96] One of the consequences of an ideological motivation is that, in contrast to groups motivated by other goals, such as nationalist-separatism, it perpetuates a world view and thus lends an international, as well as a more narrow perspective to the cause. This is clearly supported by the example of the RAF, which from the mid 1980s focused its efforts in an attempt to build a West European Guerrilla organisation, an alliance with other Marxist-Leninist European terrorists, such as Action Direct internationale (ADi) or the Belgian Cellules Communistes Combattantes (CCC). The co-operation between the RAF and ADi resulted in the murders of General Rene Audran in Paris and Ernst Zimmermann, a German manager in the munitions industry, in Munich on 1 February 1985; an attack on the US Air Base in Frankfurt; and the murder of the Director-General of the French Renault Works, Georges Besse, on 17 November 1986. All the murder victims could be perceived to have been members of the European Military-Industrial Complex. The CCC was less involved in such collaborative efforts: the only evidence of practical co-operation is that the explosive used by the RAF in its failed December 1984 attack on the NATO School in Oberammergau was stolen by the CCC in June from a quarry in Belgium. However, the arrests of the leading members of AD in February 1987 and the CCC in December 1985 largely finished those groups as viable organisations. After that, the RAF focused on its relationship with the Red Brigades, which by 1985 had split into two 'positions': the BR-PCC (Red Brigades for the Construction of the Fighting Communist Party) which was internationalist and anti-imperialist, and the UCC (the Union of Fighting Communists) which was proletarian and focused on the class struggle. However, the attempt to create a pan-European terrorist movement, directed predominantly against NATO, was only half-heartedly pursued and so failed.[97] This fact was acknowledged in the RAF's statement of 10 April 1992, in which they announced the cessation of their violence in exchange for improvements in the prison conditions of those RAF members being held by the German state. Part of the statement was as follows:

> We were faced with the fact that we had failed to accomplish our objective, namely to achieve a breakthrough in the joint international struggle for liberation. The liberation struggles were generally too weak to hold their own against the imperialist war, which was extended to all levels.[98]

The ability of the Red Brigades to justify their actions was enhanced by the belief that they were battling against oppression, on behalf of the exploited workers, for whom there were ever diminishing opportunities for liberty and justice. Within Italian society, violence was a norm, not an aberration; fascist violence was being perpetrated against the weaker members of society. The ruling elite would do anything to maintain their power; their code was arbitrarily imposed rules of law and morality. To disrupt or overthrow such a code, even using violence, was justifiable. This growing awareness about the intrinsic nature of Italian society was focused by a series of events that appeared to confirm the first generation members of the Red Brigades in their belief that there was a need to act, to protect themselves and others from the threat of fascism. The catalyst for members of the nascent group was the bombing of a bank in the Piazza Fontana in Milan on 12 December 1969, in which 16 people died and 88 were injured. The attack was perpetrated by conservative terrorists, intent on ensuring that left-wingers were blamed and clamped down upon, both of which occurred, confirming the left-wing group in the opinions of society.[99]

Martyrs played an important role in the perpetuation of the Italian terrorism, in common with most other terrorist organisations, including the West German groups, for whom imprisoned members were a vital source of inspiration and publicity, and who became increasingly critical to the group's identity and sense of purpose.[100] Mara Cagol, a founder member of the Red Brigades, was killed in a shootout with police in June 1975. The group's tribute was clearly designed to inspire and motivate others to join the cause:

> Let all sincere revolutionaries honour the memory of Mara, reflecting on the political lesson she gave by means of her choice, her work, her life. Let a thousand arms reach out to pick up her gun ... Mara is a flower which has bloomed, and the Red Brigades will continue to cultivate this flower of liberty until victory comes.

Adriana Faranda and Valerio Morucci, prominent second generation leaders of the Red Brigades, were examples of people attracted
by this campaign. During 1975, both were active in the radical group
Formazioni Armante Comuniste. In the autumn of 1976, they were
offered the command of the newly formed Rome column of the Red
Brigades by Mario Moretti. Faranda went to the Arts Faculty of
Rome university and gradually became radicalised, as her need to feel
involved meshed with her growing social conscience. Initially participating in mainstream political protest, she became more drastic as it
became clear that dissent was ineffective. Increasingly convinced that
society was too corrupt to be recovered, she believed that 'to bring
about a radical transformation the only possible way was through
revolution, which necessitated violence'. Morucci also started in the
Arts Faculty of Rome University in 1968. He spent much of the early
1970s in a series of increasingly radical organisations, such as Potere
Operaio, in which he was a part of the hard-line semi-covert wing, as
he grew increasingly frustrated at the lack of political will to transform Italian society, a reform it clearly needed.[101]

Unlike right-wing terrorists, left-wing groups have little experience
of 'split delegitimisation': the government, establishment and enemy
are all one and the same. As a result, such left-wing groups are more
likely than reactionary terrorists to regard themselves as 'outsiders'
and to be irretrievably hostile to the authorities from the outset,
driven on by revolutionary ideology. Such implacable opposition
might have an escalatory impact on the level of violence they are
willing to employ against a state in which they have no stake.
However, this is not obviously so, even in the most extreme cases.
Although it is not typical of left-wing terrorist groups, both the Red
Brigades and their contemporary West German organisations, such
as Baader-Meinhof, shared a strong, adverse reaction against fascism
and Nazism, as a major component of their initial radicalism and
subsequent alienation from the Italian and West German establishment. In part, it reflected a generational difference, believing that
these establishments represented the remnants of the far-right
regimes of 25 years before, thinly cloaked under democratic
respectability.[102] Every clash the group had with authority was taken
to represent further proof of an attempt by the right-wing establishment to repress the freedoms of the organisation and the people.
Baumann commented that 'The three deaths in Stammheim [the
suicide of three leaders of the Baader-Meinhof gang] were regarded
as confirmation by these groups that fascism has now broken out

openly.'[103] Although none of its current membership had been active
before 1984,[104] even in 1992, in the RAF's penultimate communiqué,
Germany's Nazi past figured prominently in the group's justification
for the original decision to use violence:

> Our movement was possible...in this country, where the society
> has not come to grips with the realities of Auschwitz and its Nazi
> past, and where Nazis were reinstated in all sectors of government
> and business, and where instead communists and antifascists were
> persecuted, and rearmament was forced on the society against the
> opposition of many who wanted a real break with the fascist past.[105]

Even when a state does have nuclear power, it is not invariable that
left-wing groups within that state target the industry, as a core part of
their campaign, even if the rejection of the state's establishment is as
total as was the case in both the Italian and German examples. Italy
formerly had four reactor sites (Latina, Garigliano, Caorso and Trino
Vercellese); yet, according to a chronology of nuclear incidents based
on the RAND-St Andrews Database, between 1968 and 1986, a
period of intense terrorist activity in Italy, there were very few
confirmed incidents that could even conceivably be described as
perpetrated by terrorists, and only one of those appeared to have an
anti-nuclear motive. That was the May 1979 attack on the National
Nuclear Energy Centre in which intruders poured gasoline on a
computer within the Centre and then returned fire when a night
watchman discovered them and started shooting. No group claimed
credit for the attack and a motive was never established.[106]

West Germany's example provides an interesting counterweight to
the Italian one. Baumann believed that it was entirely plausible that
the RAF might engage in an act of nuclear terrorism. In an interview
with Encounter, he said:

> I am not suggesting that at the present moment the groups have
> concrete plans or even ideas of that kind. But such things are in
> accordance with the logic of the age and the logic of the
> group...Henceforth there are no limits...Now [the RAF have] got
> to do something that will certainly work. And what can that be
> except an ultimate thing like that [nuclear terrorism]?...They are
> clever people, and they have vast amounts of money. A primitive
> atomic bomb could also be made. But a raid on a stockpile is more
> likely...If you had a thing like that under your control you can

make the Federal Chancellor dance the can-can on a table on colour television.[107]

However, such a possibility came to nothing, and there is little other evidence of a serious attempt to perpetrate such an attack. It could, therefore, possibly be dismissed as idle speculation by someone who was, at the time of the interview, an alienated former member of a rival terrorist organisation. Despite the apparent interest of left-wing terrorists in the potential of nuclear terrorism, the overwhelming majority of nuclear incidents, in West Germany, recorded by the RAND-St Andrews Database for the years 1969 to 1986, were perpetrated by genuinely single-issue anti-nuclear groups. Apart from the assassinations of Heinz Karry, economics minister of Hesse, in 1981 and of Karl-Heinz Beckurts, a senior executive of Siemans, in 1986, most of the other events appear to have been relatively low-level and directed against property, not people.[108]

Clearly, anti-nuclear violence is not necessarily a factor in left-wing terrorism, even when it might be an option and where the terrorist depiction of their adversaries comes close to demonisation. There has to be another element to explain the actions of left-wing groups such as Action Direct in France and Direct Action in Canada, or national-ist-separatist groups such as ETA in Spain. Despite the dominance of left-wing motivations in anti-nuclear violence, this type of group is singularly unlikely to be responsible for a high-level act of nuclear terrorism. Critically, left-wing groups' actions are mitigated by bounded morality. While their morality may not be clear to, or shared by, the majority of the population, it exists in a way that is a genuine constraint on the scope of left-wing groups' campaigns. Curiously, the basis for left-wing organisations' self-imposed limitations is their perception of their audience's morality, in terms of what actions by the terrorists will be tolerated. This morality is crucial in legitimising the actions of left-wing terrorists. It is this that separates them in their own minds from criminals; it justifies their consistent infringement of widely accepted moral and legal boundaries in society. They can claim to be fighting a defensive and 'just' war against an oppressive and overbearing state.[109] Furthermore, since a great deal of left-wing violence is perpetuated by a 'revolutionary vanguard', in the name of the people, against the government and elite of a state, such groups are reluctant to commit acts that needlessly injure 'innocent' people.[110] Horst Mahler, one of the founders of the Baader-Meinhof group, said of their targeting: 'Of course, it was not "the people", the little man who is innocent and not involved in any repression that we would kill. The main point in our struggle was to be some kind of sabotage and punishment of responsible personages for cruelties against the people.'[111] Direct Action displayed a ruthlessness and contempt towards their enemies, but were equally appalled when their attacks wounded innocent people. The Tupamaros sought to be the 'armed vanguard' of the Uruguayan left, a perspective that led it to treat terrorism as just one tactic amongst several on the road to political power. The group never ceased to be aware that terrorism could be potentially damaging to the revolution, so constantly sought to avoid unnecessary violence and especially injury to people other than their targets.[112] This point is so important as to bear re-emphasis: the targeting and actions of left-wing groups are restricted by proportionality and justice; attacks that are disproportionate or unjust are counter-productive, risking a government clamp-down, as well as alienating the terrorists from their audience and potential sympathisers. Consequently, while they may be capable of mass-destructive terrorism, left-wing groups are unlikely to engage in such actions. The likelihood of nuclear terrorism, determined by such considerations as tactics and targeting, and shaped by factors like ideology, psychology and opportunity, is the focus of the next section.

# 5  The Likelihood of
Nuclear Terrorism

## THE FEASIBILITY OF NUCLEAR TERRORISM

The implications of the increased opportunity to proliferate arising from the collapse of the Soviet Union are far from clear when it comes to applying them to nuclear terrorism. However, both in terms of intent and capability, any act of nuclear terrorism would be 'a quantum leap' from conventional weapons terrorism.[1]

Setting off a nuclear-yield bomb would require that a group somehow acquire a weapon, possibly through state-sponsorship, but more likely by stealing one, an extremely difficult proposition and a relatively unlikely one, given the presumed need of terrorists or states for anonymity and complete security at such a delicate stage of their operations. The more likely option would be that they build a bomb; since this would require fissile material it would seem to preclude all but the most well-off or state-sponsored terrorist groups. If terrorists were intent on building a nuclear-yield device, their biggest technical difficulty would probably be the acquisition of fissile material. The design for a crude nuclear device has been publicly accessible for 25 years and relies on technology that, while challenging in the 1940s, is almost certainly no longer so, particularly if terrorists are content with a crude nuclear weapon, of variable and uncertain yield. Easiest to construct would be a gun-type assembly using HEU. A less than critical mass quantity of uranium (probably around 15kg) would be fired down a cylinder, using a high explosive charge, into another less than critical mass quantity of uranium (about 40kg) at the other end of the cylinder and which had been hollowed out so that the smaller quantity of uranium fitted snugly, forming a supercritical mass and creating a nuclear explosion. Although such a device requires a relatively large amount of HEU and a thick-walled cylinder, probably about 50cm long, the device would not be impossibly heavy and could certainly be transported by van.[2]

The status of plutonium as the material for a terrorist weapon is much debated. The conventional wisdom is that a group would have to use weapons-grade plutonium, machined into a sphere and surrounded by shaped conventional explosives that, when detonated simultaneously, to the micro-second, compresses the sphere and creates a super-critical mass. The degree of engineering required to achieve this would make the building of such a device, if not impossible, at least very difficult for terrorists. However, the idea that constructing such a plutonium nuclear-yield device would be difficult, or even that it is compulsory to use weapons-grade material, is disputed. R.W. Selden, of the Lawrence Livermore Laboratory, has argued that 'The concept of...plutonium which is not suitable for explosives is fallacious.' Hans Blix, Director General of the International Atomic Energy Agency, said: 'The Agency considers high burn-up reactor-grade plutonium and in general plutonium of any isotopic composition...to be capable of use in a nuclear explosive device. There is no debate on the matter in the Agency's Department of Safeguards.'[3] The views of neither Selden nor Blix can be lightly dismissed. If a terrorist group were to steal plutonium oxide (plutonium from spent fuel elements is often stored at reprocessing plants as plutonium oxide), it could be converted to plutonium metal in 'a straightforward chemical process'. By using a close to critical mass (about 8kg of metal), it would not be necessary to shape the conventional high explosive to achieve a super-critical mass. Instead, the desired effect could be achieved by stacking the explosives around the plutonium and using 50–60 detonators to create a symmetrical shock wave. An electronic circuit that generated a high-voltage square wave would enable the detonators to be fired simultaneously enough to achieve the desired result. Furthermore, plutonium oxide could also be used for a crude nuclear device by placing a close to critical mass, about 35kg of reactor-grade plutonium in the form of plutonium oxide crystals, in a spherical container and surrounding it with a large quantity of conventional high explosive. The simultaneous detonation of this explosive would almost certainly result in significant energy from nuclear fission. Even if it did not work, the result would be a singularly unpleasant radiological dispersal device, since the explosion would cause the plutonium oxide to be scattered over a wide area. There are some potential risks to building a crude nuclear bomb, but fairly elementary precautions, such as the use of a neutron counter, would minimise the danger of radiological hazards or accidentally achieving criticality. A crude device could be built by a small group using the open literature, and without requiring testing of components, for a fraction of a million dollars.[4]

Balanced against that is the argument that states such as Iran and Iraq have been actively pursuing a nuclear weapons capability for years and have still not succeeded. This mainly reflects their difficulty in obtaining sufficient fissile material. However, there is widespread recognition that:

> Adding to this threat [the proliferation of weapons of mass destruction] is the emergence of low-technology nuclear devices and radioactive material dispersal weapons, based on diverted or stolen material (nuclear smuggling).[5]

While terrorism other than a nuclear-yield bomb, such as a radiological device, is more likely, the severity of the former means that the extent of the problem of a radiological device is not proportionate to a full scale terrorist nuclear weapon; consequently, most of the focus has been on the nuclear-yield device.[6]

It still seems unlikely that most terrorist organisations would seek to enrich material for a yield-producing device; it is simply too complex and requires considerable expertise and unnecessary cost to achieve. Furthermore, enrichment would be unnecessary in many cases: a crude nuclear-yield bomb can be made with material that is not weapons-grade and even low-grade fissile material would have considerable utility as the basis for a radiological device. Materials in this category can be more easily stolen from nuclear, industrial and research facilities than can weapons-grade material.[7] Such a radiological device would be extremely easy to construct: elements such as cobalt-60 or cesium-137 need a fierce fire to disperse them, so an effective device would probably use a mixture of high explosive and incendiary material with the radiological material wrapped around them or even simply next to them. A firebomb of this variety is, technologically, well within the reach of many terrorist organisations.[8] Since the materials for radiological terrorism are so widely available (cesium-137, for example, is commonly used in hospitals for X-rays), it is by far the most likely form of nuclear device, as well as the least catastrophic. However, it would still have considerable value as a terrorist weapon, since the mere fact of being 'nuclear' would almost certainly ensure that it had an impact on the public's imagination and fear, and thus on a governmental response, far in excess of the danger it poses. The response to the Three Mile Island accident in 1979 provides an example: the risk to the public was minimal, but the outcry and fear were considerable. Radiological devices are not ideal for creating mass casualties, particularly in the short-term, but they would have vast impact and could, potentially, pose a considerable problem for an extended period. Once aware of the problem, it would probably be possible to clean up the radiological effects of a device, but restoring public confidence would be very difficult.[9] Suppose that terrorists put radioactive material in the main ventilation system of the World Trade Center or the New York subway. Even if all of the material was successfully removed and the contamination dealt with, how easy would it be to persuade people to return to work in the WTC or to use the subway again? Clearly, the disruption would be immense. The decision as to whether or not to use a nuclear-yield device, or a radiological weapon, or neither, must be largely dependent not only on the type of terrorist group concerned, but also on the type of target selected. An attack requiring the destruction of an enormous area, such as an army base, or the death of as many people as possible, might conceivably justify the use of a full-scale nuclear weapon. However, in terms of destructive capability, a radiological device is unlikely to improve significantly on conventional weapons. This, then, leads to the question: why would one use such a weapon, since it would require so much more effort, especially in acquiring nuclear material, than would conventional terrorism?[10] Part of the answer must lie in its publicity value, and the fear it is capable of engendering. At the moment, it is still possible to argue that massive conventional attacks attract just as much coverage as previous non-conventional actions: the publicity around the WTC and Oklahoma attacks, the assault on the Marine Barracks in Beirut or the destruction of Pan-Am 103 was just as intense as that surrounding the sarin attack in Tokyo by Aum. Several such devastating attacks in the past 15 years have not diminished this fact. However, radiological terrorism is potentially attractive to a terrorist because it sets them apart from other groups; it takes terrorism to a new level, and it evokes the word 'nuclear' and all that that conjures in the minds of the public. Perversely, given the immense destructiveness associated with nuclear weapons, radiological terrorism offers terrorists the opportunity to obtain vast publicity *without* necessarily having to kill many people, at least not visibly or immediately. However, the sorts of group that might consider this an advantage are those whose strategy is based on an element of rationality, those that do have an earthly objective, and therefore those that are likely to be reluctant to potentially commit themselves to being considered responsible for continuing to kill people decades after the attack. The effects of a radiological weapon are largely dependent on the type of material used: while weapons-grade plutonium might cause limited damage, other elements such as cesium or even radioactive waste are potentially lethal very rapidly. In 1987, in Goiana, Brazil, two adults broke open a cesium source found abandoned in a clinic and allowed children to play with the glowing material inside. Within days, four people died and 249 others were contaminated. There was public hysteria and thousands of cubic metres of soil had to be removed for decontamination.[11]

## THE PSYCHOLOGY OF NUCLEAR TERRORISM

The decision to resort to weapons of mass destruction, would likely be more a result of group dynamics than any individual's choice, although this applies more in secular groups than religious groups or cults where the influence of a single person, such as Shoko Asahara the leader of Aum Shinrikyo, can be decisive. Their belief that the world is out to destroy them is not merely a paranoid delusion since, while this view may initially be caused by internal psychological convictions, it becomes self-fulfilling once the group begins to engage in terrorist acts. This would be especially so if a group were to engage in terrorism employing WMD, since it would elicit an extremely strong response from the government threatened, possibly endangering the existence of the group itself. However, fear of repression is scarcely a disincentive to those desperate groups that believe they have little chance of survival anyway or to those motivated by apocalyptic religious beliefs.[12]

A possible motivation for nuclear terrorism would be the group's belief that it has nothing to lose. The core priority of the organisation is survival; acts justify and call attention to its existence. If the group felt that it was fading, dissolving into factions or being usurped for prominence by another group, it might launch an act of nuclear terrorism to regain its status. The moral constraints against using terrorism are eroded by the use of ideology and rhetoric to polarise 'them' from 'us' and to reinforce the pressure to conform. If an act, no matter how heinous, furthers the group cause then it must be good by definition. The cause of society's ills is perceived to lie outside the group, often with the establishment. To destroy the source of those ills is therefore the height of morality.

Mass murder is a relatively rare terrorist phenomenon, since in most cases, killing a handful is just as effective for achieving group goals.[13] There have been no instances to date where terrorists have resorted to nuclear weapons for mass destruction. There are a number of important reasons for this: terrorists are technologically conservative, preferring to use tried and tested methods to achieve their aims; they have yet to reach 'their killing potential' using conventional weaponry, so have little need to be innovative.[14] This is reinforced by the fact that the organisational dynamics of many terrorist groups mitigate the sudden escalation of means into the nuclear domain because that would cause intense debate and risk schism.[15] Most terrorist groups have latent defectors; the group is likely to be split at the decision to 'go nuclear' between those who want to escalate and those who do not want to. Such polarisation increases the likelihood of splitting and therefore raises the risk of betrayal.[16] Since the primary goal of the organisation is survival, such controversies are avoided.

Do circumstances exist where terrorists would seek to kill many people? Jenkins has argued that 'terrorists want a lot of people watching not a lot of people dead.'[17] Causing mass casualties would be counter-productive; if this were not so, if such an act did not alienate the terrorist's constituency of supporters, then a major limitation would have been removed. Particularly for groups that operate across state boundaries, the disapproval of the targeted population is a reward not a disincentive. Two related examples are the attack by Baruch Goldstein at the Cave of the Patriarchs in Hebron on 24 February 1994, and the attack by Hamas member Salah Abdel-Rahim Hassan Assawi on a bus in Tel Aviv on 19 October 1994. In the first attack, 30 Muslim worshippers were killed; in the second, 22 Israelis. Both Goldstein and Assawi were opponents of the September 1993 Israeli-Palestinian Peace Accord; each sought, by an act of terrorism beyond the usual level of violence, to encourage an adverse reaction in the population as a whole, making further concessions impossible and derailing the entire Peace Process.[18] The levels of violence were not constrained by what might be deemed 'acceptable' to the targeted audience, so much as accentuated by the terrorists' desire that they be as unacceptably high as possible. However, it is questionable whether nuclear weapons would be appropriate as 'spoilers' since such an action depends on an individual or group claiming responsibility, the implications of which, in the context of a nuclear-yield bomb, are likely to be severe and possibly counter-productive if it meant that there would be increased outside intervention to compel an agreement.[19] Another possible scenario for a terrorist use of a nuclear-yield device is an attack on an ally of the US, rather than on a US target, for 'demonstration purposes', with the clear possibility of a further attack, to compel compliance by the US administration. Supposedly, such a high-profile action would place a huge amount of pressure on the US government without necessarily producing the same degree of counter-productive sentiments and over-powering desire for revenge that an attack on US soil would engender.[20] The subsequent reaction to such an assault is not clear: the scale of the threat and the trend towards international co-operation on terrorism might well mean that the intelligence and security force efforts to deal with the situation might be no less as a result of an attack in Japan or Canada than for one in the United States. Furthermore, restating a pledge made by the United States, Britain and the USSR in the 1968 UN Security Council Resolution 255 'to provide or support immediate assistance, in accordance with the Charter' in the event of nuclear aggression or the threat of it, in 1995 all five Nuclear Weapon States (NWS) gave non-specific promises to take measures to restore international peace and security, in the event of a nuclear attack on a Non-Nuclear Weapon State (NNWS). However, they stopped short of guaranteeing a nuclear or even a military response.[21] Although this should not be regarded as binding, it does show a clear, long-standing, commitment to regarding nuclear use or the threat of it as a problem that transcends state boundaries. Therefore, the fear of the possible repercussions may be just as much a factor when terrorists contemplate using nuclear weapons outside the US as within it. One, more justifiably worrying, factor that might encourage a terrorist use of non-conventional weaponry is that, particularly in some parts of the world, even secular terrorism is perceived in abso-lutist terms, more readily associated with religious motivations for violence. The Armenian example has already been cited, but it applies equally to parts of South Asia. Some groups are willing to define their enemies in very broad terms as anyone belonging to a rival sect, organisation or community, and to target them indiscrimin-ately as a consequence.[22]

However, despite examples such as Hebron and Tel Aviv, it largely seems that Jenkins' point, about the objectives of terrorists, is still valid: 'simply killing a lot of people has seldom been one terrorist objective...terrorists operate on the principle of the minimum force necessary. They find it unnecessary to kill many, as long as killing a few suffices for their purposes.'[23] No attacks, to date, could be regarded as approaching mass-destructive terrorism, despite their occasionally nuclear component. There have, though, been other incidents, some of which are discussed below, that show an alarming trend towards using a radiological weapon.

Most terrorist violence is symbolic: aimed at drawing attention to the group and its cause rather than destroying people or property unnecessarily. Consequently, most of such violence is directed against inanimate objects: fatal attacks accounted for only about 29 per cent of all assaults in 1995. However, this figure is rising: in 1994 it was 27 per cent of incidents and it was only 19 per cent in the 1980s and 17 per cent in the 1970s. Most attacks are still against targets with symbolic importance for the terrorist, so that diplomatic, business, airline, military and finally civilian targets are the most frequent. It is extremely rare for terrorists to contemplate the infliction of mass casualties such as might be caused by a nuclear incident. Of over 8,000 international terrorist incidents since 1968, fewer than 60 show any indication of terrorists seeking to use non-conventional means.[24]

However, terrorism is becoming increasingly lethal: in the 1980s terrorist incidents rose by a third compared to the 1970s, but the result was a twofold increase in fatalities as a result of these attacks.[25] While fatalities from international terrorism peaked at 800 in 1987, followed by 663 in 1988, 661 in 1983 and 467 in 1993,[26] the percentage of incidents that involved at least one fatality in 1995 was higher than at any time since 1968.[27] This could be partially explained by the fact that a few incidents, such as the bombing of the US Marine Barracks in Beirut in 1983, the 1985 bombing of the Air India jet, and the bombing of Pan Am flight 103 over Lockerbie in 1988, each resulted in the deaths of hundreds of people causing terrorism as a whole to appear increasingly lethal. However, such figures also reflect a trend that has three key elements: the 'amateurisation' of terrorism, the contrastingly improved professionalism of other terrorists, and the rise of religious terrorism.

Previously, terrorist groups were largely seen as well-defined bodies with a coherent (although sometimes loose) command and control structure[28] that spent the bulk of their time focused on their cause and planning future actions. The World Trade Center attack in February 1993 compelled these assumptions to be re-examined. It was a one-off operation conducted on an *ad hoc* basis by a group of like-minded individuals who shared similar frustrations, friends and religious beliefs. They were only indirectly connected to a controlling body making it very hard for the authorities to trace them beforehand. This would be significant for the likelihood of nuclear terrorism for two reasons: the lack of tight controls may mean that there are fewer constraints for terrorists to cause mass casualties and the use of cut-outs would mean that state sponsorship of nuclear terrorism could not be ruled out, so long as the state concerned could continue to plausibly deny all knowledge of the attack.[29] Acting Director of Central Intelligence, William Studeman, testified in April 1995 that:

a new Islamic extremist threat is on the rise. These groups – often *ad hoc* – are even more dangerous in some ways than the traditional groups because they do not have a well established organizational identity and they tend to decentralize and compartment their activities. They also are capable of producing and using more sophisticated conventional weapons as well as chemical and biological agents. They are less restrained by state sponsors or other benefactors than are the traditional groups. These groups appear disinclined to negotiate, but instead seek to take revenge on the United States and Western countries by inflicting heavy civilian casualties...

Both the traditional Islamic terrorists and the new breed have filled their ranks with militants who trained in the Afghan war, where they learned the value of violence in defeating a major power. They are well funded. Some have developed sophisticated international networks that allow them great freedom of movement and opportunity to strike, including in the United States. They also are attracting a more qualified cadre with greater technical skills.[30]

In the past, it was easier to argue that terrorism was clearly instrumental, at least in part: groups sought legitimacy and 'a seat at the table'. However, now it is possible to see organisations that: 'don't seem to care about establishing legitimacy, but just want to strike a blow in anger and kill as many people as possible...For them, the calculation of the right level of violence seems to have no upper bounds.'[31] To brand most terrorism in this way would be an overgeneralisation: many groups retain as much rationality and calculated instrumentalism as ever, but it does have some validity for a number of other organisations, such as Aum Shinrikyo.

Religious terrorists appear to have a higher level of lethality than most other types of group: between 1982 and 1996, Shia groups were responsible for eight per cent of terrorist attacks but 28 per cent of deaths arising from such attacks. Religious terrorism is widespread: from Islamic groups to White Supremacists in the US, ultra-Orthodox

Jews in Israel, or Sikhs in India. As has already been noted, religion enhances the likelihood of violence being employed by some groups because it has the ability to inspire total loyalty and commitment, a prime factor in the utilisation of force as a valid means. Such organisations may seek to remove whole sections of society and are not constrained by the political, practical or moral factors that limit others' actions.[32] Whereas, in secular terrorism, violence usually begins as an instrument and may become an end in itself, in religious terrorism, violence can be an end in itself, a sacramental act or divine duty carried out in response to a theological imperative.[33] It would be a mistake, though, to assume that religious motivations equate to highly violent terrorism and secular motivations to acts of low violence. This is obviously not so: both the Liberation Tigers of Tamil Eelam and Sendero Luminoso are examples of secular terrorists that have been responsible for massacres. However, religion does more readily offer a justification for highly destructive terrorism than do secular motives.

Cults and millenarian groups are the most likely of religious groups to resort to high-level violence because, in the former case, they are the most likely to be controlled by a single leader and to be isolated from moderating outside influences. Undiluted authority can be rigorously imposed with devastating effects to both the cult members and the wider world. Millenarian groups believe that the world will end imminently with the descent from heaven of a redeemer, a messiah. They may be encouraged to use extensive violence if it offers the prospect of speeding the process. Post cites a Jewish sect that formed a group within the Gush Emunim organisation. It planned to destroy the El Aksa Mosque and the Mosque of Omar (the Dome of the Rock), both in Jerusalem. The former is the third holiest site in Islam, but the Jewish terrorists argued that it stood on Temple Mount, the holiest place in Judaism. As Kabbalist millenarians, they believed that the coming of the Messiah would be delayed for a thousand years unless they helped to promote the world's redemption, scheduled for the year 6000 in the Jewish calendar, and that the destruction of the mosques was wholly justifiable and necessary. Post argues that such acts would surely have caused a world-wide jihad and made the possibility of nuclear terrorism against Israel permissible in the eyes of some Islamic groups.[34] However, this fails to distinguish between motivation and intent; it is the latter that is vital to any assessment of the likelihood of nuclear terrorism since possible motivations for such an act are so numerous that it does little to assist in a helpful analysis of the situation. A similar case involves White Supremacists in the United States who allegedly sought to engage in mass indiscriminate killing. The federal grand jury indictment stated that they met in 1983 at Aryan Nations headquarters in Idaho and there plotted to overthrow the federal government and establish a separate Aryan state within the United States. They planned to assassinate federal officials, politicians and Jews, and to bomb and pollute municipal water supplies. When, in April 1984, federal agents raided a supremacist compound in Arkansas, they found 30 gallons of cyanide intended for this mass poisoning. This program of action was in line with that prescribed in *The Turner Diaries*.[35] White Supremacists continue to experiment with WMD: in April 1993 there was an attempt by Thomas Lewis Lavy to smuggle 130 grams of ricin (a nerve agent) into Canada from Alaska. The Lavy example is significant because although he had links to White Supremacist and survivalist groups, he acted alone in bringing in enough ricin to kill thousands of people. When he was arrested, he was carrying four guns, 20,000 rounds of ammunition and at least two pieces of survivalist literature: 'The Poisoner's Handbook' and 'Silent Death'.[36] In May 1995, Larry Wayne Harris, a former member of the Aryan Nations, was arrested for mail-ordering three vials of bubonic plague bacteria for $240 from the American Type Culture Collection. Harris claimed he was working on an antidote for plague and was 'concerned about an imminent invasion from Iraq of super-germ-carrying rats'.[37] Harris was arrested again in February 1998 for possession of anthrax, but was finally charged only with violating the terms of his probation from the earlier offence. He and William Leavitt, who was arrested with Harris, claimed they had been working on a vaccine for anthrax.[38]

Professional terrorists have become increasingly ruthless, as well as more sophisticated and operationally competent. Each group learns from the mistakes of its predecessors making it harder for state authorities to detect and destroy them. Although most groups prefer off-the-shelf weaponry with which they are familiar and confident, some groups are also adept at adapting or improvising their weaponry: the WTC bombers used readily available fertiliser as the main component of their device. Such innovation from freely available resources makes it impossible for governmental forces to guard against every eventuality and protect every target. Conventional explosives such as semtex, used to destroy the Pan Am flight over Lockerbie, are sufficiently powerful that relatively little is required to inflict considerable damage: theoretically, a quantity the size of a fist would be enough to blow a hole in the side of an aircraft.[39] Therefore, even when it is not a viable option to plant a truckbomb, there are conventional explosives available to terrorists that negate the necessity of escalating to non-conventional weaponry. This would seem to mitigate against the higher-level forms of nuclear terrorism: as yet the materials for it are not easily available and vast damage can be achieved using more conventional means, even against major targets, since they cannot be comprehensively guarded all the time.[40]

The psychological constraints are almost certainly less extreme for the use of a nuclear hoax or the seizure of a nuclear weapon than for the detonation of one. A credible hoax might be an attractive option because it would require high-level decision-making by the threatened state, which might be regarded by the group as a success in itself since it conveys prestige and status upon the group, thus making them a major actor. DeLeon, Hoffman, Kellen and Jenkins argued that a combination of propaganda, coercion and destruction would be a probable motivation for nuclear terrorism.[41] Since both the public and government agencies are so sensitised to the potential of nuclear weapons, even a credible nuclear hoax, posing no danger to an area, could potentially cause panic, create vast disruption to daily life and commerce and result in casualties as terrified residents fled from the area.[42] Even if the physical damage caused by the incident were minimal, the psychological ramifications for the public and government and the cache for the terrorists would be considerable.[43] On 15 April 1995, having already established that they were capable of such action by attacking the underground with chemical weapons on 20 March, Aum Shinrikyo threatened further attacks in Tokyo. The threat was taken seriously; there was widespread alarm and the city remained at a standstill on what would ordinarily have been a busy working day.[44]

One difficulty with a high-level act of nuclear terrorism is that of credibility: terrorists have to prove to governments that they are capable of the acts that are being threatened. They also have to persuade the government that it is worth negotiating, that a settlement can be reached without the threat being consummated. This is not always feasible: no government could agree to dissolve itself, nor could policy be permanently altered because it would require retaining a perpetual threat and one government condition would certainly be the surrender of the nuclear capability. These problems would not be insoluble for a terrorist group, merely complicating factors and constraints on what was possible. However, such high-level acts might be unnecessary, since there is plenty of low-level nuclear terrorism that could potentially give almost as much leverage to the terrorists.[45] Shortly after the WTC bombing in February 1993, the FBI investigated whether a group of Iranians was planning a nuclear attack on New York. They were allegedly going to smuggle radioactive material into the city and distribute it around Manhattan. The FBI was concerned, too, that the proliferation of fissile material out of the former USSR would result, not in a terrorist nuclear bomb, but in a nuclear-enriched conventional explosion.[46] The Chechen case in Moscow in November 1995 may represent the first stage in a move towards a terrorist 'dirty' bomb, a conventional device with a highly radioactive coating, the sort of weapon that the FBI feared could be used in Manhattan. The CIA are also concerned that non-fissile, radioactive materials could be used in a terrorist device designed to create psychological or economic trauma or to contaminate buildings or localised areas. Such a bomb could make whole areas no-go zones without requiring the cost, difficulty or risk that is entailed by a nuclear bomb. Such a device would also be less likely to cause massive casualties, so the political risks of using one are less than for a nuclear bomb.[47]

## AN ASSESSMENT OF THE FUTURE RISK OF NUCLEAR TERRORISM

Low-level nuclear terrorism is already a reality: on 23 November 1995, Chechen guerrilla leader, Shamyl Basayev, informed the Russian television network, NTV, that four cases of radioactive cesium had been hidden around Moscow. NTV discovered the 32 kilo case, giving off 310 times the background amount of radioactivity in Ismailovo Park. Basayev had repeatedly threatened to attack Moscow with nuclear or chemical weapons, and had already proved his ability to create 'terrorist spectaculars' by taking 1,500 people hostage in Budennovsk in June. Russian officials largely dismissed the nuclear threat, claiming that the material was cesium-137, used in X-ray equipment or some industrial processes, capable only of emitting 100 times the background amount of radioactivity.[48] Western experts also dismissed the threat, doubting that the Chechens had access to weapons-grade material.[49] However, the Russian authorities took the threat seriously, sending emergency search teams out around the city with Geiger counters.[50] Basayev was intent on displaying capability and ensuring that his threats to launch further attacks against Moscow, unless Russia withdrew from Chechenya, were taken seriously.[51] His attack was plausible because the state of the Russian nuclear industry made it impossible to rule out that the Chechens did have access to fissile material.

Aum's attack in Tokyo was far more serious. At about 8am, the morning rush hour, sarin, a lethal nerve-gas agent, was simultaneously released on five underground trains, all bound for central government ministries.[52] Twelve people were killed and about 5,500 were injured in the attack.[53] This attack followed another in Matsumoto on 24 June 1994, in which seven died and over 200 were treated for the effects of sarin.[54] Blame for both incidents was levelled at the Aum Shinrikyo cult, led by Shoko Asahara. Subsequent police raids uncovered vast amounts of raw materials for making sarin at various cult buildings.[55] The chemical fingerprints at these facilities, along with the quantity and variety of chemicals stored there, leave little doubt that Aum Shinrikyo was responsible for the attacks.[56]

While the immediate timing of the Tokyo attack may have reflected the fact that the cult was under investigation by the Japanese authorities,[57] more significantly, the cult displayed clear millenarian tendencies: Asahara had predicted that the world would end in 1997, in an Armageddon-type finale that the cult planned to further by bringing down the Japanese establishment.[58] Yoshihiro Inoue, the cult's 'Intelligence Minister', stated at the trial of Asahara that 'If things had gone as planned, the Aum Shinrikyo would have released 50 tonnes of sarin in Tokyo and ten tonnes each in Washington and New York... We regarded the world outside as evil, and destroying the evil was salvation.'[59] The cult even contemplated developing nuclear weapons, investigating methods of enriching uranium, but chose not to pursue the option.[60] Nuclear weaponry, appearing to incorporate cosmic energy and possessing the ability to destroy human life on earth, seems to transfer world-destroying capabilities from the deity to humans and thus make the terrorist the arbiter of human destiny in the place of God, making it possibly attractive to millenarian groups, such as Aum Shinrikyo.[61] Furthermore, 'if destabilizing society or drawing attention to one's cause is the goal, a mushroom cloud outranks truck bombs and sarin attacks'.[62] There can be no doubt that the fascination that exists with nuclear weapons is starting to have an impact on the tactical decisions of would-be attackers. Three New Yorkers were arrested in June 1996 for plotting to kill the chief investigator for Brookhaven and two officials of the local Republican Party by planting radioactive material in their food and in their cars. Rather than trying to use the five cases of radium that they stole from a defence contractor, it would have been far more straightforward and effective to rely on conventional means for the assault.[63] In the past, there have been a few isolated incidents of radiological poisoning, but it does seem to be becoming a more widespread phenomenon, and one that, whereas in the past, was largely the province of disaffected workers able to exploit their access to nuclear material, is increasingly the tactic of attackers with a political motive.

The Tokyo attack was unusual not because it was an attempt to kill hundreds of people, although in this century fewer than a dozen incidents have resulted in over 100 deaths,[64] but rather because of the method chosen. Tokyo was by far the most serious sub-state actor use of non-conventional weaponry. However, most terrorist groups do not want to cause mass-killings; and conventional means remain sufficient to achieve their objectives. There is the added disincentive for using high-level non-conventional weapons that the results are highly unpredictable and radiological, chemical or biological effects continue to occur over a long time, denying the immediacy that many terrorists seek and providing a residue of counter-productive publicity long after the event. However, this should not be overstated as a reason against terrorist use of WMD because this element of uncertainty exists, to some extent, with any weapon and where the objective is to maximise casualties, the whole concept of uncertainty is largely meaningless.[65]

It is worth properly considering chemical and biological weapons as alternatives to nuclear devices. Both have the potential to cause a range of effects, varying from mass-murder to incapacitating a small portion of the population. Aum undoubtedly sought to cause as many fatalities as possible, but were betrayed in their objective by the poor quality of the sarin and the dispersal device that they employed.[66] However, prior to Aum's assault, even if they had the opportunity and the resources to launch such an attack, terrorists have abstained from doing so. The ramifications of Aum's attack on future uses of nuclear, chemical or biological weapons by terrorists is far from clear.[67]

The factors that mitigate against most terrorists, and especially those with left-wing or nationalist-separatist motivations, resorting to nuclear weapons apply equally to both biological and chemical weapons. Aum represented a new type of terrorist group, being both apocalyptic and, in part, criminal, since they sought to extort money from both members and non-members to promote the activities of the organisation. However, even groups such as Aum are not certain to resort to these weapons again. Possibly, the cult represented a unique combination of factors, motivated by revenge, apocalyptic desires and material greed. It would be unwise, though, to preclude the possibility that they were not unique and may represent the pattern of future attempts to produce mass-destructive terrorism. Many terrorist groups mimic other groups' actions, so the fact that one chemical attack has occurred would significantly increase the likelihood of another such incident.[68]

Despite Aum, terrorists' use of either chemical or biological agents is a rarity. This is partly a result of the same factors that have restricted the terrorist use of nuclear devices: a fear of the response by both governments and potential supporters, and a belief that such an act would be not only unnecessary, given the potential of conventional weapons, but also disproportionate and counter-productive. This is especially so, given the abhorrence with which chemical and biological weaponry are widely regarded.[69] Furthermore, and certainly compared to conventional weapons with which terrorist are familiar, chemical or biological weapons would present a significant risk to the terrorists themselves, arising from the toxic nature of the materials being handled. This is one of the most significant barriers to terrorist use of biological weapons in particular.[70] Weaponising the biological agent would be problematic, given that dispersal in a water supply would be ineffective and that an open air dispersal method would pose as great a risk to the terrorist as to the target audience.[71] The possibility of self-sacrifice might not be a significant disincentive to some groups, but it may represent a barrier at the production stage. While there is ample evidence of suicidal terrorists being willing to die delivering their weapon and attacking the enemy in the process, there is little proof that any terrorists favour taking risks that are not absolutely necessary in manufacturing their weapon. To die killing an adversary may be one, acceptable, thing; to die mixing chemicals or preparing a biological agent may be quite another.

Assuming that the terrorists were unused to dealing with such weapons, there would also be additional technical hurdles to be overcome and heightened uncertainty about the likely effects of an attack with either chemical or biological weapons, due, in large part, to the importance of weather conditions in the effective dissemination of such agents. To be sure of causing the desired effect, terrorists would probably have to obtain and release significantly greater quantities of the material than would be the case under optimum conditions. This obviously heightens other difficulties, such as the uncertainty over the effect of the attack and the problems associated with acquiring the requisite amounts of the agent.[72] Particularly in the case of biological weapons, this leaves the possibility that the effects could range from non-existent to a pandemic.[73] Consequently, terrorists might be more inclined to channel their efforts into other types of weapons. Finally, especially in the case of biological weapons, the effects tend not to be immediate, but rather require an incubation period from hours to days, depending on the type of agent used. Chemical agents also vary considerably in the rapidity of their effects: some nerve agents are almost instantaneous, whereas others, such as sulphur mustard, take between three and eight hours following exposure to cause pain and blistering. This robs terrorists of the spectacular effects that might be achieved using other weapons. Consequently, Tucker argues, a biological attack is unlikely to appeal to a group seeking to use their terrorism as a means of drawing attention to themselves and their cause.[74] However, this assumes that media and public attention can be obtained only through immediate and devastating attacks; it is more persuasive to suggest that any terrorist attack using biological weapons would, by its very nature, attract attention and that, as large numbers of people became sick, there would be considerable interest in the cause of the outbreak.

Both chemical and biological weapons would have some appeal for a terrorist group intent on a non-conventional attack because, certainly compared to a nuclear weapon, chemical and biological weapons have the potential to be cheap and are lethal in small quantities, easing the problems of production, concealment, transportation and delivery. A biological weapon attack would almost certainly be undetectable, both because it is odourless, colourless and tasteless and because its effects would not be manifest for hours or even days, depending on the agent used. Therefore, the likelihood would be that if the attack was conducted covertly, its perpetrators would have ample time to make their escape, increasing the possibility that they might 'get away with it'. In addition, due to the possibility of pre-testing and in spite of the various uncertainties, they are still likely to be more reliable than a nuclear weapon.[75] Furthermore, the lead time between 'desiring and acquiring' a useful capability is much shorter for chemical weapons than for their nuclear equivalent: Shoko Asahara ordered his cult to develop chemical weapons in 1993, only slightly over a year before the Tokyo attack. Thus, the most immediate terrorist threat is from a chemical or biological weapon, although, if the prospects for nuclear non-proliferation were to deteriorate significantly, this would compel a rapid reassessment of the situation especially in light of the greater scope for destruction of nuclear weapons than chemical or biological ones.[76] However, while these advantages undoubtedly do apply when chemical and biological weapons are compared to a nuclear-yield device, they are much less obvious when the comparison is with a radiological dispersal device, since all of these factors are equally applicable to a weapon using highly radioactive material, such as cobalt-60; thus it would be unwise to exclude the possibility of this variety of nuclear terrorism now.

Terrorists intent on acquiring a chemical or biological weapon capability would have a number of possible avenues of obtaining the required material. Probably not amongst those options is state sponsorship. The arguments against transferring control of a state's nuclear, chemical or biological capability to a client group are basically the same: an unwillingness to abdicate control over both the material and the group, and a fear of the possible repercussions from attacked states. Roberts disagrees with this assessment, arguing that it would be more feasible for an aggressor state to be able to deny responsibility for an epidemic of a naturally occurring disease, as might be caused by a biological attack. Consequently, the risks of retaliation from the victim state would be lessened, and the willingness of the state to sponsor mass-destructive terrorism thereby increased.[77] This does not preclude the possibility that terrorists might covertly acquire their capability from a state's stockpile. In addition to states such as Iraq, Iran, Syria, Libya and North Korea, all of which possess such a supply, Russia alone has, by its own admission, 40,000 metric tons of chemical-warfare agents. These are stored at seven declared sites, at least four of which have recently been found to have lax security, closely replicating the situation at a number of storage sites for nuclear material. Terrorists' other option would be to manufacture the chemical or biological weapons themselves. Although this would not be an easy process, depending on the agents being manufactured, neither would it be an impossible one, particularly for groups that, like Aum, had sufficient financial and technical resources. Organisations such as the Australia Group of States do attempt to impose some restrictions and export-controls on the sale of chemical and biological weapons-usable materials and equipment. However, these are an ineffective barrier to proliferation because restrictions are limited to targeted states, so it is possible, through legitimate front companies, for determined states or terrorist groups to obtain the necessary materials.

Aum had particular difficulty in finding an effective means of delivery for their chemical weapons. This problem is especially acute due to the highly hazardous nature of the agents. This risk could be minimised by using 'binary' chemical weapons, since they are easier to produce, transport and use. This means that two precursor chemicals are stored separately and then mixed to form the agent immediately before use. There are methods to achieve this mixing process automatically or by remote-control, but, for Aum, these proved too technologically difficult or unreliable. The most likely possibility is that terrorists would have to manually mix the precursor chemicals, an extremely hazardous procedure and one that partly defeats the purpose of separating the chemicals initially.[78]

Biological agents have the potential to be extremely effective and potent weapons. Since pathogenic micro-organisms are able to rapidly multiply within a host, only small quantities of the agent are required to cause widespread casualties over an extended area, especially if it is disseminated through the air in the form of an aerosol. Furthermore, many animal pathogens, such as anthrax or brucellosis, are highly lethal when inhaled, but are not passed from one individual to another. Therefore, they have the advantage that it would be possible for the terrorists to partially control the extent of the attack, using such agents. However, other types of potential biological weaponry are contagious, such as pneumonic plague bacteria or haemorrhagic fever viruses such as Ebola, and could be used with the objective of causing mass casualties from an epidemic. Aum certainly considered this possibility: members of the cult were sent to Zaire in 1992, ostensibly to minister to the victims of the Ebola virus, as part of their 'African Salvation Tour', but, in reality, to collect samples of the disease to aid production of biological weapons.[79] Once back in Japan, the cult was unable to cultivate its samples into a usable form.

The production of biological agents is certainly not an insurmountable problem for terrorists. Most of the material and equipment are readily available because they have other, legitimate, commercial applications. Even lethal agents, such as anthrax, can currently be openly obtained by sending a letter on the letterhead of a university or research institute to commercial vendors. Biological agents also have the advantage that they can be grown in a short time, even using low-technology equipment; there would thus be no need for terrorists to stockpile it for long periods before an attack. The cultivation process would not be especially dangerous, compared to that for chemical weapons. The use of masks and vaccinations against the agent would probably be sufficient protection at this stage of the process. Later parts of the manufacturing process would be more risky: concentrating the agent in a continuous-flow centrifuge, drying it in a spray or freeze-dryer, and milling the dried cake into a fine powder would all entail greater danger and would require more protective measures.[80] These parts of the process would be necessary if terrorists sought to maximise the effectiveness of their biological agent because most biological weapons rely on inhalation of the material, rather than penetration of the skin. Therefore, ideally, the biological agent needs to be contained in an aerosol and to consist of particles small enough (a diameter of about one to five microns or thousandths of a millimetre) to remain suspended in the atmosphere for long periods. This would be technologically difficult to achieve, so terrorists might well choose instead to prepare the agent in liquid form and then refrigerate it until use, a considerably easier, if less efficient method. As with nuclear weaponry, there is some concern that affluent terrorists might be able to acquire the services of scientists who had worked on a state's biological weapons program, in particular that of Russia. There has been speculation that President Yeltsin's 1992 decision to eliminate the Russian program has resulted in hundreds of unemployed scientists, all with the knowledge that would greatly enhance the development of a biological weapons capability by sub-state actors.

The effects of a biological weapons attack would be hard to gauge because, like chemical weapons, the result depends heavily on a number of external factors, such as the weather. Even under the best of conditions there is considerable uncertainty as to the result: Aum apparently launched two biological attacks in Tokyo with no effect at all.[81] Clearly, chemical and biological weapons, as well as nuclear ones, are not straightforward to use, which is a major reason that makes a massive conventional attack a more realistic option for the majority of terrorists. The devastation caused by fertiliser bombs at the WTC and Oklahoma suggests that even when groups are less concerned about a counter-productive impact on their audience, conventional weaponry is still enough. Furthermore, it is cheaper, easier to access, harder for the authorities to detect, and given most terrorists' unfamiliarity with non-conventional weapons, probably safer to use as well.

The increased availability of fissile material has probably had relatively little impact on the likelihood of a terrorist nuclear bomb: it would still be difficult and expensive to build, and the credibility of all but a cult group using such a device remains low. Aum may have investigated the possibility of building a nuclear bomb, but they were still a long way off achieving it, and consequently chose a more straightforward method of creating terror. However, fissile material availability has made the feasibility and thus the credibility of a threat or hoax involving radiological terrorism a much more real possibility, one that will have to be taken seriously and would give considerable leverage to any group using such a threat. This may mean that the arguments against any secular sub-state use of non-conventional means are lessened. Religious terrorism is undoubtedly on the increase, but, for the above reasons, the attack in Moscow and possibly the threat in New York, not the attack in Tokyo is the most likely model for nuclear terrorism in the near future. However, this is not to deny the importance of the attack. Aum set a precedent, being the first terrorist attempt at an act of mass-destruction using non-conventional means: 'it breaks a taboo and has psychological import. Others will ask whether such tactics should be adopted by them. It is now more likely that at least some will say yes.'[82] According to Bruce Hoffman, 'We've definitely crossed a threshold. This is the cutting edge of high-tech terrorism for the year 2000 and beyond. It's the nightmare scenario that people have quietly talked about for years coming true.'[83]

# 6 Conclusion

The issue of mass-destructive terrorism has, in the post-Cold War era, caused concern to an unprecedented degree. This sentiment was aptly expressed by former United States Senator Sam Nunn who has argued that: 'Combating the proliferation of nuclear, chemical, and biological weapons is the most pressing issue that we face today.'[1] Indeed, Senator Nunn has contended, rogue nation's or terrorist groups' possession of nuclear weapons 'could pose a clear and present danger to our society'.[2] Particularly in the case of nuclear terrorism, the impetus for such concern is often cited as being the collapse of the Soviet Union which has led to increased opportunities for proliferation. However, it is the argument of this thesis that the real driving force behind the heightened danger of nuclear terrorism lies not with the increased opportunities for micro-proliferation, but rather with the changing nature of political violence and the psychological and organisational characteristics of terrorism itself. It is these that are the true factors that would make terrorists resort to nuclear weapons.

While the ostensible source of this concern is relatively new, arising from the opportunities for nuclear smuggling, the fact of it is not. Nuclear terrorism has been a source of regular academic and policy-oriented discussion from the early 1970s onwards. This strongly suggests that the danger stems from more than simply the fact that terrorists now have a better chance to acquire fissile materials and then use it.

In fact, the very nature of terrorist behaviour is at the core of this problem. It is a conflict between the psychological and instrumental instincts of terrorists. At a psychological level, terrorism is essentially about the search for, and then the reaffirmation of, identity. It is violence that defines the group and the individual within that group. It is the aspect that sets them apart from other types of group or individual. Although there is no 'terrorist personality', no psychological profile that would describe all perpetrators of political violence, there are clearly characteristics that are common to many groups and individuals that make heightened levels of violence not only more likely, but, from an organisational perspective, even highly desirable.

Individuals tend to initially join terrorist groups because it offers an opportunity to belong, an identity as part of the organisation, and

because it offers an outlet to channel their frustrations and anger at
society or some element within that society. They find themselves
finally accepted, usually after a progression through several other
groups, amongst similarly minded individuals. This progression has
an impact on the willingness of groups to use extremes of violence in
a number of important ways. Since individuals tend to become
members of terrorist organisations only after they have rejected, and
moved on from, membership of less violent groups, there is a very real
extent to which they 'have nowhere else to go'. This, combined with
the fact that the terrorist group offers an identity, a sense of belonging, means that the individual's primary concern is to remain within
the organisation. As a result, they are far more likely to accept the
absolutist and violent characteristics of the group than they might
otherwise. Their psychological and emotional well-being are intimately associated with the group and with the members within it. This
not only partially explains why individuals join such organisations, but
also why, once they are members, they are able to engage in violent
acts. The group enables them to feel powerful and fulfilled as individuals. The group's violence compels recognition from their society
and government. Not only must it acknowledge their existence for the
first time, but the government must also deal with the group. The
bigger the problem the group creates through its actions, the more
urgently the government must try to overcome them, tacitly recognising them as 'a player' in the process. The individual is emotionally,
intellectually and psychologically tied to the group. As well as making
it less likely that they would seek to leave the organisation, it also
ensures that individuals have a stake in preserving the identity, the
character, and above all, the existence of the group. It is from this that
the need to maintain violence as a tactic, and even to escalate it,
comes.

At the same time, the emotional and ideological justifications of
the organisation protect its members from suffering the psychological costs of imposing violence on its victims. The moral imperative
for the action is altered by using the norms and values of the group
to make such attacks a desirable duty, rather than an abhorrence. By
emphasising the necessity of the action, in the face of the enemy's
gross misdeeds, terrorism is justified, within the group's moral framework. The worthy end, the group's objective, permits the violent
means since it is perpetrated in pursuit of the higher good.
Furthermore, when the victims of the terrorist act are depicted as
representatives of the enemy, rather than as individuals, they are

depersonalised, dehumanised, so that the consequences of the violence are psychologically easier to accept for the individual terrorist. They are able to disengage from the realities of their actions by redefining the framework in which it occurs. This is important because it means that morality, at either a group or an individual level, could not, by itself, be regarded as a restraint on mass-destructive terrorism. There is no moral absolute that would prohibit the use of such weapons in all circumstances. If a sufficiently important end were sought by the group, all means, including nuclear terrorism, might be justifiable.

At the same time, anarchic-ideologue groups, especially ones that are compelled by a lack of support to exist underground, tend to contain members that are much more dependent on the organisation and are consequently much more affected by the dynamics of the group. A good example is the SLA, in which the pressures of being cut off from the rest of society, and the interactions between the members of the group, had a profound impact on the range of actions that the SLA pursued. An important example of this was their need to perform acts of terrorism on a regular basis, to reaffirm the group's importance, defined by the publicity and attention it received. The individual's need for feelings of power and authority over others was transferred onto the group as well. It had to be constantly planning or perpetrating acts of terrorism to satisfy its members' psychological requirements. Group dynamics therefore perpetuated existing patterns of behaviour, identity and action: the continued use of violence.

The need to preserve the group's organisational integrity and identity manifests itself in a number of critical ways. It ensures that any challenge, either internal or external, to the group is likely to be regarded adversely by its members. This applies equally to dissent or attempts to leave by individuals within the terrorist organisation, and to any attempt by factions within the group to mitigate the level of violence that the organisation employs. Such challenges threaten to split the group because they dispute the norms of the organisation. They are equated with treason within the group because they risk destroying the organisation. As the survival of the group becomes paramount, the instrumental objectives of the organisation become subverted. Since violence defines the group and sets it apart from other organisations, to cease or reduce the level of violence that the terrorists use is to lower the group to the status of other non-violent organisations. Such groups were previously psychologically unsatisfactory for the individual, so they have a stake in maintaining the organisation in its present state. Consequently, even if the group does achieve its declared goal, it may not disband.

This inability to alter the character of the group has an impact not only on the type of action, violence, that the terrorist organisation employs, but also on the level of that violence. Terrorism rarely achieves its intended goal. However, even when the utility of terrorism, as an instrument with which to achieve strategic objectives, has declined, many groups remain committed to the military option. Faced with the failure of their campaign, terrorist groups face a series of unpalatable choices, all of which may ultimately risk the destruction of the group. Since terrorist organisations define themselves in terms of their violence, and since, as has been shown, they are singularly poor in their ability to pursue twin-track strategies, their solution to the threat of extinction is likely to be further violence. In such circumstances, it is not unreasonable to suggest that an escalation of violence is the most plausible outcome. Such an assertion is supported by examples such as the IRA's campaign, particularly in the 1970s, or the Tamil Tigers in recent years. In the latter example, as Sri Lankan government forces compelled a Tamil retreat, the violence of Tiger attacks in Colombo has increased, culminating in the devastating bombings of 31 January 1996, and 15 October 1997. One group that is an exception to this trend towards escalation is the RAF, which did not attempt a violent recovery to stem its decline. However, in this respect, the RAF is not strictly comparable to other organisations, since it collapsed due to the increasing irrelevance of its ideology and removal of its main campaign objectives, following the release of prisoners under the Kinkel initiative of 1992.

As a group declines, it may be tempted to attempt a 'spectacular', such as the Tamil bombings, to achieve publicity and thus to reassert its cause and attract much-needed support from potential sympathisers, impressed with the group's capability and commitment to its objectives. While the need for publicity is by no means universal, it is a common motivation for many organisations. It emphasises their power and importance, so reinforces the psycho-dynamics of terrorism that make such groups attractive to their members in the first instance. This need to set themselves apart, to use a 'spectacular', means that terrorists must either resort to new tactics, or to new levels of violence. The series of hijackings of airliners in 1968 by the PFLP was an example of the former; an act of mass-destructive terrorism would be an example of both.

Instrumentally, terrorist groups base their tactical and targeting decisions not only on their capabilities, but also, to a crucial extent, on their strategic objectives. For many organisations, these both form very considerable barriers to any use of non-conventional weaponry. Terrorist groups all use an element of rational choice in their pursuit of goals. Although the group's instrumental decisions may be constrained or partially determined by psychology, this rationality does exist. It is crucially tied to proportionality, to the way that means are tied to ends. The scale of terrorist demands and their perception of their enemy are clearly linked to the lengths to which they are likely to be willing to go in pursuit of their campaign. A group that defines an entire society as its opponent and wishes to purify the world in preparation for a messianic arrival is far more likely to be willing to regard high levels of violence against that society as acceptable than would a group that purports to fight on behalf of that society against an oppressive and exploitative government. Obviously then, the motivation of the organisation plays a central role in determining their willingness to engage in high level acts of terrorism.

While it might be argued that major incidents of nuclear terrorism have not occurred as a result of terrorists' inability to acquire the means to do so, in fact, it appears that the majority of groups choose not to. They are tactically conservative, preferring the weapons with which they are familiar. Rather than adopting entirely new techniques, most terrorists appear to prefer to adapt and improve their existing ones, as the RAF did in its use of bombs to attack dignitaries travelling in moving cars. In such examples, it seems clear that such a radical departure as the use of non-conventional weaponry, though not unprecedented, is highly improbable. This is partly because more straightforward conventional attacks have a higher probability of success, requiring fewer technical skills, resources or risks than would presumably be entailed in producing a non-conventional weapon.

Despite psychological escalatory pressures, there have been few incidents of mass-destructive terrorism, and no major nuclear terrorism incidents, to date. This is largely because, until relatively recently, the prevalent types of terrorism, while containing these escalatory pressures, were also, paradoxically, self-moderating. Heavily dependent on the support, or at least on the perceived support, of a wider audience, terrorist groups largely had to restrict their actions to those that were tolerable to this audience. The role of an individual's identity, in determining terrorist action, is fundamentally different, depending on the type of group of which they are a member, and this is reflected in their respective willingness to engage in acts of mass destruction. In the case of nationalist-separatist groups, such as the IRA or ETA, an individual's violence can be seen to be an effort to promote their national identity. It is an attempt to earn the approbation of their community, to 'prove' their loyalty, by attacking the enemies of their people. Even if the wider community does not wholly support the methods of the terrorists, they may have some sympathy for their objectives. Although not universally applicable to nationalist-separatist groups, there does tend to be some support for the group in the wider community. This support is vital, emotionally and often logistically, to the terrorists and their actions are, to a considerable extent, geared to a level that will enable them to maintain that support. When the group oversteps the boundaries of 'acceptable' violence, it may not necessarily denounce the attack or apologise, but they will often issue a statement explaining that it was not their intention to cause considerable loss of life. An example of this might be Irgun's bombing of the King David Hotel in Jerusalem in 1946. Consequently, assuming that their national community's desire for mass-destructive terrorism remains small, the likelihood of nationalist-separatist terrorists using nuclear terrorism remains small too.

In contrast to national-separatists, anarchic-ideologues, left-wing terrorists such as the Red Brigades or the RAF, perpetrate violence as a rejection of the values of their community. It is far more likely that their terrorism will be perceived wholly negatively by their society. Left-wing terrorism is usually an attack on the 'establishment' of a community, and on the political, military and economic leadership in particular. Ideologically, left-wing terrorism is perpetrated on behalf of 'the people', to liberate them from oppression. This means though, that any action that injures innocent victims, members of 'the people', is unjustifiable, disproportionate and counter-productive. Consequently, an act, such as nuclear terrorism, that threatens the lives of hundreds or even thousands of innocents is extremely unlikely.

However, where it was once the case that nationalist-separatist and anarchic-ideologue violence were the predominant varieties of terrorism, other types have become increasingly prevalent today. The change has not been rapid or total, but its effect on the nature of contemporary terrorism, and thus on the likelihood of terrorists using nuclear weapons, has been profound. Amongst the most significant of these developments has been the growth in religious-motivated terrorism. Religion may be the oldest cause of political violence, but in the modern era, it has been largely overshadowed by secular motivations. In 1968, no international terrorist group could be described as religious; by 1980, only two of 64 could be classed as non-secular. However, in the 1990s, the proportion had risen markedly: in 1992, 11 of 48 terrorist groups were religious, in 1994, 16 of 49, and in 1995, 25 of 58 active international terrorist organisations were predominantly religious in character or motivation.[3]

There are two interrelated consequences of the increase in religious terrorism, both of which are significant for the likelihood of nuclear terrorism. Firstly, the nature of religion, as a motivation for terrorism, means that it is more likely to support, and even demand, higher levels of violence than secular-oriented terrorism, although extremely destructive secular terrorist groups also exist. Secondly, as part of the increase in religious violence, there has been a growth in terrorism driven by messianic beliefs or millenarianism, both of which may inspire heightened levels of violence.

Terrorism in general is becoming increasingly lethal: in 1995, 29 per cent of incidents resulted in at least one fatality, the highest percentage since 1968. During the 1980s, the number of terrorist incidents rose by roughly 30 per cent, compared to the 1970s; fatalities rose by 100 per cent in the same period. Religious terrorism accounts for a disproportionate amount of this. There are a number of reasons for this. In the case of religious terrorism, violence is perceived to be part of an all-encompassing struggle between good and evil. The stakes involved legitimise the means used by religious terrorists to defend their faith and even justify acts of self-sacrifice in that protection. Although much religious violence is aimed at preserving purity within that religion, it is also directed against external sources of corruption which threaten to erode that purity. It is entirely possible that, in order to protect their faith from such an influence, adherents might resort to extreme levels of violence, especially given the totalist nature of many religious terrorist beliefs.

However, the organisational dynamics that apply to secular terrorism also have a role to play in religious terrorism and it is therefore reasonable to suggest that many of the same escalatory pressures also exist. A critical difference is that whereas these pressures are somewhat moderated by instrumental considerations in nationalist-separatist and anarchic-ideologue terrorism, these considerations have a less effective mitigating role in religious violence. As with nationalist-separatists, religious terrorists use their violence as a means of establishing their identity within their community.

However, whereas in secular terrorism, the rewards of victory are finite, in religious terrorism they are infinite: national determination, compared to paradise. Furthermore, religious terrorism is sanctioned by figures who draw their justifications from the highest sources, interpreted in holy texts. Consequently, not only is the absolutist and uncompromising aspect of the terrorist magnified, but the possibility of unconditional support from their community is also increased. Secular groups, such as nationalist-separatists, that find that a 'natural constituency's' support is critical to their continuation, are much more likely to be moderate in their actions because that support is conditional, so there has to be some proportionality between their goals and the means used to attain those. In the case of religious terrorists, that necessity for moderation is removed, thus the likelihood of high levels of violence is increased. This is especially so since the organisational pressures that inhibit moderate action or de-escalation in secular terrorism also apply to religious terrorism, but with the added aspect that any compromise may be perceived as a betrayal not only of the goal or the group, but of an entire faith and perhaps of God as well.

The danger of non-conventional terrorism is especially acute in the case of messianic or millenarian groups since, in some cases, they may come to believe that their role and duty is to speed the end of the world, to facilitate redemption. Since the ultimate result will be the higher good, the salvation of the righteous and the punishment of the faithless, any action that promotes this situation, including a wholesale destruction of the corrupting elements of society, may be justified. This problem of religious-inspired violence is even greater now, as the millennium approaches and the numbers of millenarian groups increase. Not all messianic belief results in terrorism, but for that which does, that violence may well be at an apocalyptic level. Aum Shinrikyo offers the clearest example of this.

Significantly, although groups such as the RAF talked about using nuclear weapons, it has been non-traditional, often amateur, types of organisations, such as Aum, that have come closest to using weapons of mass destruction. These include various White Supremacist plots in the United States to use chemical or biological agents, and the attempt by followers of Baghwan Shree Rajneesh to use salmonella to debilitate an entire town. In common with Aum and groups, such as the bombers of the World Trade Center and the Kabbalist millenarians who tried to destroy the El Aksa Mosque and the Mosque of Omar in Jerusalem, who have used conventional weaponry for a mass-destructive act of terrorism, these organisations all have a significant religious content. Clearly, not all large-scale terrorist attacks are perpetrated by religious terrorists; for example, the Tamil Tigers, responsible for a series of massive bombings in Sri Lanka, are predominantly driven by nationalism. Neither are all uses of non-conventional weaponry by religious terrorists (the Chechen threat in Moscow in December 1995 is one secular example); but virtually all attempts to cause mass casualties with non-conventional weapons, and the majority of attempts to do so with conventional weapons, have been by terrorists for whom religion is a key component in their motivation.

The collapse of the Soviet Union has significantly increased the opportunities for terrorists, particularly well-funded or state-sponsored ones, to acquire fissile materials. The question remains, however, whether terrorists would necessarily seek to exploit this, given the technological conservatism that has already been discussed. This is particularly so since building and using nuclear-yield, chemical or biological weapons, although not impossible, is also far from straightforward. However, these difficulties should not be over-estimated as a barrier to micro-proliferation. In all probability, it is the acquisition of fissile materials that is the greatest obstacle for terrorists seeking to construct a nuclear bomb, which, since a device of uncertain and variable yield can be built using more easily obtained non-weapons-grade material, is certainly not an insuperable problem. Such a weapon could be built, at modest expense, using the open literature, and with minimal risk of detection, since it would be unnecessary to test the components.[4]

However, this should not mask the fact that the level of difficulty required to construct such a weapon is still considerably above that of a large conventional device that would be capable of causing mass casualties. The bomb used at Oklahoma consisted of little more than nitrate fertiliser and benzene. Why then, would non-conventional weaponry be attractive to terrorists? Certainly, their destructive potential would be beyond that of any conventional device, but there are other reasons too. In the case of nuclear weapons, it would have considerable value as a terrorist instrument, since the mere fact of being 'nuclear' would almost certainly ensure that it had vast coercive power, having a considerable impact on the public's imagination and fear, and thus on a governmental response. Being 'nuclear', it would also convey added prestige and status on the perpetrators. Finally, it would set them apart from other groups, in a way that even the use of biological or chemical weapons could not.

Much of the material potentially available to terrorists through the 'grey market' has been of non-fissionable quality. This has opened a further possibility: that of radiological terrorism. This would consist of either leaving radiation-emitting material to contaminate an area, as the Chechen separatists claimed to have done in 1995, or of wrapping conventional explosives in a radiological agent, to create a 'dirty bomb'. In both cases, such a weapon would offer many of the same benefits to the terrorist as a full-scale nuclear-yield device, whilst also being more credible and easier for the terrorist to build and use.

There can be no doubt that the attraction of using nuclear weapons has had some impact on the tactical decisions of would-be terrorists. The RAF talked about using a nuclear bomb because they perceived it to be the 'ultimate thing'.[5] However, while there are concrete examples of radiological terrorism, such as the three men accused of using radioactive material against Republican Party officials and the chief investigator for Brookhaven in New York,[6] or the Russian Mafiya's assassination of a Moscow businessman using gamma ray emitting pellets,[7] there are few clear-cut cases, apart from Aum, of terrorists trying to construct a nuclear-yield weapon. Instead, most examples of non-conventional attempts to cause mass casualties have involved chemical or biological weapons, as Aum ultimately used, or the alleged plot by the World Trade Center bombers to use sodium cyanide simultaneously with a conventional bomb, so as to kill any survivors of the explosion.[8] This suggests that chemical and biological weapons are more readily accessible than nuclear-yield weapons for mass-destructive terrorism. Although both chemical and biological weapons share the problem, with nuclear-yield weapons, of having an uncertain effect, they have the advantage of being cheaper to produce and may be lethal in small quantities, easing the production process. Furthermore, although this process is not simple, particularly in 'weaponising' the agent, chemical and biological weapons could be produced more rapidly and require less specialist equipment and expertise than a nuclear weapon would necessitate. Consequently, a chemical or biological weapon is a more likely method than a nuclear-yield device for terrorists to achieve an attack in which mass casualties are the primary objective. However, where the objective is to set the group apart from others and to guarantee that the group continues to be noticed, to be acknowledged as an important entity, radiological terrorism, combining the coercive advantage of being 'nuclear' with ease of production and access to raw materials may be the most likely form of non-conventional terrorism.

The collapse of the Soviet Union has undoubtedly made the opportunities for nuclear terrorism significantly greater but even if these increased chances for micro-proliferation had not existed, the threat of nuclear terrorism would still be significantly greater than it was fifteen years ago. The key point is that terrorism is growing in its lethality. How individual groups achieve that is partly an instrumental decision, based on the objectives of the group, and partly a matter of opportunism. Mass-destructive terrorism is now the greatest non-traditional threat to international security, and of these, nuclear terrorism poses a real danger. A terrorist use of a nuclear-yield device is the most devastating type of terrorism conceivable and a radiological attack is the most likely variety of non-conventional terrorism. It is a danger that cannot be ignored; since it is not the current proliferation problems, but rather the current psycho-dynamics of terrorist groups combined with the nature of terrorism in the 1990s that make the threat so potent, it will not recede in the foreseeable future.

# Notes

CHAPTER 1: INTRODUCTION

1. David Fischer's response to Thomas Davies, 'What Nuclear Means and Targets Might Terrorists Find Attractive?', in Paul Leventhal & Yonah Alexander (eds), *Nuclear Terrorism: Defining The Threat* (Washington DC: Pergamon, 1985), pp. 85–6.
2. Kyle Olson, Testimony to: US Senate Committee on Global Affairs, Permanent Subcommittee on Investigations, Global Proliferation of Weapons of Mass Destruction, 104th Congress, 1st Session, 31 October and 1 November 1995, p. 104.
3. 'Sceptical Bear Ill-Disposed to Having Its Claws Clipped', *Financial Times*, 15 January 1996, 4.
4. Graham T. Allison, Testimony to: The Senate Committee On Foreign Relations Subcommittee on European Affairs, 23 August 1995.
5. Alexander Rahr, 'Soviet Fear of Nuclear Terrorism', *Report on the USSR*, vol. 2, no. 13 (30 March 1990), 11.
6. William Potter, 'Before the Deluge? Assessing the Threat of Nuclear Leakage from the Post-Soviet States', *Arms Control Today*, October 1995, 13.
7. Phil Williams & Paul Woessner, 'Nuclear Material Trafficking: An Interim Assessment', *Transnational Organized Crime*, vol. 1, no. 2 (Summer 1995), 211–12.
8. Potter, 'Before the Deluge...', 12.
9. Leonard Spector, Director, Nuclear Non-Proliferation Project, Carnegie Endowment for International Peace, Washington, DC, *Interview with Author*, 15 November 1996, Washington, DC.
10. John Sopko, 'The Changing Proliferation Threat', *Foreign Policy*, vol. 105 (Winter 1996–7), 10.
11. Williams & Woessner, 'Nuclear Material Trafficking...', 211–12.
12. John Barry, 'Future Shock', *Newsweek*, 24 July 1995, 34–7.
13. Graham T. Allison, Testimony to: US Senate Committee on Government Affairs, Permanent Subcommittee On Investigations, Global Proliferation of Weapons of Mass Destruction, 104th Congress, 2nd Session, 13 March 1996.
14. Holly Yeager, 'Warning: Nuclear Theft Peril Rising; Stockpiles of Bomb Material are Growing but Security is Lagging in the Former Soviet Union, Experts Say', *The Orange County Register*, 14 March 1996, A03.
15. Williams & Woessner, 'Nuclear Material Trafficking...', 212.
16. Rensselaer Lee III, 'Post-Soviet Nuclear Trafficking: Myths, Half-Truths, and the Reality', *Current History*, October 1995, 345.
17. A. Robitaille & R. Purver, 'Smuggling Special Nuclear Materials', Canadian Security Intelligence Service, *Commentary*, no. 57 (May 1995).
18. Richard Beeston, 'Russian "Secret City" Admits Uranium Stolen By Civilians', *The Times*, 25 August 1994, 8.

19. John Deutch, Testimony to: US Senate Committe on Government Affairs, Permanent Subcommittee On Investigations, Global Proliferation of Weapons of Mass Destruction', 104th Congress, 2nd Session, 20 March 1996.

20. Robitaille & Purver, 'Smuggling Special Nuclear Materials…'

21. International Physicians for the Prevention of Nuclear War, 'Crude Nuclear Weapons: Proliferation and the Terrorist Threat', IPPNW Global Health Watch, Report no. 1, 1996, 18–20.

22. Oleg Bukharin, 'The Future of Russia's Plutonium Cities', *International Security*, vol. 21, no. 4 (Spring 1997), 140.

23. 'Uranium, Plutonium, Pandemonium', *The Economist*, 5 June 1993, 105.

24. Bukharin, 'The Future of Russia's…', 134.

25. Mark Franchetti, 'US Atom Workers Help Russia', *The Sunday Times*, 20 July 1997.

26. Rensselaer W. Lee, 'Recent Trends in Nuclear Smuggling', in Phil Williams (ed.), *Russian Organized Crime: The New Threat?* (London: Frank Cass, 1997), p. 112.

27. Lee, 'Post-Soviet Nuclear Trafficking…', 345.

28. William Potter, 'Exports and Experts: Proliferation Risks from the New Commonwealth', *Arms Control Today*, January/February 1992, 34.

29. David E. Kaplan & Andrew Marshall, *The Cult at the End of the World: The Incredible Story of Aum*, (London: Random House, 1996), pp. 73–6.

30. Thomas Cochran, Senior Scientist, Natural Resources Defense Council, Washington, DC, *Interview with Author*, 21 November 1996, Washington, DC.

31. Richard Falkenrath, Executive Director, Center for Science and International Affairs, JFK School of Government, Harvard University, *Interview with Author*, 12 November 1996, Cambridge, Mass.

32. US General Accounting Office, 'Nuclear Nonproliferation: Status of US Efforts to Improve Nuclear Material Controls in Newly Independent States', March 1996.

33. James L. Ford, 'Nuclear Smuggling: How Serious A Threat?', *Institute for National Strategic Studies*, Strategic Forum, no. 59 (January 1996). See too Paul N. Woessner, 'Chronology of Radioactive and Nuclear Smuggling Incidents: July 1991–June 1997', *Transnational Organized Crime*, vol. 3, no. 1 (Spring 1997), 114–209.

34. Rensselaer Lee III, Address to: Institute For National Security Studies, Center for Strategic Leadership, 'Report of the Executive Seminar on Special Material Smuggling', 13 September 1996, 21.

35. Kaplan & Marshall, *The Cult…*, pp. 110–12 and 126; Frank Barnaby, *Instruments of Terror* (London: Vision Paperbacks, 1996), pp. 129–30; Campbell, 'Excerpts from Research Study "Weapons of Mass Destruction and Terrorism: Proliferation by Non-State Actors"', *Terrorism and Political Violence*, vol. 9, no. 2 (Summer 1997), 36.

36. Sopko, 'The Changing Proliferation…', 11.

37. Cochran, *Interview…*

38. Phil Williams & Paul Woessner, 'The Real Threat Of Nuclear Smuggling', *Scientific American*, vol. 274, no. 1 (January 1996), 26–7.

39. 'Germany's Plutonium Sting Was Sham – TV Report', *Reuters*, 15 February 1996.
40. Potter, 'Before The Deluge...', 12.
41. Woessner 'Chronology...', or the CIA's chronology of incidents from November 1993 to March 1996 in Gordon C. Oehler, 'The Continuing Threat from Weapons of Mass Destruction', Testimony to the Senate Armed Services Committee, Appendix A, 27 March 1996.
42. Deutch, *Testimony...*
43. Tim McGirk, 'A Year Of Looting Dangerously', *The Independent*, 24 March 1996.
44. Lee, Address, 23.
45. William Potter, Testimony to: US Senate Committe on Government Affairs, Permanent Subcommittee on Investigations, Global Proliferation of Weapons of Mass Destruction, 104th Congress, 2nd Session, 13 March 1996.
46. Williams & Woessner, 'Nuclear Material Trafficking...', 208–9.
47. Deutch, *Testimony...*
48. Bernd Schmidbauer, 'Illegaler Nuklearhandel und Nuklear-terrorismus', *Internationale Politik,* vol. 50, no. 2, (February 1995).
49. Lee, 'Post-Soviet Nuclear Trafficking...', 345.
50. Potter, 'Before The Deluge...', 12.
51. Geoffrey York, 'Unhappy Russian Workers Threaten Nuclear Disaster', *The Globe & Mail*, 2 July 1997, 1–2.
52. Lee, 'Post-Soviet Nuclear Trafficking...', 346.
53. Potter, 'Before The Deluge...', 14.
54. Deutch, *Testimony...*
55. Lee, 'Recent Trends...', pp. 111, 114.
56. Williams & Woessner, 'Nuclear Material Trafficking...', 215–17.
57. Sopko, 'The Changing Proliferation...', 6–7.
58. See: Roger Boyes, 'Bonn Uncovers Nuclear Leaks At Military Bases', *The Times*, 25 August 1994, 8.
59. Jennifer G. Mathers, 'Corruption In the Russian Armed Services', *The World Today*, vol. 51, Nos. 8–9 (August–September 1995), 169–70.
60. James Adams & Carey Scott, 'US Fears Grow as Russia Loses Nuclear Grip', *The Sunday Times*, 27 October 1996, A19.
61. Turbiville, 'Mafia In Uniform...', 17.
62. Andrew Veitch, 'Nuclear Smuggling', Transcript of *Channel 4 Television 7pm News*, 15 February 1995.
63. Potter, 'Before The Deluge...', 10.
64. Graham T. Allison & Richard Falkenrath, 'The World's Biggest Problem?', *Prospect*, (February 1996), 83.
65. Spector, *Interview...*
66. Oleg Bukharin, 'Nuclear Safeguards and Security in the Former Soviet Union', *Survival*, vol. 36, no. 4 (Winter 1994–5), 53.
67. Rose Gottemoeller, 'Preventing a Nuclear Nightmare', *Survival*, vol. 38, no. 2 (Summer 1996), 172.
68. Stella Rimington, 'Security and Democracy: Is There a Conflict?', The Richard Dimbleby Lecture 1994, BBC Educational Development, 1994, 9.

69. Markus Wolf with Anne McElvoy, 'When Carlos the Jackal Turned Nasty', *The Sunday Times*, 15 June 1997.
70. Falkenrath, *Interview* ...
71. Floyd Clarke, Former Deputy Director, FBI, *Interview with Author*, 20 November 1996, Washington, DC.
72. Williams & Woessner, 'Nuclear Material Trafficking...', 222.
73. 'Thinking The Unthinkable', *New Scientist*, Editorial, 11 May 1996, 3.
74. Deutch, *Testimony* ...
75. S. Kendall, 'Colombia Measures the Cost of Violence', *Financial Times*, 12 November 1996.
76. James Adams, *The Financing of Terror* (Sevenoaks: New English Library, 1986).
77. Samuel Porteous, 'The Threat from Transnational Crime: An Intelligence Perspective', *Canadian Security Intelligence Service, Commentary*, no. 70 (Winter 1996), 5–6.
78. Charles Hanley, 'Increasingly Guerrillas Financed by Drugs', *Toronto Star*, 29 December 1994, A19.
79. Bruce Hoffman, 'Terrorism and WMD: Some Preliminary Hypotheses', *The Nonproliferation Review*, vol. 4, no. 3 (Spring/Summer 1997), 45–7.

## CHAPTER 2: PSYCHOLOGICAL AND INSTRUMENTAL TERROR

1. Martha Crenshaw, 'The Psychology of Political Terrorism', in Margaret Herman (ed.), *Political Psychology – Contemporary Problems and Issues* (San Francisco: Jossey-Bass, 1986), p. 383.
2. Robert P. Clark, 'Patterns in the Lives of ETA Members', *Terrorism: An International Journal*, vol. 6, no. 3 (1983), 425.
3. Maxwell Taylor, *The Terrorist* (London: Brassey's, 1988), p. 137
4. See Walter Ellis, 'Rebel Consumed by Blood Lust and Republican Rage', *The Times*, 12 February 1994, 6.
5. *The Sunday Times Magazine*, cover, 3 September 1995.
6. Menachem Begin, *The Revolt: Story of the Irgun* (New York: Henry Schuman Incorporated, 1951), pp. 103–5.
7. Taylor, *The Terrorist*, pp. 73–7.
8. Albert Bandura, 'Mechanisms of Moral Disengagement', in Walter Reich (ed.), *Origins of Terrorism: Psychologies, Ideologies, Theologies, States of Mind* (Cambridge: Cambridge University Press, 1990), p. 164.
9. Joseph Margolin, 'Psychological Perspectives in Terrorism', in Yonah Alexander & Seymour Finger (eds) *Terrorism: Interdisciplinary Perspectives* (New York: John Jay Press, 1992), pp. 271–4.
10. Crenshaw, 'The Psychology of Political Terrorism', p. 385.
11. Jerrold M. Post, 'Terrorist Psycho-Logic: Terrorist Behaviour as a Product of Psychological Forces', in Reich, *Origins Of Terrorism* ..., p. 27.
12. Begin, *The Revolt*, pp. 212–30.
13. Maria McGuire, *To Take Arms*, (London: MacMillan, 1973), pp. 102–3. McGuire's book has to be treated with some caution: it is evident that

she did not see action with the IRA, and it is not clear whether she even belonged to the organisation, rather than to its political wing, Sinn Fein. Consequently, the extent to which she was privy to Army Council decisions is also debatable. However, her book remains important because it does offer an unprecedented insight into the Republican movement. M. L. R. Smith, *Fighting For Ireland? The Military Strategy of the Irish Republican Movement* (London: Routledge, 1995), pp. 112–13.

14.  Maxwell Taylor & Ethel Quayle, *Terrorist Lives* (London: Brasseys, 1994) p. 33.
15.  Patricia Steinhoff, 'Kozo Okamoto', *Asian Survey*, vol. 16, no. 9 (September 1976), 830–45.
16.  Jane Alpert, *Growing Up Underground* (New York: William Morrow, 1981), pp. 178–219.
17.  Yitzhak Shamir, *Summing Up: An Autobiography* (London: Weidenfeld & Nicolson, 1994), pp. 42–3.
18.  Ibid., pp. 19–20.
19.  Post, 'Terrorist Psycho-Logic...' pp. 25–6.
20.  Alpert, *Growing Up Underground*, pp. 17–18.
21.  Post, 'Terrorist Psycho-Logic...' pp. 25–6.
22.  Taylor, *The Terrorist*, p. 88.
23.  Eileen McDonald, *Shoot The Women First* (New York: Random House, 1991), pp. 233–4.
24.  Jeanne N. Knutson, 'The Terrorists Dilemmas: Some Implicit Rules of the Game', *Terrorism: An International Journal*, vol. 4 (1980), 199.
25.  Bandura, 'Mechanisms of Moral...', p. 173.
26.  Begin, *The Revolt*, p. 46.
27.  Gustave Morf, *Terror in Quebec: Case Study of the FLQ* (Toronto: Clark Irwin, 1970).
28.  Crenshaw, 'The Psychology of Political Terrorism', p. 387.
29.  Abraham Kaplan, 'The Psychodynamics of Terrorism', *Terrorism: An International Journal*, vol. 1, nos. 3/4, 245.
30.  Sean O'Callaghan, 'The Killer Who Said Sorry: Confessions of a Gunman who Betrayed the IRA', *Sunday Times*, 15 December 1996, section 3, 2.
31.  Erik H. Erikson, *Childhood and Society* (New York: Norton, 1963), and *Identity: Youth and Crisis*, (New York: Norton, 1968).
32.  Erikson, *Identity...*, p. 232.
33.  Crenshaw, 'The Psychology of Political Terrorism', p. 392.
34.  Konrad Kellen, 'Terrorists – What are They Like? How Some Terrorists Describe their World and Actions', *RAND N-1300-SL* (November 1979), 15.
35.  Taylor & Quayle, *Terrorist Lives*, p. 35.
36.  Patty Hearst, *Patty Hearst* (London: Corgi Books, 1988), p. 55.
37.  Begin, *The Revolt*, p. 55.
38.  Taylor, *The Terrorist*, p. 165.
39.  Khachig Toloyan, 'Martyrdom as Legitimacy: Terrorism, Religion and Symbolic Appropriation in the Armenian Diaspora', in Paul Wilkinson & Alexander Stewart (eds), *Contemporary Research on Terrorism* (Aberdeen: Aberdeen University Press, 1987).

40. Ibid., pp. 92–3.
41. Martha Crenshaw, 'An Organizational Approach to the Analysis of Political Terrorism', *Orbis*, vol. 29 (Fall 1985), 469.
42. Jerrold M. Post, 'Current Understanding of Terrorist Motivation and Psychology: Implications for a Differentiated Antiterrorist Policy', *Terrorism*, vol. 13, no. 1 (1989), 66.
43. Nicholas Bethell, *The Palestine Triangle: The Struggle for the Holy Land, 1935–48* (New York: G. P. Putnam's Sons, 1979), p. 161.
44. Taylor, *The Terrorist*, p. 165.
45. Crenshaw, 'An Organizational Approach...', 470.
46. Kellen, 'Terrorists – What Are They Like?...', 34.
47. Erikson, *Identity*..., p.119.
48. Leila Khaled, *My People Shall Live* (London: Hodder & Stoughton, 1973), pp. 31–2.
49. Erikson, *Childhood*..., p. 189.
50. Jerrold M. Post, 'Rewarding Fire with Fire: Effects of Retaliation on Terrorist Group Dynamics', *Terrorism*, vol. 10, no. 1 (1987), 25.
51. Post, 'Terrorist Psycho-Logic...', pp. 29–30.
52. Susan Stern, *With the Weathermen: The Personal Journal of a Revolutionary Woman* (New York: Doubleday & Company Inc, 1975).
53. Crenshaw, 'The Psychology of Political Terrorism', p. 388.
54. Stern, *With The Weathermen*, p. 41.
55. Jerrold M. Post, 'Notes on a Psychodynamic Theory of Terrorist Behaviour', *Terrorism: An International Journal*, vol. 7, no. 3 (1984), 245.
56. Patrick Seale, *Abu Nidal: A Gun for Hire* (New York: Random House, 1992), pp. 57, 99.
57. Hearst, *Patty Hearst*, pp. 143–4.
58. Fernando Lopez-Alves, 'Political Crises, Strategic Choices, and Terrorism: The Rise and Fall of the Uruguayan Tupamaros', *Terrorism and Political Violence*, vol. 1, no. 2 (April 1989), 208–9.
59. Leonard Weinberg & William Eubank, 'Leaders and Followers in Italian Terrorist Groups', *Terrorism and Political Violence*, vol. 1, no. 2 (April 1989), 157.
60. Martha Crenshaw, 'Questions to be Answered, Research to be Done, Knowledge to be Applied', in Reich, *Origins Of Terrorism*..., p. 250.
61. Hearst, *Patty Hearst*, p. 66.
62. Taylor & Quayle, *Terrorist Lives*, p.189.
63. Seale, *Abu Nidal*, pp. 9–27.
64. Jerrold M. Post, 'Hostilité, Conformité, Fraternité: The Group Dynamics of Terrorist Behaviour', *International Journal of Group Psychotherapy*, vol. 36, no. 2 (April 1986), 214–15.
65. Ibid., Clark, 'Patterns...', 433.
66. Anne McElvoy, 'The Trapping of a Tigress', *The Times Magazine*, 9 September 1995, 23–6.
67. Sean MacStiofain, *Revolutionary in Ireland* (London: Gordon Cremonesi, 1975.)
68. McGuire, *To Take Arms*, pp. 71–2.
69. Crenshaw, 'Questions to be Answered...', pp. 250–3.

70. Toloyan, 'Martyrdom as Legitimacy...', pp. 93–6.
71. Taylor & Quayle, *Terrorist Lives*, pp. 20–1.
72. Begin, *The Revolt*, p. 153 and David C. Rapoport, 'Terror and the Messiah: An Ancient Experience and Some Modern Parallels', in David C. Rapoport & Yonah Alexander (eds), *The Morality of Terrorism: Religious and Secular Justifications*, 2nd edn (New York: Columbia University Press, 1989), pp. 31–3.
73. Bassam Abu-Sharif & Uzi Mahnaimi, *Tried By Fire* (London: Little, Brown & Co., 1995), pp. 65–6.
74. Ibid., pp. 69–72 and 78–9.
75. Taylor, *The Terrorist*, p. 153.
76. O'Callaghan, 'The Killer...', 1.
77. Kellen, 'Terrorists – What Are They Like?...', 24.
78. Taylor & Quayle, *Terrorist Lives*, pp. 39–40.
79. Alison Jamieson, 'Entry, Discipline and Exit in the Italian Red Brigades', *Terrorism and Political Violence*, vol. 2, no. 1 (Spring 1990), 1–3.
80. Clark, 'Patterns in the Lives...', 427, 439–43.
81. Crenshaw, 'The Psychology of Political Terrorism', p. 389.
82. Taylor & Quayle, *Terrorist Lives*, p. 44.
83. Kellen, 'Terrorists – What Are They Like?...', 18–19.
84. Bassam Abu-Sharif & Uzi Mahnaimi, *Tried By Fire*, p. 50.
85. Clark, 'Patterns in the Lives...', 443.
86. Alpert, *Growing...*, pp. 196–7.
87. Crenshaw, 'An Organizational Approach...', 478.
88. Khaled, *My People...*, p. 109.
89. Shamir, *Summing...*, pp. 22–3.
90. McGuire, *To Take Arms*, p. 62.
91. Begin, *The Revolt*, p. 73.
92. Joseph E. Vorbach, 'Monte Melkonian: Armenian Revolutionary Leader', *Terrorism and Political Violence*, vol. 6 no. 2 (Summer 1994).
93. Steinhoff, 'Kozo Okamoto', 830–9.
94. Alpert, *Growing Up Underground*, pp. 106 and 200–26.
95. Deborah M. Galvin, 'The Female Terrorist: A Socio-Psychological Perspective', *Behavioural Sciences and the Law*, vol. 1, no. 2 (1983), 20.
96. MacDonald, *Shoot...*, p. 232. However, there are flaws in MacDonald's analysis and methodology that may limit the usefulness of her conclusions. See Bruce Hoffman's review of *Shoot the Women First* in *The Oral History Review*, vol. 22, no. 1 (Summer 1995), 126–9.
97. Galvin, 'The Female Terrorist...', 23–5.
98. McDonald, *Shoot...*, pp. 231–2.
99. Kaplan, 'The Psychodynamics...', 245.
100. Bassam Abu-Sharif & Uzi Mahnaimi, *Tried By Fire*, p. 58.
101. Ibid., pp. 80–2.
102. Shamir, *Summing...*, pp. 30–1.
103. As'ad AbuKhalil, As'ad, 'Internal Contradictions in the PFLP: Decision Making and Policy Orientation', *The Middle East Journal*, vol. 41, no. 3 (Summer 1987), 363–4.
104. Hearst, *Patty Hearst*, p. 259.

105. Ibid., p. 385.
106. Irving L. Janis, *Victims of Groupthink* (Boston: Houghton-Mifflin, 1972), pp. 191–2.
107. Seale, *Abu Nidal*, pp. 258–9.
108. Ibid., pp. 285–6.
109. Post, 'Hostilité...', 216.
110. Bandura, 'Mechanisms of Moral...', p. 175.
111. Hearst, *Patty Hearst*, pp. 385–6.
112. Clark, 'Patterns in the Lives...', 436.
113. Hearst, *Patty Hearst*, p. 214.
114. Post, 'Terrorist Psycho-Logic...', p. 35.
115. Crenshaw, 'Questions to be Answered...', p. 18.
116. McGuire, *To Take Arms*, pp. 106–7.
117. Jamieson, 'Entry, Discipline...', 15.
118. Post, 'Terrorist Psycho-Logic...', p. 34.
119. Stern, *With the Weathermen*, p. 88.
120. Martha Crenshaw, *Terrorism and International Co-operation* (New York: Institute for East-West Security Inc., 1989), p. 16.
121. Post, 'Terrorist Psycho-Logic...', p. 35.
122. Ibid., pp. 37–8.
123. J. Bowyer Bell, *Terror Out of Zion* (New York: St. Martin's Press), p. 66.
124. Albert Hirschman, *Exit, Voice and Loyalty* (Cambridge, Mass: Harvard University Press, 1970), p. 93.
125. Seale, *Abu Nidal*, pp. 9–27.
126. Shamir, *Summing...*, pp. 20–1.
127. Hearst, *Patty Hearst*, pp. 244–5.
128. Hirschman, *Exit, Voice...*, p. 93.
129. Jamieson, 'Entry, Discipline...', 13.
130. MacStiofain, *Revolutionary...*, pp. 128–43.
131. Begin, *The Revolt*, p. 74.
132. Hirschman, *Exit, Voice...*, pp. 98–100.
133. McGuire, *To Take Arms*, pp. 146–7.
134. John Horgan and Max Taylor, 'The Provisional Irish Republican Army: Command and Functional Structure', *Terrorism and Political Violence*, vol. 9, no. 4 (Winter 1997), 25.
135. Jamieson, 'Entry, Discipline...', 14.
136. Crenshaw, 'An Organizational Approach...', 486.
137. Ronald Crelinstein, 'The Internal Dynamics of the FLQ During the October Crisis of 1970', *Journal of Strategic Studies*, vol. 10, no. 4 (1987), 62.
138. Ibid., 68–9.
139. Peter Janke (ed.), *Terrorism and Democracy* (London: Macmillan, 1992), pp. 42–57.
140. Vorbach, 'Monte Melkonian...', 182–3.
141. Post, 'Rewarding Fire...', 28.
142. Robert W. White & Terry Falkenberg White, 'Revolution in the City: On the Resources of Urban Guerrillas', *Terrorism and Political Violence*, vol. 3, no. 4 (Winter 1991), 111.

143. Post, 'Rewarding Fire...', 28.
144. K. Zawodny, 'Internal Organizational Problems and the Sources of Tensions of Terrorist Movements as Catalysts of Violence', *Terrorism: An International Journal*, vol. 1, no. 3/4 (1978), 280–1.
145. Kaplan, 'The Psychodynamics...', 246.
146. Alpert, *Growing Up Underground...*, p. 188.
147. Galvin, 'The Female Terrorist...', 29–30.
148. Ibid., pp. 240–1.
149. McGuire, *To Take Arms*, pp. 74–5.
150. Leila Khaled, *My People Shall Live*, p. 133.
151. Bandura, 'Mechanisms of Moral...', p. 164.
152. Ibid., p. 176.
153. Hearst, *Patty Hearst*, pp. 361–2.
154. O'Callaghan, 'The Killer...', 1.
155. Hearst, *Patty Hearst*, pp. 224–5.
156. Bandura, 'Mechanisms of Moral...', pp. 185–6.
157. McGuire, *To Take Arms*, p. 9.
158. McElvoy, 'The Trapping...', 26.
159. Smith, *Fighting For Ireland...*, pp. 72–3.
160. Martha Crenshaw, 'The Strategic Development of Terrorism', *Paper for the 1985 Annual Meeting of the American Political Science Association*, New Orleans, 29 August–1 September 1985, 1.
161. Lopez-Alves, 'Political Crises...', 204.
162. Magnus Ranstorp, *Hizb'allah in Lebanon: The Politics of the Western Hostage Crisis* (London: Macmillan Press, 1997), pp. 88–108.
163. Crenshaw, 'The Strategic...', 2–7.
164. Wilkinson, *Terrorism and the Liberal State* (London: Macmillan, 1979), p. 106.
165. Tim Pat Coogan, *The IRA*, (London: Fontana, 1987), p. 693.
166. Christopher Hewitt, 'Terrorism and Public Opinion: A Five Country Comparison', *Terrorism and Political Violence*, vol. 2, no. 2 (Summer 1990), 146.
167. David C. Rapoport, 'Fear and Trembling: Terrorism in Three Religious Traditions', *American Political Science Review*, vol. 78, no. 3 (September 1984), 659.
168. Andrew Silke, 'Honour and Expulsion: Terrorism in Nineteenth-Century Japan', *Terrorism and Political Violence*, vol. 9, no. 4 (Winter 1997).
169. Bruce Hoffman, 'Intelligence and Terrorism: Emerging Threats and New Security Challenges in the Post-Cold War Era', *Intelligence and National Security*, vol. 11, no. 2 (April 1996), 207.
170. Coogan, *The IRA*, pp. 646–7.
171. James Adams, *Trading in Death: The Modern Arms Race* (London: Pan, 1991), pp. 8–10.
172. See Bruce Hoffman, 'Terrorist Targeting: Tactics, Trends, and Potentialities', in Paul Wilkinson (ed.), 'Technology and Terrorism', *Terrorism and Political Violence*, Special Edition, vol. 5, no. 2 (Summer 1993).
173. White & White, 'Revolution in the City...', 104–5.

174. Edgar O'Ballance, *Islamic Fundamentalist Terrorism, 1979–95: The Iranian Connection* (London: Macmillan, 1997), p. 187.
175. Leonard Downie Jr, 'IRA Bomb Kills Lord Mountbatten', *Washington Post*, 28 August 1979, A1, A8.
176. Walter Laqueur, 'Postmodern Terrorism', *Foreign Affairs*, vol. 75, no. 5 (September/October 1996), 25.
177. Paul Wilkinson, 'Beleaguered in Lima', *Times Higher Educational Supplement*, 21 February 1997, 18. In contrast, there were only two international terrorist barricade and hostage situations of any sort in 1994 and four such incidents in 1995. Bruce Hoffman and Donna Kim Hoffman, 'The Rand-St Andrews Chronology of International Terrorism, 1994', *Terrorism and Political Violence*, vol. 7, no. 4 (Winter 1995), 226; Bruce Hoffman and Donna Kim Hoffman, 'The Rand-St Andrews Chronology of International Terrorist Incidents 1995', *Terrorism and Political Violence*, vol. 8, no. 3 (Autumn 1996), 95.
178. Wainstein, 'The Cross...', 2–4, 38–9.
179. Hoffman & Hoffman, 'The Rand-St Andrews...1995', 87, 91n and 95.
180. Hoffman & Hoffman, 'The Rand-St Andrews...1994', 226.
181. Michael Field, 'Haig Escapes Assassination by a Second', *Daily Telegraph*, 26 June, 1979, 1; Ferdinand Protzman, 'Head of Top West German Bank is Killed in Bombing by Terrorists', *New York Times*, 1 December 1989.
182. Hans Horchem, 'The Decline of the Red Army Faction', *Terrorism and Political Violence*, vol. 3, no. 2 (Summer 1991), 65.
183. Brian Jenkins, 'The Terrorist Mindset and Terrorist Decisionmaking: Two Areas of Ignorance', *Rand P-6340*, California (June 1979), 4–5.
184. *The Economist*, 'Arming the IRA: The Libyan Connection', 31 March 1990, 19–22.
185. James Adams & Liam Clarke, 'War Without End', *Sunday Times*, 17 June 1990.
186. Jeffrey Ian Ross, 'The Rise and Fall of Quebecois Separatist Terrorism: A Qualitive Application of Factors from Two Models', *Studies in Conflict and Terrorism*, vol. 18, no. 4 (October–December 1995), 288.
187. Lopez-Alves, 'Political...', 214–15.
188. Ronald Crelinsten, 'What the Peruvian Hostage-takers Wanted to Achieve', *The Globe & Mail*, 31 December 1996, A19.
189. The *New York Times*, *The Times* and the *Globe & Mail* all carried the Sri Lanka bombing on their front pages on 1 February 1996. However, in each case, by 2 February, the story had been relegated to a small article on an inside page. In contrast, the siege in Lima continued to receive front-page coverage even after the situation had settled down to a long, drawn-out stalemate between the terrorists and the Peruvian security forces.
190. Bell, *Terror...*, pp. 62–3, 75.
191. Bethell, *The Palestine...*, p. 181.
192. Bell, *Terror...*, pp. 89–100. Shamir, *Summing...*, pp. 52–4.
193. Williams & Woessner, 'The Real Threat...', 30.
194. Mark Galeotti, 'Mafiya: Organized Crime in Russia', *Jane's Intelligence*

*Review*, Special Report, no. 10 (June 1996), 11.
195. Ze'ev Iviansky, 'Individual Terror: Concept and Typology', *Journal of Contemporary History*, vol. 12 (1977), 47.
196. David Ronfeldt & W. Sater, 'The Mindsets of High-Technology Terrorists: Future Implications from an Historical Analog', *RAND*, California, March 1981.
197. Iviansky, 'Individual Terror...', 45.
198. Sam Nunn, Congressional Record – US Senate, 28 September 1996, S11756.
199. Laqueur, 'Postmodern...', 35.
200. Amory & L. Hunter Lovins, 'The Fragility of Domestic Energy', *The Atlantic Monthly* (November 1983), 118–26.
201. Stewart Tendler, 'How Police Watched the "A Team"', *The Times*, 3 July 1997, and 'The Men Who Tried to Shut London', *The Times*, 3 July 1997.
202. Laqueur, 'Postmodern...', 27–8.
203. Begin, *The Revolt*, p. 52.
204. Cited in Bethell, *The Palestine...*, p. 157.
205. Ibid., p. 161.
206. David Fromkin, 'The Strategy of Terrorism', *Foreign Affairs*, vol. 53, no. 4 (July 1975), 687–91.
207. Nicholas O. Berry, 'Theories on the Efficacy of Terrorism', *Conflict Quarterly*, vol. 7, no. 1 (Winter 1987), 10–14.
208. Wilkinson, *Terrorism and the Liberal State*, pp. 50–1.
209. Smith, *Fighting for Ireland*, p. 60.
210. Ibid., p. 127.
211. Adrian Guelke cited in Martha Crenshaw, 'How Terrorism Declines', *Terrorism and Political Violence*, vol. 3, no. 1 (Spring 1991).
212. Crenshaw, 'How Terrorism Declines', 80–1.
213. Jamieson, *The Heart Attacked: Terrorism and Conflict in the Italian State* (London: Marion Boyars Publishers, 1989), p. 23.
214. Lopez-Alves, 'Political...', 228–9.
215. Ross, 'The Rise...', 292–4.
216. Jeffrey Ian Ross & Ted Robert Gurr, 'Why Terrorism Subsides', *Comparative Politics*, vol. 21, no. 4 (July 1989).
217. Crenshaw, 'How Terrorism Declines'.
218. Wayne G. Reilly, 'The Management of Political Violence in Quebec and Northern Ireland: A Comparison', *Terrorism and Political Violence*, vol. 6, no. 1 (Spring 1994), 46–56.
219. Lopez-Alves, 'Political...', 217–22.
220. Hewitt, 'Terrorism...', 143–70.
221. Smith, *Fighting for Ireland*, pp. 106–8, 114–15 and 219–20.
222. Ibid., pp. 14–19, 21–2, 152–7 and 170–8.
223. Ibid,. p. 224.
224. David Blundy, 'Inside the IRA', *The Sunday Times*, 3 July 1977.
225. Lopez-Alves, 'Political...', 226–9.
226. Smith, *Fighting for Ireland*, pp. 194, 197–200 and 211–14.
227. Roger Boyes, 'Germany's Terrorists Aim to Swap Guns for Amnesty', *The Times*, 22 April 1998.

228. Dennis Pluchinsky, 'Germany's Red Army Faction: An Obituary', *Studies in Conflict and Terrorism*, vol. 16, no. 2 (April–June 1993), 142–4.
229. Bruce Λ. Scharlau & Donald Philips, 'Not the End of German Left-Wing Terrorism', *Terrorism and Political Violence*, vol. 4, no. 3 (Autumn 1992), 114.
230. Bethell, *The Palestine...*, p. 161.

CHAPTER 3: RELIGIOUS TERROR

1. Hoffman, 'Terrorism and WMD...', p. 48.
2. Richard E. Rubenstein, *Alchemists of Revolution: Terrorism in the Modern World* (New York: Basic Books, 1987), pp. 132–4.
3. Ranstorp, *Hizb'allah...*, p. 55.
4. Magnus Ranstorp, 'Terrorism in the Name of Religion', *Journal of International Affairs*, vol. 50, no. 1 (Summer 1996), 48.
5. Ibid., 46–50.
6. Bruce Hoffman, 'The Contrasting Ethical Foundations of Terrorism in the 1980s', *Terrorism & Political Violence*, vol. 1, no. 3 (July 1989), 389.
7. Mark Juergensmeyer, 'The Logic Of Religious Violence', in David C. Rapoport (ed.), *Inside Terrorist Organizations* (London: Frank Cass & Company Limited, 1988), p. 183.
8. Ranstorp, 'Terrorism in the Name...', 44.
9. Rapoport, 'Fear & Trembling...', 659.
10. Bruce Hoffman, '"Holy Terror": The Implications of Terrorism Motivated by a Religious Imperative', *Studies in Conflict and Terrorism*, vol. 18, no. 4 (1995), 272.
11. David C. Rapoport, 'Some General Observations on Religion and Violence', in Mark Juergensmeyer (ed.), 'Violence and the Sacred in the Modern World', *Terrorism and Political Violence*, Special Issue, vol. 3, no. 3 (Autumn 1991), 120–1.
12. Ranstorp, 'Terrorism in the Name...', 52.
13. Ibid., 54–5.
14. See Juergensmeyer, 'The Logic...', pp. 180–2.
15. Rapoport, 'Some General...', 128–9.
16. Mark Juergensmeyer, 'Editor's Introduction: Is Symbolic Violence Related to Real Violence?', in Juergensmeyer (ed.), 'Violence and the Sacred...', 2–3.
17. Juergensmeyer, 'The Logic...', p. 186.
18. Martin Kramer, 'Sacrifice and Fratricide in Shiite Lebanon', in Juergensmeyer (ed.), 'Violence and The Sacred...' 38–40.
19. Ron Ben-Yishal, 'Anatomy of a Suicide', *Yediot Ahronot*, 27 January 1995, Supplement, 7 and 23.
20. *Sunday Times*, 'Wedded to Death in a Blaze of Glory', 10 March 1996.
21. Ranstorp, *Hizb'allah...*, p. 38.
22. June Leavitt, 'Maze of Terror: A Settler's Diary. Fear and Faith in a West Bank Settlement', *US News and World Report*, 18 April 1994, 58.
23. Taylor, 'The Terrorist', pp. 118–19.

24. Raphael Cohen-Almagor, 'Vigilant Jewish Fundamentalism: From the JDL to Kach (or "Shalom Jews, Shalom Dogs")', *Terrorism and Political Violence*, vol. 4, no. 1 (Spring 1992), 51–2.
25. Juergensmeyer, 'The Logic...', p. 173.
26. Emmanuel Sivan, 'The Mythologies of Religious Radicalism: Judaism and Islam', in Juergensmeyer (ed.), 'Violence and the Sacred...', 84.
27. Kramer, 'Sacrifice...', 43–5.
28. Kaplan & Marshall, *The Cult*..., pp. 32–7, 62 and 114.
29. Cited in Peter Janke, 'Terrorism: Trends and Growth?', *RUSI Journal*, August 1993, 25.
30. *Washington Post*, 'World Trade Center Bombing Statement', 25 March 1995.
31. Ehud Sprinzak, 'Violence and Catastrophe in the Theology of Rabbi Meir Kahane: The Ideologization of Mimetic Desire', in Juergensmeyer (ed.), 'Violence and the Sacred...', 51, 54–6.
32. Frantz Fanon, *The Wretched Of The Earth* (London: Penguin Books, 1967).
33. Meir Kahane, *Forty Years* (Miami Beach: Institute of the Jewish Idea, 1983), p. 36.
34. Sprinzak, 'Violence...', 63–6.
35. Juergensmeyer, 'The Logic...', p. 187.
36. Ben-Yishal, 'Anatomy of a Suicide'.
37. *Sunday Times*, 'Wedded to Death'.
38. US Senate Committe on Government Affairs, Permanent Subcommittee On Investigations, 'Global Proliferation of Weapons of Mass Destruction', 104th Congress, 1st Session, US Congress, Hearings held 31 October and 1 November 1995, 656.
39. Taylor & Quayle, *Terrorist Lives*, pp. 219–20.
40. Timur Kuran, 'Sparks and Prairie Fires: A Theory of Unanticipated Political Violence', *Public Choice*, vol. 61 (1989), 41–74
41. Thomas Friedman, *From Beirut to Jerusalem* (New York: Doubleday, 1989), pp. 251–321.
42. Richard D. Hecht, 'The Political Cultures of Israel's Radical Right: Commentary on Ehud Sprinzak's "The Ascendance of Israel's Radical Right"', *Terrorism and Political Violence*, vol. 5 no. 1 (Spring 1993), 135–7.
43. Hoffman, '"Holy Terror"...', 272.
44. Rapoport, 'Fear and Trembling...', 674.
45. Erich Fromm, *The Anatomy of Human Destructiveness* (London: Penguin Books, 1977), p. 243.
46. Jerrold M. Post, 'Fundamentalism and the Justification of Terrorist Violence', *Terrorism*, vol. 11, no. 5, 370.
47. Rapoport, 'Fear and Trembling...', 660.
48. Post, 'Fundamentalism...', 369.
49. Hecht, 'Israel's Radical Right...', 143, 154–7.
50. Ranstorp, 'Terrorism in the Name...', 61.
51. Rapoport, 'Fear and Trembling...', 662, 673.
52. Ben-Yishal, 'Anatomy...'
53. Cited in Cohen-Almagor, 'Vigilant...', 54–5.

54.  Dick Anthony & Thomas Robbins, 'Religious Totalism, Violence and Exemplary Dualism: Beyond the Extrinsic Model', in Michael Barkun (ed.), *Terrorism and Political Violence*, 'Millennialism and Violence' Special Issue, vol. 7, no. 3 (Autumn 1995), 13–18.
55.  Ibid., 10–50.
56.  Kaplan & Marshall, *The Cult...*, pp. 26–9, 91.
57.  Kramer, 'Sacrifice...', 40–1.
58.  Magnus Ranstorp, 'Hizbollah's Command Leadership: Its Structure, Decision-Making and Relationship with Iranian Clergy and Institutions', *Terrorism and Political Violence*, vol. 6, no. 3 (Autumn 1994), 304.
59.  Mattew Kalman, 'Sharif Said Killed for Refusing to Make Bomb', *The Globe & Mail*, 15 April 1998, A11.
60.  Crenshaw, 'An Organizational...', 481–2.
61.  Bell, *Terror...*, p. 85.
62.  Hoffman, '"Holy Terror"...', 273.
63.  Guenter Lewy, *Religion and Revolution* (New York: Oxford University Press, 1974), pp. 13–14, 26–7.
64.  Ibid., pp. 32–6.
65.  Eliezer Don-Yehiya, 'Jewish Messianism, Religious Zionism And Israeli Politics: The Impact and Origins of Gush Emunim', *Middle Eastern Studies*, vol. 23, no. 2 (April 1987), 222–3.
66.  Sprinzak, 'Violence...', 53.
67.  Lewy, *Religion...*, pp. 38–41.
68.  Rapoport, 'Fear and Trembling...', 665.
69.  Post, 'Fundamentalism...', 370.
70.  Lewy, *Religion...*, pp. 51–2.
71.  David C. Rapoport, 'Why Does Religious Messianism Produce Terror?', in Wilkinson & Stewart (eds), *Contemporary Research on Terrorism*.
72.  Jean E. Rosenfeld, 'Pai Marire: Peace and Violence in a New Zealand Millenarian Tradition', in Barkun (ed.), *Millennialism...*, 86.
73.  Rosenfeld, 'Pai Marire...', 96–7.
74.  Rapoport, 'Why Does Religious...', p. 79.
75.  Jeffrey Kaplan, 'The Context of American Millenarian Revolutionary Theology: The Case of the "Identity Christian" Church of Israel', *Terrorism and Political Violence*, vol. 5, no. 1 (Spring 1993), 31, 56.
76.  Rosenfeld, 'Pai Marire...', 97.
77.  Rapoport, 'Some General...', 132–3.
78.  Rapoport, 'Why Does Religious...', pp. 83–5.
79.  Kaplan & Marshall, *The Cult...*, pp. 14–16, 29–34, 46–8, 222.
80.  Rapoport, 'Why Does Religious...', pp. 76–7.
81.  Hoffman, '"Holy Terror"...', 281–2.
82.  Rapoport, 'Why Does Religious...', p. 77.

CHAPTER 4: IDEOLOGICAL TERRORISM

1.  Steve Bruce, 'The Problems of "Pro-State" Terrorism: Loyalist Paramilitaries in Northern Ireland', in Paul Wilkinson (ed.), *Terrorism: British Perspectives* (Aldershot: Dartmouth Publishing, 1993), p. 205.

2. Peter Taylor, *States of Terror: Democracy and Political Violence*, (London: Penguin/BBC Books, 1993), pp. 285–6.
3. C. J. M. Drake, 'The Phenomenon of Conservative Terrorism', *Terrorism and Political Violence*, vol. 8, no. 3 (Autumn 1996), 35.
4. Bruce, 'The Problem...', pp. 204–6.
5. Ehud Sprinzak, 'Right-Wing Terrorism in a Comparative Perspective: The Case of Split Delegitimization', in Tore Bjorgo (ed.), *Terror from the Extreme Right* (London: Frank Cass, 1995), pp. 26–30.
6. Rubenstein, *Alchemists*..., pp. 127–8.
7. Paul Wilkinson, *The New Fascists* (London: Pan Books, 1983), pp. 133–7.
8. Ibid.
9. Paul Wilkinson, 'Violence and Terror and the Extreme Right', *Terrorism and Political Violence*, vol. 7, no. 4 (Winter 1995), 82.
10. Drake, 'The Phenomenon...', 29.
11. James Dalrymple, 'Nightmare USA', *The Sunday Times Magazine*, 3 September 1995, 34.
12. Warren Kinsella, *Web of Hate: Inside Canada's Far Right Network* (Toronto: HarperCollins Publishers Limited, 1994), pp. 393–410.
13. Rubenstein, *Alchemists*..., p. 129.
14. Sprinzak, 'Right-Wing...', 17.
15. Leonard Weinberg, 'On Responding to Right-wing Terrorism', *Terrorism and Political Violence'*, vol. 8, no. 1 (Spring 1996), 82.
16. Sprinzak, 'Right-Wing...', pp. 17–26.
17. Sprinzak, 'The Case...', p. 33.
18. Peter Merkl, 'Radical Right Parties in Europe and Anti-Foreign Violence: A Comparative Essay', in Bjorgo (ed.), *Terror*..., p. 105.
19. Sprinzak, 'The Case...', pp. 36–7.
20. Jeffrey Kaplan, 'Right-Wing Violence in North America', in Bjorgo (ed.), *Terror*..., p. 56.
21. Merkl, 'Radical Right...', pp. 109–10.
22. David Van Biema, 'When White Makes Right', *Time*, 9 August 1993, 39.
23. Helene Loow, 'Racist Violence and Criminal Behaviour in Sweden: Myths and Realities', in Bjorgo (ed.), *Terror*..., pp. 122–3.
24. Weinberg, 'On Responding...', 83.
25. Sprinzak, 'The Case...', pp. 38–9.
26. Jeffrey Ian Ross, 'Research Note: Contempoary Radical Right-Wing Violence in Canada: A Quantitive Analysis', *Terrorism and Political Violence*, vol. 4, no. 3 (Autumn 1992), 74–5.
27. Kaplan, 'The Context...', pp. 38–9.
28. Steven E. Salmony & Richard Smoke, 'The Appeal and Behaviour of the Ku Klux Klan in Object Relations Perspective', *Terrorism: An International Journal*, vol. 11 (1988).
29. Van Biema, 'When...', 40.
30. Weinberg & Eubank, 'Leaders...', 156–76.
31. Leonard Weinberg, 'Italian Neo-Fascist Terrorism: A Comparative Perspective', in Bjorgo (ed.), *Terror*..., pp. 221–3.
32. Jeffey S. Handler, 'Socioeconomic Profile of an American Terrorist:

1960s and 1970s', *Terrorism: An International Journal*, vol. 13 (1990).
33. Loow, 'Racist...', pp. 132–3.
34. Helmut Willems, 'Development, Patterns and Causes of Violence Against Foreigners in Germany: Social and Biographical Characteristics of Perpetrators and the Process of Escalation', in Bjorgo (ed.), *Terror...*, pp. 168–73.
35. Ingo Hasselbach with Tom Reiss, 'How Nazis Are Made', *New Yorker Magazine*, 8 January 1996, 39–41.
36. Ingo Hasselbach, 'Fantasy Fuhrer', *The Guardian Weekend*, 10 February 1996, 14.
37. Loow, 'Racist...', p. 126.
38. Hasselbach with Reiss, 'How...', 48.
39. Loow, 'Racist...', p. 128.
40. Hasselbach with Reiss, 'How...', 36.
41. Hasselbach, 'Fantasy...', 15.
42. Hasselbach with Reiss, 'How...', 53.
43. Ibid., 51.
44. Hasselbach, 'Fantasy...', 18–19.
45. Hasselbach with Reiss, 'How...', 54–6.
46. Stewart Tendler & Roger Boyes, 'Letter Bombs Turn British Neo-Nazis into Terrorists', *The Times*, 20 January 1997.
47. Hasselbach with Reiss, 'How...', 37, 47 and 51.
48. Weinberg, 'On Responding...', 85–8.
49. Kaplan, 'The Context...', 42–3, 57.
50. Michael Barkun, 'Millenarian Aspects of "White Supremacist" Movements', *Terrorism and Political Violence*, vol. 1, no. 4 (October 1989), 412, 425–30.
51. Kaplan, 'Right Wing...', pp. 66–7, 80–1.
52. Dalrymple, 'Nightmare...', 39.
53. Brian Levin, Testimony to: US House of Representatives Judiciary Committee, Subcommittee On Crime, 'The Nature and Threat of Violent Anti-Government Groups in America', 104th Congress, 1st Session, 2 November 1995, 64.
54. Michael Barkun, 'Religion, Militias and Oklahoma City: The Mind of Conspiratorialists', *Terrorism and Political Violence*, vol. 8, no. 1 (Spring 1996), 50.
55. Brent Smith, Testimony to: US House of Representatives Judiciary Committee, Subcommittee On Crime, 'The Nature and Threat of Violent Anti-Government Groups in America', 104th Congress, 1st Session, 2 November 1995, 21.
56. Barkun, 'Religion...', 52.
57. Martin Durham, 'Preparing for Armageddon: Citizen Militias, the Patriot Movement and the Oklahoma City Bombing', *Terrorism and Political Violence*, vol. 8, no. 1 (Spring 1996), 70.
58. Smith, Testimony..., 21.
59. Durham, 'Preparing...', 67.
60. Bruce Hoffman, 'American Right-Wing Extremism', *Jane's Intelligence Review*, vol. 7, no. 7 (July 1995), 329–30.
61. Durham, 'Preparing...', 75.

62. Barkun, 'Religion...', 61.
63. Kenneth Stern, Testimony to: US House of Representatives Judiciary Committee, Subcommittee On Crime, 'The Nature & Threat of Violent Anti-Government Groups in America', 104th Congress, 1st Session, 2 November 1995, 50.
64. Jamieson, *The Heart...*, pp. 20–1.
65. Hoffman, 'The Contrasting...', 366–7.
66. Rubenstein, *Alchemists...*, pp. 131–2.
67. Hoffman, 'The Contrasting...', 367.
68. Sopko, 'The Changing...', 9.
69. Richard Clutterbuck, *Terrorism in an Unstable World* (London: Routledge, 1994), p. 167.
70. Ibid., pp. 171–2.
71. Konrad Kellen, 'Appendix: Nuclear-Related Terrorist Activities by Political Terrorists', in Leventhal & Alexander (eds), *Preventing Nuclear Terrorism* (Lexington, Mass.: Lexington Books, 1987), pp. 129–30.
72. Matthew L. Wald, 'Gate Crasher Shakes Up Nuclear Debate', *New York Times*, 11 February 1993, A16.
73. Bruce Hoffman, *Report of Dr Bruce Hoffman for Ontario Court (General Division) on the Likelihood of Nuclear Terrorism in Canada* (July 1993), 4–5.
74. 'FBI Seizes Nuclear Protester in Car Bombing at A-Weapons Lab', *Los Angeles Times*, 8 April 1988, A32.
75. 'Anti-Nuclear Group Damaged Railways – German Police', *Reuters*, 14 November 1994.
76. Bruce Hoffman, Thomas C. Tompkins, Bonnie Cordes, Peter deLeon, Sue Ellen Moran, 'The Changing Threat to US Nuclear Programmes', *RAND*, May 1985, 27–9.
77. Frank J. Prial, 'Antitank Rockets are Fired at French Nuclear Reactor', *New York Times*, 20 January 1982, A3.
78. Hoffman, Tompkins, Cordes, deLeon, Moran, 'The Changing...', pp. 32–3.
79. James M. Jasper & Jane D. Poulsen, 'Recruiting Strangers and Friends: Moral Shocks and Social Networks in Animal Rights and Anti-Nuclear Protests', *Social Problems*, vol. 42, no. 4 (November 1995), 498–503.
80. Ruud Koopmans & Jan Willem Duyvendak, 'The Political Construction of the Nuclear Energy Issue and Its Impact on the Mobilization of Anti-Nuclear Movements in Western Europe', *Social Problems*, vol. 42, no. 2 (May 1995).
81. Jasper & Poulsen, 'Recruiting...', 504.
82. James Scaminaci III & Riley E. Dunlap, 'No Nukes! A Comparison of Participants in Two National Anti-Nuclear Demonstrations', *Sociological Inquiry*, vol. 56, no. 2 (Spring 1986) 276.
83. David Kowalewski & Karen L. Porter, 'Ecoprotest: Alienation, Deprivation, or Resources?', *Social Science Quarterly*, vol. 73, no. 3 (September 1992).
84. Brent L. Smith, *Terrorism in America: Pipe Bombs and Pipe Dreams*

(Albany, NY: State University of New York Press, 1994), p. 126.
85. Smith, *Terrorism in America...*, pp. 26–7 and 125–7.
86. Michel Wieviorka, *The Making of Terrorism* (Chicago: University of Chicago Press, 1993), p. 118.
87. Richard Wigg, 'Atomic Power Station is Sabotaged in France', *The Times*, 16 August 1975, 3.
88. Wieviorka, *The Making...*, pp. 166–8, 174.
89. Ian Mulgrew, 'The Defiant Squamish Five: Down to Earth with a Thud', *The Globe & Mail*, 19 June 1984, 7.
90. 'Sun Receives "Blast" Letter', *Vancouver Sun*, 2 June 1982, A1, 2.
91. Direct Action, 'Statement Regarding the October 14 Litton Bombing', 17 October 1982.
92. Laqueur, *The Age of Terrorism* (Boston: Little, Brown, 1987), p. 289.
93. Aliaga, *Terrorism in Peru* (Edinburgh: Janati, 1994), pp. 32–5, 47.
94. Lopez-Alves, 'Political...', 216.
95. Jamieson, *The Heart...*, pp. 52–5.
96. Docom, 1981 or 1982, cited in Laqueur, *The Age...*, p. 302.
97. Horchem, 'The Decline...', 67–9.
98. Translation of Red Army Faction's 10 April 1992 communiqué in: Pluchinsky, 'Germany's...', 148.
99. Jamieson, *The Heart...*, pp. 53, 59–60.
100. Pluchinsky, 'Germany's...'
101. Jamieson, *The Heart...*, pp. 89, 103–5.
102. See Jillian Becker, *Hitler's Children: The Story of the Baader-Meinhof Gang*, 3rd edn (London: Pickwick, 1989).
103. Kellen, 'Terrorists...', 61–2.
104. Pluchinsky, 'Germany's...', 142.
105. Translation of Red Army Faction's 29 June 1992 communiqué in ibid., 154.
106. RAND-St Andrews Database.
107. Peter Neuhauser, 'The Mind of a German Terrorist', *Encounter*, vol. 51, no. 3 September 1978, 87.
108. Rand-St Andrews Database.
109. Bonnie Cordes, 'When Terrorists Do the Talking: Reflections on Terrorist Literature', in Rapoport (ed.), *Inside...*, p. 157.
110. Hoffman, 'The Contrasting...', 363–4.
111. Elizabeth Pond, 'Remorseful Terrorist Looks Back', *Christian Science Monitor*, 29 August 1978, 13.
112. Lopez-Alves, 'Political...', 203–6.

CHAPTER 5: THE LIKELIHOOD OF NUCLEAR TERRORISM

1. Clarke, *Author's...*
2. International Physicians for the Prevention of Nuclear War, pp. 6–8.
3. R. W. Selden, 'Reactor Plutonium and Nuclear Explosives', Lawrence Livermore Laboratory, 1976, and H. Blix, 'Letter to the Nuclear Control Institute, Washington DC', 1990, both cited in ibid., p. 8.
4. Ibid., pp. 8–10.

5. D. Cobb & W. Kirchner, Testimony to: US Senate Governmental Affairs Committee, Permanent Subcommittee On Investigations, 'Reducing the Threat of Nuclear, Biological, and Chemical Proliferation and Terrorism', 104th Congress, 2nd Session, 13, 20, and 22 March 1996, 4.
6. Falkenrath, *Author's*...
7. Louis Freeh, Testimony to: US Senate Governmental Affairs Committee, Permanent Subcommittee On Investigations, 'International Organized Crime and Its Impact on the United States', 103rd Congress, 2nd Session, 25 May 1994, 62.
8. Barnaby, *Instruments of Terror*, pp. 172–4.
9. Spector, *Author's*...
10. Brad Thayer & Robert Newman, Research Fellows, Center for Science and International Affairs, JFK School of Government, Harvard University, Interview with Author, 12 November 1996, Cambridge, Mass.
11. Sopko, 'The Changing...', 7–8.
12. Ron Purver, 'Understanding Past Non-Use of CBW by Terrorists', Conference on 'ChemBio Terrorism: Wave of the Future?' Sponsored by the Chemical and Biological Arms Control Institute, Washington DC, 29 April 1996, 7–8.
13. Brian Jenkins, 'The Likelihood of Nuclear Terrorism', *RAND P-7119*, July 1985, 6.
14. Hoffman, 'Terrorist Targeting...', 23.
15. Hoffman, 'An Assessment of the Potential Threat to Canadian Nuclear Power Plants', Ontario Court (General Division), 25 April 1993, 9.
16. Jenkins, 'The Likelihood...', 8.
17. Jenkins, 'Will Terrorists Go Nuclear?', 4–5.
18. Friedman, *From Beirut to Jerusalem,* pp. 559–60.
19. Thayer & Newman, *Author's*...
20. David I. Ross, 'Canada and the World at Risk: Depression, War and Isolationism in the 21st Century?', *International Journal*, vol. LII, no. 1 (Winter 1996–7), 13.
21. E. Johanson, 'Nuke Vote', *Voice of America*, 11 April 1995.
22. Paul Leventhal & Brahma Challaney, 'Nuclear Terrorism: Threat, Perception, and Response in South Asia', *Terrorism*, vol. 11 (1988), 458–9.
23. Jenkins, 'The Likelihood...', 6.
24. RAND-St Andrews Chronology of International Terrorism.
25. Bruce Hoffman, 'Testimony Before the US Senate Committee on Environment and Public Works, Subcommittee on Clean Air and Nuclear Regulation', *RAND*, March 1993, 7.
26. Hoffman & Hoffman, 'The Rand-St Andrews...1994', 185.
27. Ibid.
28. Crenshaw, 'An Organizational Approach...'.
29. Hoffman, 'Responding to Terrorism Across the Technological Spectrum', *RAND*, April 1994, 13–16.
30. William O. Studeman, Testimony of the Acting Director of Central Intelligence to the House Judiciary Committee Hearings on the Omnibus Counterterrorism Act of 1995, 6 April 1995.

31.	Cited in Robert Taylor, 'All Fall Down', *New Scientist*, 11 May 1996, 32–3.
32.	Hoffman, 'Responding...', 9–12.
33.	Hoffman, '"Holy Terror"...', 272.
34.	Jerrold M. Post, 'Prospects for Nuclear Terrorism: Psychological Motivations and Constraints', in Leventhal & Alexander (eds), *Preventing Nuclear Terrorism*, pp. 99–100.
35.	Hoffman, '"Holy Terror"...', 277–8.
36.	See: 'Arrest Follows 1993 Poison Seizure', *The Globe & Mail*, 23 December 1995, A13.
37.	Sopko, 'The Changing...', 4–6.
38.	Tim Appleby, Brian Milner & David Roberts, 'Two US Men Charged with Possessing Anthrax', *The Globe & Mail*, 20 February 1998, pp. A1, A11.
39.	Vitali Vitaliov Pardubice, 'Semtex Sales Go Through the Roof', *The Sunday Times*, 29 September 1996, A16.
40.	Hoffman, 'Responding...', 21–6.
41.	Peter DeLeon, Bruce Hoffman with Konrad Kellen & Brian Jenkins, 'The Threat of Nuclear Terrorism: A Reexamination', *RAND*, January 1988, 3.
42.	Clarke, *Author's...*
43.	Hoffman, 'An Assessment...', 4.
44.	Kaplan & Marshall, *The Cult...*, p. 271.
45.	Jenkins, 'The Likelihood...', 10–11.
46.	'FBI probed Iranian Nuclear Attack Plan', *United Press International*, 18 February 1996.
47.	See Oehler, 'The Continuing...'
48.	*Agence France Presse*, 23 November 1995.
49.	Mark Hibbs, 'Chechen Separatists Take Credit for Moscow Cesium-137 Threat', *Nuclear Fuel*, vol. 20, no. 25 (5 December 1995), 5.
50.	Phil Reeves, 'Moscow Tries to Play Down Radioactive Chechen Feat', *The Irish Times*, 25 November 1995, 11.
51.	Stephane Orjollet, 'Nuke Package Raises Fear of Chechen Attacks – But How Real Are They?', *Agence France Presse*, 24 November 1995.
52.	'Six Die, 3,200 Hurt in Gas Attack', *The Japan Times*, 21 March 1995, 1.
53.	Gwen Robinson, 'Diary Blames Asahara for Subway Attack', *The Times*, 18 April 1995, 10.
54.	Jonathan Annells & James Adams, 'Did Terrorists Kill with Deadly Nerve Gas Test?', *The Sunday Times*, 19 March 1995.
55.	'Sarin Raw Material Seized in Raid', *The Japan Times*, 23 March 1995, 1.
56.	'All Three Sarin Cases Tied to Same Group', *The Japan Times*, 26 March 1995, 1.
57.	Gwen Robinson & Michael Binyon, 'Police Raid May Have Triggered Nerve Gas Attack', *The Times*, 21 March 1995, 10.
58.	'Doomsday Cult Plotted Urban War on Japan – Report', *The Daily Telegraph*, 26 May 1995.
59.	Robert Whymant, 'Cult Planned Gas Raids on America', *The Times*, 29 March 1997.

60. Kaplan & Marshall, *The Cult...*, pp. 190–2, 208.
61. Barkun, 'Millenarian...', 431.
62. Douglas Waller, 'Nuclear Ninjas: A New Kind of SWAT Team Hunts Atomic Terrorists. An Exclusive Look at their Operation', *Time*, vol. 147, no. 2 (8 January 1996), 38–40.
63. John T. McQuiston, 'Third Man Held in Plot to Use Radium to Kill N.Y. Officials', *New York Times*, 14 June 1996, B2.
64. Jenkins, 'The Likelihood...', 7.
65. Purver, 'Understanding...', 3–4.
66. Jonathan B. Tucker, 'Chemical/Biological Terrorism: Coping with a New Threat', *Politics and the Life Sciences*, vol. 15, no. 2 (September 1996), 167.
67. Richard Falkenrath, 'Chemical/Biological Terrorism: Coping with Uncertain Threats and Certain Vulnerablities', *Politics and the Life Sciences*, vol. 15, no. 2 (September 1996), 201–2.
68. Brad Roberts, 'Terrorism and Weapons of Mass Destruction: Has the Taboo Been Broken?', *Politics and the Life Sciences*, vol. 15, no. 2 (September 1996), 216–17.
69. Tucker, 'Chemical/Biological...', 169.
70. Ron Purver, 'Chemical and Biological Terrorism: The Threat According to the Open Literature', Canadian Security Intelligence Service, June 1995, 42.
71. W. Mullins cited in Ibid.
72. Graham S. Pearson, 'Chemical/Biological Terrorism: How Serious a Risk?', *Politics and the Life Sciences*, vol. 15, no. 2 (September 1996), 210–11.
73. Purver, 'Chemical and Biological...', 41.
74. Tucker, 'Chemical/Biological...', 169.
75. Purver, 'Chemical and Biological...', 96.
76. John Deutch, *Conference on Nuclear, Biological, Chemical Weapons Proliferation and Terrorism*, 23 May 1996.
77. Roberts, 'Terrorism...', 216.
78. Ibid., 170–2.
79. Kaplan & Marshall, *The Cult...*, pp. 96–7.
80. Tucker, 'Chemical/Biological...', 174.
81. Kaplan & Marshall, *The Cult...,* pp. 94–6.
82. Cited in Ron Purver, 'The Threat Of Chemical/Biological Terrorism', Canadian Security Intelligence Service, *Commentary*, no. 60 (August 1995).
83. Cited in Kaplan & Marshall, *The Cult...*, p. 289.

## CHAPTER 6: CONCLUSION

1. Nunn, *Author's...*
2. Nunn, *Congressional...*, S11761.
3. Hoffman, 'Terrorism and WMD...', 48.
4. International Physicians for the Prevention of Nuclear War, 6–10.

5.   Neuhauser, 'The Mind of a German Terrorist', *Encounter*, 87.
6.   McQuiston, 'Third Man Held In Plot To Use Radium to Kill N.Y.
     Officials'.
7.   Williams and Woessner, 'The Real Threat...', 30.
8.   Hoffman, 'Terrorism and WMD...', 50.

# Select Bibliography

AUTHOR'S CORRESPONDENCE

Clarke, Floyd, Formerly Deputy Director FBI, Interview with Author, 20 November 1996, Washington DC.
Cochran, Thomas, Natural Resources Defense Council, Washington DC, Interview with Author, 21 November 1996, Washington DC.
Falkenrath, Richard, Executive Director, Center for Science and International Affairs, Harvard University, Interview with Author, 12 November 1996, Cambridge, Mass.
Newman, Robert, Center for Science and International Affairs, Harvard University, Interview with Author, 12 November 1996, Cambridge, Mass.
Spector, Leonard, Director, Nuclear Non-Proliferation Project, Carnegie Endowment for International Peace, Washington DC, Interview with Author, 15 November 1996, Washington DC.
Thayer, Brad, Center for Science and International Affairs, Harvard University, Interview with Author, 12 November 1996, Cambridge, Mass.


OFFICIAL SOURCES

Allison, Graham T., Testimony to the Senate Committee on Foreign Relations, Subcommittee on European Affairs, Hearings Held 23 August 1995.
Nunn, Sam, 'Statement to the US Senate', Congressional Record – Senate, S11754, 28 September 1996.
Oehler, Gordon C., 'The Continuing Threat from Weapons of Mass Destruction', Testimony to the Senate Armed Services Committee, 27 March 1996.
Studeman, William O., Testimony of the Acting Director of Central Intelligence to the House Judiciary Committee Hearings on the Omnibus Counterterrorism Act of 1995, 6 April 1995.
US Congress, US Senate Governmental Affairs Committee, Permanent Subcommittee on Investigations, 'International Organized Crime and Its Impact on the United States', 103rd Congress, 2nd Session, 25 May 1994.
US Congress, US Senate, Governmental Affairs Committee, Permanent Subcommittee on Investigations, 'Global Proliferation of Weapons of Mass Destruction', 104th Congress, 1st Session, 31 October and 1 November 1995.
US Congress, 104th Congress 1st Session, 'The Nature and Threat of Violent Anti-Government Groups in America', US House of Representatives Judiciary Committee, Subcommittee On Crime, 'The Nature and Threat of Violent Anti-Government Groups in America', 104th Congress, 1st Session, 2 November 1995.

US Congress, US Senate Committee on Governmental Affairs, Permanent Subcommittee on Investigations, 'Global Proliferation of Weapons of Mass Destruction', 104th Congress, 2nd Session, 13, 20 and 22 March 1996, Parts I–III.

US General Accounting Office, 'Nuclear Nonproliferation: Status of US Efforts to Improve Nuclear Material Controls in Newly Independent States', GAO/NSIAD/RCED-96-89, March 1996.

REPORTS

Hoffman, Bruce, 'An Assessment of the Potential Threat to Canadian Nuclear Power Plants', Ontario Court (General Division), 25 April 1993.

—— *Report of Dr Bruce Hoffman for Ontario Court (General Division) on The Likelihood of Nuclear Terrorism in Canada*, July 1993.

—— 'Responding to Terrorism Across the Technological Spectrum', *RAND*, April 1994.

—— 'Testimony Before US Senate Committee on Environment and Public Works, Subcommittee on Clean Air and Nuclear Regulation', *RAND*, March 1993.

Hoffman, Bruce, Thomas C. Tompkins, Bonnie Cordes, Peter deLeon, Sue Ellen Moran, 'The Changing Threat to US Nuclear Programmes', *RAND*, May 1985.

Institute for National Security Studies, Center for Strategic Leadership, 'Report of the Executive Seminar on Special Material Smuggling', 13 September 1996.

International Physicians for the Prevention of Nuclear War, 'Crude Nuclear Weapons: Proliferation and the Terrorist Threat', *IPPNW Global Health Watch*, Report no. 1, 1996.

Jenkins, Brian, 'The Likelihood of Nuclear Terrorism', *RAND-7119*, July 1985.

—— 'The Terrorist Mindset and Terrorist Decisionmaking: Two Areas of Ignorance', *RAND P-6340*, June 1979.

—— 'Will Terrorists Go Nuclear?', *RAND P-5541*, November 1975.

Kellen, Konrad, 'On Terrorists and Terrorism', *RAND N-1942-RC*, December 1982.

—— 'Terrorists – What Are They Like? How Some Terrorists Describe their World and Actions', *RAND N-1300-SL*, November 1979.

deLeon, Peter, Bruce Hoffman with Konrad Kellen, Brian Jenkins, 'The Threat of Nuclear Terrorism: A Reexamination', *RAND N-2706*, January 1988.

Purver, Ron, 'Chemical and Biological Terrorism: The Threat According to the Open Literature', *Canadian Security Intelligence Service*, June 1995.

Ronfeldt, David and W. Sater, 'The Mindsets of High-Technology Terrorists: Future Implications from an Historical Analog', *RAND*, March 1981.

Turbiville, Graham H. Jr., 'Mafia in Uniform: The "Criminalization" of the Russian Armed Forces', *Foreign Military Studies Office*, Fort Leavenworth, Kansas, July 1995.

Wainstein, Eleanor S., 'The Cross and Laporte Kidnappings, Montreal, October 1970', *RAND R-1986-DOS/ARPA*, October 1976.

## LECTURES

Crenshaw, Martha, 'The Strategic Development of Terrorism', 1985 Annual Meeting of the American Political Science Association, New Orleans, 29 August–1 September 1985.

Deutch, John, *Conference on Nuclear, Biological, Chemical Weapons Proliferation and Terrorism*, 23 May 1996.

Purver, Ron, 'Understanding Past Non-Use of C.B.W. by Terrorists', Conference on 'ChemBio Terrorism: Wave of the Future?', Sponsored by the Chemical and Biological Arms Control Institute, Washington DC, 29 April 1996.

Rimington, Stella, 'Security and Democracy – Is There a Conflict?', The Richard Dimbleby Lecture 1994, BBC Educational Developments, 1994.

## BOOKS AND ARTICLES

AbuKhalil, As'ad, 'Internal Contradictions in the PFLP: Decision Making and Policy Orientation', *The Middle East Journal*, vol. 41, no. 3 (Summer 1987).

Abu-Sharif, Bassam & Uzi Mahnaimi, *Tried By Fire* (London: Little, Brown & Co., 1995).

Adams, James, *The Financing of Terror* (Sevenoaks: New English Library, 1986).

—— *Trading in Death: The Modern Arms Race* (London: Pan Books Limited, 1991).

Alexander, Yonah & Seymour Finger (eds), *Terrorism: Interdisciplinary Perspectives* (New York: John Jay Press, 1977).

Aliaga, Jorge, *Terrorism in Peru* (Edinburgh: Jananti, 1994).

Allison, Graham, & Richard Falkenrath, 'The World's Biggest Problem?', *Prospect* (February 1996).

Alpert, Jane, *Growing Up Underground* (New York: William Morrow & Company, 1981).

Barkun, Michael, 'Millenarian Aspects of White Supremacist Movements', *Terrorism and Political Violence*, vol. 1, no. 4 (October 1989).

—— (ed)., 'Millennialism and Violence', *Terrorism and Political Violence*, Special Issue, vol. 7, no. 3 (Autumn 1995).

—— 'Religion, Militias and Oklahoma City: The Mind of Conspiratorialists', *Terrorism and Political Violence*, vol. 8, no. 1 (Spring 1996).

Barnaby, Frank, *Instruments of Terror* (London: Vision Paperbacks, 1996).

Becker, Jillian, *Hitler's Children: The Story of The Baader-Meinhof Gang*, 3rd edition (London: Pickwick, 1989).

Begin, Menachem, *The Revolt: Story of the Irgun* (New York: Henry Schuman, 1951).

Bell, J. Bowyer, *Terror Out of Zion* (New York: St Martin's Press, 1977).

Berry, Nicholas O., 'Theories on the Efficacy of Terrorism', *Conflict Quarterly*, vol. VII, no. 1 (Winter 1987).

Bethell, Nicholas, *The Palestine Triangle: The Struggle for the Holy Land, 1935–48* (New York: G. P. Putnam's Sons, 1979).

Bjorgo, Tore (ed)., *Terror from the Extreme Right* (London: Frank Cass, 1995).

Bukharin, Oleg, 'The Future of Russia's Plutonium Cities', *International Security*, vol. 21, no. 4 (Spring 1997).

—— 'Nuclear Safeguards and Security in the Former Soviet Union', *Survival*, vol. 36, no. 4 (Winter 1994–95).

Campbell, James K., 'Excerpts from Research Study "Weapons of Mass Destruction and Terrorism: Proliferation By Non-State Actors"', *Terrorism and Political Violence*, vol. 9, no. 2 (Summer 1997).

Clark, Robert P., 'Patterns in the Lives of ETA Members', *Terrorism: An International Journal*, vol. 6, no. 3 (1983).

Clutterbuck, Richard, *Terrorism in an Unstable World* (London: Routledge, 1994).

Cohen-Almagor, Raphael, 'Vigilant Jewish Fundamentalism: From the JDL to Kach (or "Shalom Jews, Shalom Dogs")', *Terrorism and Political Violence*, vol. 4, no. 1 (Spring 1992).

Coogan, Tim Pat, *The IRA* (London: Fontana, 1987).

Crelinsten, Ronald D., 'The Internal Dynamics of the FLQ During the October Crisis of 1970', *Journal of Strategic Studies*, vol. 10, Part 4 (1987).

Crenshaw, Martha, 'How Terrorism Declines', *Terrorism and Political Violence*, vol. 3, no. 1 (Spring 1991).

—— 'An Organisational Approach to the Analysis of Political Terrorism', *Orbis*, no. 29 (Fall 1985).

—— *Terrorism and International Co-operation* (Institute For East-West Security Studies, Occasional Paper Series II, 1989).

Don-Yehiya, Eliezer, 'Jewish Messianism, Religious Zionism and Israeli Politics: The Impact and Origins of Gush Emunim', *Middle Eastern Studies*, vol. 23, no. 2 (April 1987).

Drake, C. J. M., 'The Phenomenon of Conservative Terrorism', *Terrorism and Political Violence*, vol. 8, no. 3 (Autumn 1996).

Durham, Martin, 'Preparing for Armageddon: Citizen Militias, the Patriot Movement and the Oklahoma City Bombing', *Terrorism and Political Violence*, vol. 8, no. 1 (Spring 1996).

Erikson, Erik H., *Childhood and Society* (New York: Norton, 1963).

—— *Identity: Youth and Crisis*, (New York: Norton, 1968).

Falkenrath, Richard A., 'Chemical/Biological Terrorism: Coping with Uncertain Threats and Certain Vulnerabilities', *Politics and the Life Sciences*, vol. 15, no. 2 (September 1996).

Fanon, Frantz, *The Wretched of the Earth* (London: Penguin Books, 1967).

Ford, James L., 'Nuclear Smuggling: How Serious a Threat?', *Institute for National Strategic Studies*, Strategic Forum, no. 59 (January 1996).

Friedman, Thomas, *From Beirut to Jerusalem* (New York: Doubleday, 1995).

Fromkin, David, 'The Strategy of Terrorism', *Foreign Affairs*, vol. 53, no. 4 (July 1975).

Fromm, Erich, *The Anatomy of Human Destructiveness* (London: Penguin Books, 1977).

Galeotti, Mark, 'Mafiya: Organized Crime in Russia', *Jane's Intelligence Review*, Special Report no. 10 (June 1996).

Galvin, Deborah M., 'The Female Terrorist: A Socio-Psychological Perspective', *Behavioural Science and the Law*, vol. 1, no. 2 (1983).

Gottemoeller, Rose, 'Preventing a Nuclear Nightmare', *Survival*, vol. 38, no. 2 (Summer 1996).

Handler, Jeffrey S., 'Socioeconomic Profile of an American Terrorist: 1960s and 1970s', *Terrorism: An International Journal*, vol. 13 (1990).

Hearst, Patty, *Patty Hearst* (London: Corgi Books, 1988).

Hecht, Richard D., 'The Political Cultures of Israel's Radical Right: Commentary on Ehud Sprinzak's *The Ascendance of Israel's Radical Right*', *Terrorism and Political Violence*, vol. 5, no. 1 (Spring 1993).

Herman, Margaret (ed)., *Political Psychology: Contemporary Problems and Issues* (San Francisco: Jossey Bass, 1986).

Hewitt, Christopher, 'Terrorism and Public Opinion: A Five Country Comparison', *Terrorism and Political Violence*, vol. 2, no. 2 (Summer 1990).

Hirschman, Albert, *Exit, Voice and Loyalty: Response to Decline in Firms, Organisations and States* (Cambridge, Mass.: Harvard University Press 1970).

Hoffman, Bruce, 'American Right-Wing Extremism', *Jane's Intelligence Review*, vol. 7, no. 7 (July 1995).

—— 'The Contrasting Ethical Foundations of Terrorism in the 1980s', *Terrorism and Political Violence*, vol. 1, no. 3, (July 1989).

—— 'Holy Terror: The Implications of Terrorism Motivated by Religious Imperatives', *Studies in Conflict and Terrorism*, vol. 18 (1995).

—— 'Intelligence and Terrorism: Emerging Threats and New Security Challanges in the Post-Cold War Era', *Intelligence and National Security*, vol. 11, no. 2 (April 1996).

—— 'Review of E. MacDonald's "Shoot The Women First"', *The Oral History Review*, vol. 22, no. 1 (Summer 1995).

—— 'Terrorism and WMD: Some Preliminary Hypotheses', *The Nonproliferation Review*, vol. 4, no. 3 (Spring/Summer 1997).

Hoffman, Bruce & Donna Kim Hoffman, 'The RAND-St Andrews Chronology of International Terrorism, 1994', *Terrorism and Political Violence*, vol. 7, no. 4 (Winter 1995).

—— 'The RAND-St Andrews Chronology of International Terrorist Incidents, 1995', *Terrorism and Political Violence*, vol. 8, no. 3 (Autumn 1996).

Horchem, Hans Josef, 'The Decline of the Red Army Faction', *Terrorism and Political Violence*, vol. 3, no. 2 (Summer 1991).

Horgan, John & Max Taylor, 'The Provisional Irish Republican Army: Command and Functional Structure', *Terrorism and Political Violence*, vol. 9, no. 4 (Winter 1997).

Iviansky, Ze'ev, 'Individual Terror: Concept and Typology', *Journal of Contemporary History*, vol. 12 (1977).

Jamieson, Alison, 'Entry, Discipline and Exit in the Italian Red Brigades', *Terrorism and Political Violence*, vol. 2, no. 1 (Spring 1990).

—— *The Heart Attacked: Terrorism and Conflict in the Italian State* (London: Marion Boyars Publishers, 1989).

Janis, Irving L., *Victims of Groupthink* (Boston: Houghton-Mifflin, 1972).

Janke, Peter (ed)., *Terrorism and Democracy* (London: Macmillan 1992).

—— 'Terrorism: Trends and Growth?', *RUSI Journal* (August 1993).

Jasper, James M. & Jane D. Poulsen, 'Recruiting Strangers and Friends:

Moral Shocks and Social Networks in Animal Rights and Anti-Nuclear Protests', *Social Problems*, vol. 42, no. 4 (November 1995).

Juergensmeyer, Mark (ed)., 'Violence and the Sacred in the Modern World', *Terrorism and Political Violence*, Special Issue, vol. 3, no. 3 (Autumn 1991).

Kahane, Meir, *Forty Years* (Miami Beach: Institute of the Jewish Idea, 1983).

Kaplan, Abraham, 'The Psychodynamics of Terrorism', *Terrorism: An International Journal*, vol. 1, no. 3/4 (1978).

Kaplan, David E. & Andrew Marshall, *The Cult at the End of the World* (London: Random House, 1996).

Kaplan, Jeffrey, 'The Context of American Millenarian Revolutionary Theology: The Case of the "Identity Christian" Church of Israel', *Terrorism and Political Violence*, vol. 5, no. 1 (Spring 1993).

Khaled, Leila, *My People Shall Live* (London: Hodder & Stoughton, 1973).

Kinsella, Warren, *Web of Hate: Inside Canada's Far Right Network* (Toronto: HarperCollins, 1994).

Knutson, Jeanne N., 'The Terrorist Dilemmas: Some Implicit Rules of the Game', *Terrorism: An International Journal*, vol. 4 (1980).

Koopmans, Ruud & Jan Willem Duyvendak, 'The Political Construction of the Nuclear Energy Issue and Its Impact on the Mobilization of Anti-Nuclear Movements in Western Europe', *Social Problems*, vol. 42, no. 2 (May 1995).

Kowalewski, David & Karen L. Porter, 'Ecoprotest: Alienation, Deprivation, or Resources?', *Social Science Quarterly*, vol. 73, no. 3 (September 1992).

Kuran, Timur, 'Sparks and Prairie Fires: A Theory of Unanticipated Political Violence', *Public Choice*, vol. 61 (1989).

Laqueur, Walter, *The Age of Terrorism* (Boston: Little, Brown & Co., 1987).

—— 'Postmodern Terrorism', *Foreign Affairs*, vol. 75, no. 5 (September/ October 1996).

Lee, Rensselaer W., 'Post-Soviet Nuclear Trafficking: Myths, Half-Truths, and the Reality', *Current History* (October 1995).

Leventhal, Paul & Yonah Alexander (eds), *Nuclear Terrorism: Defining the Threat* (Washington, DC: Pergammon, 1985).

—— *Preventing Nuclear Terrorism* (Lexington, Mass.: Lexington Books, 1987).

Leventhal, Paul & Brahma Chellaney, 'Nuclear Terrorism: Threat, Perception, and Response in South Asia', *Terrorism: An International Journal*, vol. 11, no. 6 (1988).

Lewy, Guenter, *Religion and Revolution* (New York: Oxford University Press, 1974).

Lopez-Alves, Fernando, 'Political Crises, Strategic Choices and Terrorism: The Rise and Fall of the Uruguayan Tupamaros', *Terrorism and Political Violence*, vol. 1, no. 2 (April 1989).

Lovins, Amory & L. Hunter Lovins, 'The Fragility of Domestic Energy', *The Atlantic Monthly* (November 1983).

MacDonald, Andrew, *The Turner Diaries* (Arlington: National Alliance/ National Vanguard Books, 1985).

McDonald, Eileen, *Shoot The Women First* (New York: Random House, 1991).

McGuire, Maria, *To Take Arms* (London: Macmillan, 1973).

MacStiofain, Sean, *Revolutionary in Ireland* (Edinburgh: Gordon Cremonesi, 1975).

Marighella, Carlos, *Mini-Manual of the Urban Guerrilla*, 1969.

Mathers, Jennifer G., 'Corruption in the Russian Armed Forces', *The World Today*, vol. 51, nos. 8–9 (August–September 1995).

Morf, Gustave, *Terror in Quebec: Case Study of the FLQ* (Toronto: Clark Irwin, 1970).

O'Ballance, Edgar, *Islamic Fundamentalist Terrorism, 1979–95: The Iranian Connection* (London: Macmillan Press Limited, 1997).

Pearson, Graham S., 'Chemical/Biological Terrorism: How Serious a Risk?', *Politics and the Life Sciences*, vol. 15, no. 2 (September 1996).

Pluchinsky, Dennis, 'Germany's Red Army Faction: An Obituary', *Studies in Conflict and Terrorism*, vol. 16, no. 2 (April–June 1993).

Porteous, Samuel D., 'The Threat from Transnational Crime: An Intelligence Perspective', Canadian Security Intelligence Service, *Commentary*, no. 70 (Winter 1996).

Post, Jerrold M., 'Current Understanding of Terrorist Motivation and Psychology: Implications for a Differentiated Antiterrorist Policy', *Terrorism: An International Journal*, vol. 13, no. 1 (1990).

—— 'Fundamentalism and the Justification of Terrorist Violence', *Terrorism: An International Journal*, vol. 11, no. 5 (1988).

—— 'Hostilité, Conformité, Fraternité: The Group Dynamics of Terrorist Behaviour', *International Journal of Group Psychotherapy*, 36 (2) (April 1986).

—— 'Notes on a Psychodynamic Theory of Terrorist Behaviour', *Terrorism: An International Journal*, vol. 7, no. 3 (1984).

—— 'Rewarding Fire with Fire: Effects of Retaliation on Terrorist Group Dynamics', *Terrorism: An International Journal*, vol. 10, no. 1 (1987).

Potter, William C., 'Before the Deluge? Assessing the Threat of Nuclear Leakage from the Post-Soviet States', *Arms Control Today*, (October 1995).

—— 'Exports and Experts: Proliferation Risks from the New Commonwealth', *Arms Control Today* (January/February 1992).

Purver, Ron, 'The Threat of Chemical/Biological Terrorism', Canadian Security Intelligence Service, *Commentary*, no. 60 (August 1995).

Rahr, Alexander, 'Soviet Fear of Nuclear Terrorism', *Report on the USSR*, vol. 2, no. 13 (March 30, 1990).

Ranstorp, Magnus, 'Hizbollah's Command Leadership: Its Structure, Decision-Making and its Relationship with Iranian Clergy and Institutions', *Terrorism and Political Violence*, vol. 6, no. 3 (Autumn 1994).

—— *Hizb'allah in Lebanon: The Politics of the Western Hostage Crisis* (London: Macmillan Press, 1997).

—— 'Terrorism in the Name of Religion', *Journal of International Affairs*, vol. 50, no. 1 (Summer 1996).

Rapoport, David C., 'Fear and Trembling: Terrorism in Three Religious Traditions', *American Political Science Review*, vol. 78, no. 3 (September 1984).

—— (ed.), *Inside Terrorist Organisations* (London: Frank Cass & Co., 1988).

—— 'Messianic Sanctions for Terror', *Comparative Politics*, vol. 20, no. 2 (January 1988).

Rapoport, David C. & Yonah Alexander (eds), *The Morality of Terrorism: Religious and Secular Justifications*, 2nd edn (New York: Columbia University Press, 1989).

Reich, Walter (ed)., *Origins of Terrorism: Psychologies, Ideologies, Theologies, States of Mind* (Cambridge: Cambridge University Press, 1990).

Reilly, Wayne G., 'The Management of Political Violence in Quebec and Northern Ireland: A Comparison', *Terrorism and Political Violence*, vol. 6, no. 1 (Spring 1994).

Roberts, Brad, 'Terrorism and Weapons of Mass Destruction: Has the Taboo Been Broken?', *Politics and the Life Sciences*, vol. 15, no. 2 (September 1996).

Robitaille, A. & Ron Purver, 'Smuggling Special Nuclear Materials', Canadian Security Intelligence Service, *Commentary*, no. 57 (May 1995).

Ross, D., 'Canada and the World at Risk: Depression, War and Isolationism for the 21st Century?', *International Journal*, vol. LII, no. 1 (Winter 1996–7).

Ross, Jeffrey Ian, 'Research Note: Contemporary Radical Right-Wing Violence in Canada: A Quantitative Analysis', *Terrorism and Political Violence*, vol. 4, no. 3 (Autumn 1992).

—— 'The Rise and Fall of Quebecois Separatist Terrorism: A Qualitative Application of Factors from Two Models', *Studies in Conflict and Terrorism*, vol. 18, no. 4 (October–December 1995).

Ross, Jeffrey Ian & Ted Robert Gurr, 'Why Terrorism Subsides', *Comparative Politics*, vol. 21, no. 4 (July 1989).

Rubenstein, Richard E., *Alchemists of Revolution: Terrorism in the Modern World* (New York: Basic Books, 1987).

Salmony, Steven E. & Richard Smoke, 'The Appeal and Behaviour of the Ku Klux Klan in Object Relations Perspective', *Terrorism: An International Journal*, vol. 11 (1988).

Scaminaci, James III & Riley E. Dunlap, 'No Nukes! A Comparison of Participants in Two National Anti-nuclear Demonstrations', *Sociological Inquiry*, vol. 56, no. 2 (Spring 1986).

Scharlau, Bruce A. & Donald Philips, 'Not the End of German Left-Wing Terrorism', *Terrorism and Political Violence*, vol. 4, no. 3 (Autumn 1992).

Schmidbauer, Bernd, 'Illegaler Nuklearhandel und Nuklearterrorismus', *Internationale Politik*, vol. 50, no. 2 (February 1995).

Seale, Patrick, *Abu Nidal: A Gun For Hire* (New York: Random House Incorporated, 1992).

Shamir, Yitzhak, *Summing Up: An Autobiography* (London: Weidenfeld & Nicolson, 1994).

Silke, Andrew, 'Honour and Expulsion: Terrorism in Nineteenth-Century Japan', *Terrorism and Political Violence*, vol. 9, no. 4 (Winter 1997).

Smith, Brent L., *Terrorism in America: Pipe Bombs and Pipe Dreams* (Albany, NY: State University of New York Press, 1994).

Smith, M. L. R., *Fighting for Ireland? The Military Strategy of the Irish Republican Movement* (London: Routledge, 1995).

Sopko, John F., 'The Changing Proliferation Threat', *Foreign Policy*, vol. 105 (Winter 1996–7).

Steinhoff, Patricia, 'Portrait of a Terrorist: An Interview with Kozo Okamoto', *Asian Survey*, vol. 16, no. 9 (September 1976).

Stern, Susan, *With the Weathermen* (New York: Doubleday, 1975).

Taylor, Maxwell, *The Terrorist* (London: Brassey's, 1988).

Taylor, Maxwell & Ethel Quayle, *Terrorist Lives* (London; Brassey's, 1994).

Taylor, Peter, *States of Terror: Democracy and Political Violence* (London: Penguin Books/BBC Books, 1993).

Tucker, Jonathan B., 'Chemical/Biological Terrorism: Coping with a New Threat', *Politics and the Life Sciences*, vol. 15, no. 2 (September 1996).

Vorbach, Joseph E., 'Monte Melkonian: Armenian Revolutionary Leader', *Terrorism and Political Violence*, vol. 6, no. 2 (Summer 1994).

Wardlaw, Grant, *Political Terrorism* (Cambridge: Cambridge University Press, 1982).

Weinberg, Leonard, 'On Responding to Right-wing Terrorism', *Terrorism and Political Violence*, vol. 8, no. 1 (Spring 1996).

Weinberg, Leonard & William Eubank, 'Leaders and Followers in Italian Terrorist Groups', *Terrorism and Political Violence*, vol. 1, no. 2 (April 1989).

White, Robert W. & Terry Falkenberg White, 'Revolution in the City: On the Resources of Urban Guerrillas', *Terrorism and Political Violence*, vol. 3, no. 4 (Winter 1991).

Wieviorka, Michel, *The Making of Terrorism* (Chicago: University of Chicago Press, 1993).

Wilkinson, Paul, *The New Fascists* (London: Pan Books, 1983).

—— (ed.), 'Technology and Terrorism', *Terrorism and Political Violence*, Special Edition, vol. 5, no. 2 (Summer 1993).

—— (ed.), *Terrorism: British Perspectives* (Aldershot: Dartmouth Publishing, 1993).

—— *Terrorism and the Liberal State* (London: Macmillan, 1979).

—— 'Violence and Terror and the Extreme Right', *Terrorism and Political Violence*, vol. 7, no. 4 (Winter 1995).

Wilkinson, Paul & Alexander Stewart (eds), *Contemporary Research on Terrorism* (Aberdeen: Aberdeen University Press, 1987).

Williams, Phil (ed)., *Russian Organized Crime: The New Threat?* (London: Frank Cass, 1997).

Williams, Phil & Paul N. Woessner, 'Nuclear Material Trafficking: An Interim Assessment', *Transnational Organized Crime*, vol. 1, no. 2 (Summer 1995).

—— 'The Real Threat of Nuclear Smuggling', *Scientific American*, vol. 274, no. 1 (January 1996).

Woessner, Paul N., 'Chronology of Radioactive and Nuclear Smuggling Incidents: July 1991–June 1997', *Transnational Organized Crime*, vol. 3, no. 1 (Spring 1997).

Zawodny, J. K., 'Internal Organizational Problems and the Sources of Tensions of Terrorist Movements as Catalysts of Violence', *Terrorism: An International Journal*, vol. 1, no. 3/4 (1978).

# Index

*Index*